for Jim
With Blessings from [signature]
[signature]

FACE TO FACE WITH Shiva

SCIENTIFIC PERSPECTIVE OF
A SPIRITUAL EXPERIENCE

ABHINAV AGGARWAL, PH.D.

AND LENS OF ROHAN GEET GUPTA

authorHOUSE®

AuthorHouse™
1663 Liberty Drive
Bloomington, IN 47403
www.authorhouse.com
Phone: 1 (800) 839-8640

© 2016 Abhinav Aggarwal. All rights reserved.

No part of this book may be reproduced, stored in a retrieval system, or transmitted by any means without the written permission of the author.

Published by AuthorHouse 10/21/2016

ISBN: 978-1-5049-8216-0 (sc)
ISBN: 978-1-5049-8215-3 (hc)
ISBN: 978-1-5246-3884-9 (e)

Library of Congress Control Number: 2016916056

Print information available on the last page.

This book is printed on acid-free paper.

Because of the dynamic nature of the Internet, any web addresses or links contained in this book may have changed since publication and may no longer be valid. The views expressed in this work are solely those of the author and do not necessarily reflect the views of the publisher, and the publisher hereby disclaims any responsibility for them.

Author or publisher would be in no way responsible for any direct, indirect, or consequential damages resulting to any individual, community, or business out of a practice of the exercises, hypothesis, or experiments suggested in this book. If you have a medical condition, please seek appropriate medical advice to ensure that the practice of any of exercises suggested in the book is safe for you.
The facts stated out of history are not verified, and are cited only by way of an example to illustrate the point under discussion. It is neither the intent nor the objective of either the author or the publisher to pick any individual, community, or nation for criticism. All references are only as illustration and no unintended interpretation may be drawn there from.

Contents

Acknowledgements..ix
Aum Namah Shivaya – the sacred hymn xiii
Prologue...xv
Chapter 1:   The Experience 1
Chapter 2:   Getting to know Shiva.......................................7
Chapter 3:   Abstract Neural Networks (ANN)................41
Chapter 4:   Acquired Identity Syndrome 60
Chapter 5:   The secret of creation hypothesis..................66
Chapter 6:   The modes of existence 76
Chapter 7:   From respect to realization 111
Chapter 8:   The Road Ahead.. 117
Chapter 9:   Questions and Answers with Shiva 136
Chapter 10: A page out of the Future 173
Chapter 11: Meditation...181
Chapter 12: The latter day experiences 199
Epilogue...207
Suggested Prayers 210
References 222
Picture Index..223
Picture gallery 224

for Parv, Avi, Sarita, and Urmila
the divine sources of my inspiration, my guides, my joy
-Abhinav Aggarwal

for Geetika Gupta
-Rohan Geet Gupta

Acknowledgements

The author is highly indebted to several friends and volunteers who have contributed their efforts in selfless service to review and give feedback, comments, and suggestions for improvement of this manuscript, and provided pictures for the book. Note-able among such contributors are: Dr. Balbir Singh Dhillon, Prof. Bhupen Gupta (NCSU); Prof. Mo-Yuen Chow, IEEE Fellow (NCSU); Mr. Bharat Vala, Mr. Gere Stafford, Ms. Terry Dimmick, Ms. Susan Weineke, Ms. Premi, Mrs. Shanthi Deenadayalan, Mrs. Jayathi Raghu, Mr. Dinesh Gupta and friends from PEC Joshite group, Mr. Rama Kant, Dr. Shan, Mr. Carlo, and friends at WISE (World Institute for Scientific Exploration), Vikram and other volunteers at SKY meditation group, Mr. Bhukan S Rathore, and the gentleman from Flowood / Jackson, MS, whose contact details have been lost.

Picture credits are mentioned in the photo gallery, acknowledging the volunteer contributors. Unless mentioned, all pictures are courtesy of Aggarwal family archives. Most of the recent pictures were contributed by Mr. Rohan Geet Gupta, Mr. Sunil Bakhshi, Ms. Usha Harding, Mr. Virender Bhardwaj, and Mr. Pradeep Seth (cover).

Above all, I applaud my family for their unconditional support in all my endeavors. Avi, my daughter, for her reviews; Parv, my son, for his continued encouragement and contributing Alaska pictures; Sarita, my wife, for always being there; Urmila, my mother, for her leading by example and her blessings; Dr Mridu Vikram, Dr Hemla Rakesh, and Dr Anu Ish Sud – my sisters and their families for supporting my efforts.

Chapel Hill, NC, USA   Abhinav Aggarwal
June 2016

A Word from Behind the Lens

When I was approached for this photography assignment, there was a childish excitement in me. Going to familiar places, to capture where as a child I've had memories. Jammu is where I spent the happiest days of my life, I grew up with my family and my sister Geetika, and even she loved Jammu.

I hope these photographs take you to a spiritual journey that Jammu, the city of temples can provide, teleport you to being there, get a firsthand glimpse of the experience and live it.

Delhi, June 2016   Rohan Geet Gupta

Aum Namah Shivaya – The Sacred Hymn

ॐ नमः शिवाय

The following text attempts to explain the meaning and relevance of this sacred hymn (mantra), also known as the Panchaakshar (five alphabets) mantra or sometimes 'Maha Mantra' (the greatest amongst all mantras) that is chanted by all devotees – literal translation can be interpreted as "bowing in respect to the divinity - within and without."

The 'within' aspect of divinity is the mind, body, and spirit connection. The 'without' aspect of divinity is the extension of this connection to the entire world, all beings, all material and non-material, all that exists and that is yet to exist, and the entire universe of existence and non-existence. Consider Shiva as the super consciousness that manifests in the existence as a combination of three elements of consciousness, knowledge and energy, and all existence merge into it upon dissolution.

Existence is for a purpose that generates life. Each life has a mission to fulfill. Life is an instance of consciousness, with associated knowledge and energy as a manifestation. The mission of each life is to return a useful value that contributes to the enhancement of collective universal knowledge that eventually results in the evolution of consciousness. The circumstances and environment around each life are different, rendering it an absolutely unique platform to experiment throughout its span and keep on returning those useful values. If the mission of a life is fulfilled satisfactorily, upon its dissolution it merges in to the super element – the super consciousness of Shiva.

Our knowledge has boundaries that keep extending as we experience and evolve. More of unknown merges with the known as we progress to make newer discoveries. It is never possible to figure out what is unknown as there is no limit to it. While chanting 'Aum Namah Shivaya,' we encompass all the divinity of the known and the unknown, the within and without, the existence and non-existence, the bonded

Abhinav Aggarwal, Ph.D.

and the unbound. The bonded is the anchored body on the planet, and the unbound is the limitless vastness in which the spirit can potentially wander. This sacred chant integrates the mind and body with the soul, the bonded body with the unbound vastness, and opens up horizons of the infinite universe for our exploration.

As one chants 'Aum Namah Shivaya' – even if silently within the heart, it instantly brings divine peace, tranquility, and joy. It melts away the anger, hatred, jealousy, prejudice, disease, unrest, frustration, and above all, ill feelings for anyone. As one connects with the all pervading divinity through the beauty of this sacred chant, one is in all and all is in one – there is no them vs us, or me vs you, and one begins to transcend the boundaries that limit the self.

Prologue

This book gives a real life account from the author of being face to face with Lord Shiva: the highest among all kinds of known beings – from God to everything else. The experience of being face to face with Lord Shiva, an event that took place in 1970, is given in the as-is form. It was, perhaps, among rarest of the rare experiences. Ever since then, the continuous dialog between the author and Lord Shiva has been unfolding, and has provided revelation to mysteries of life and defining its very purpose.

The velocity of this experience was so intense that it put 'speed of light' to shame and the term 'light years' to less than an 'instant.' It is one of those that gradually transformed from a spiritual experience to a scientific explanation, laying the foundation for a hypothesis that all scientific experiences can eventually be traced back to being a spiritual experience. The background of it all is that Lord Shiva has been consistently communicating with my inner-self over the past 45 years. The time taken in the making of this book is the time spent in interpreting revelations – an ongoing eternal dialog.

While the experience itself was so momentary and it did freeze time as a delimiting dimension, as well as space, the velocity and intensity of it were both so powerful that it left a permanent mark on my conscience. That permanent mark has kept surfacing from time to time in several wake-up calls.

Among one of those wake-up calls was an airplane crash in 1988 that made me jump out of a burning aircraft and run as fast as I could, holding the hand of my mother who was also in the flight with me and she suffered some injuries while jumping from the chute.

Another was the events of September 11, 2001 that inspired me to write a book on the tragedy of these events (a free download from www.sfuo.org)

Though it had been decided that the unique experience was a very personal event and was not to be shared with anyone, so much so that even close family members were never told about it, one of the most interesting inspirations came from none other than a couple of Mormons who visited our apartment in Chapel Hill, North Carolina.

After they read out some inspiringly beautiful prayers from the book of 'Latter Day Saints,' they were invited to a spiritual experience, to which they kindly consented.

An abrupt remark after they actually 'experienced' something was: "Devil can make anything happen."

Obviously, this was not the kind of complement that one expected after successfully transitioning a divine and spiritual experience.

What followed was a long debate and argument on what and who is God, Spirituality, and who is right or wrong, and discussion on the very topic of religion itself, and whether one religion was superior to another. To say the least, intense provocation of the argument led to sharing the "Experience" with them.

After heat settled on the debate, the visiting Mormons were convinced that the "Experience" was none less either in velocity, intensity, or importance to the one that their Prophet had experienced. They did end up inspiring and motivating to share it with anyone and everyone that I ever came in contact with. Perhaps that itself was the very purpose of my remaining life on planet while living on the borrowed time, and the result is this book in your hands.

In retrospect, one would complement those two fine Mormon gentlemen to run into the debate that finally resulted in some positive outcomes. Eventually, everything happens for a good reason and often times has a hidden divine purpose behind it. One does need to 'let go' of argument and heat at spur of the moment, in view of a realization that all that is happening 'now' is for a higher purpose and a noble cause.

In the dilemma of being a scientist, who must find a scientific explanation to every phenomenon, I had been exploring answers to this unique experience. Over forty five years of research has now yielded a scientific hypothesis to this rare happening.

In this brief presentation, the author shares hypothesis and the experience alike. Bridging the gap between science and spirituality, physical and metaphysical, existence and manifestation, abstract and defined, through revelations inspired by Lord Shiva, this book gives scientific answers to the most unanswered questions:

Is there God? If so, who is that?

Who made God?

What is the purpose of Life? Who are we?

What can one do as an individual to make a difference in this world?
Why do tragedies happen?
Why do living beings have desires?
How do we participate in the universal divine plan?
What happens after the death?
Are we the only living beings in the universe and is there life elsewhere in this inter-galactic universe?
Are we being observed?
Am I empowered to change the universe?
What is the end-all of existence?
What is our responsibility in this life?
How is the universe managed?
Who controls the universe?
What lies beyond edge of the universe?

Atheists, believers, and scientists can all benefit by drawing insight to the reality of all that is, and discover the truth beyond science and religion.

Revelations by Lord Shiva answer most of the questions that naturally come to our mind. The readers are likely to start developing further questions in their mind as they read through initial chapters of the book, and are requested to bear with till they finish reading until end of the book, as most curiosities would be answered in later chapters. By then, following the suggested exercises, one would also be able to establish their very own, personal connection to Lord Shiva and find answers to whatever they seek to know. Finally, a state of calm stillness would be reached.

Chapter 1

The Experience

It was just about going to get dark, a pre-dusk time with its own subtle cold and serenity. I was accompanied by Mr. Rajinder Kumar Gupta (close family friend hailing from Kishtwar) to this rather isolated spot behind hustle and bustle of the crowded street at Purani Mandi (Old Market) in Jammu (in the state of Jammu and Kashmir, India). When he introduced me to Mr. Mahajan, after an initial conversation, I realized that I and Mr. Mahajan were distantly related.

Mr. Mahajan was going to perform a 'yajna,' an offering of prayers. He laid out the woods and twigs, and the 'Samagari' (a collection of naturally scented herbs that is offered in the sacred fire) that he had brought. He lit the sacred fire in the pit that he created by putting a few mud bricks around the rectangular spot of ground lying in front of me. I was seated on the side of it from where I could get a clear glimpse of the picturesque 'Trikuta' range of the Himalayas, the abode of Mata Vaishno Devi (the divine mother). Jammu is at the foothills and Trikuta range flocks north-east side of the city. Mata Vaishno Devi is one of the most revered deities for Hindus, and traditions believe this Shrine to be the holiest of all since the skull of Mata Sati fell here. Mata Sati is the consort of Lord Shiva (more details in the next chapter).

On my right was an old but solid wall made of earthen brick blocks. It was partial, and apparently some of its top may have been removed or eroded with time. To my left were some long steel rods bent in the center in horse-shoe magnet style 'U' shapes, as this place was the open ground goods yard for my cousin (Subhash Bahi Sahib) who ran a steel shop at Purani Mandi Square, very close to this vicinity.

Mr. Rajinder Gupta was seated on my left. The east was on my right, the north in my front, and the west on my left. Glancing through the corner of my eyes, I could see some ruffling of leaves of the topmost portion of majestic Peepal (sacred fig, ficus religiosa) tree towards east of my house, as it was not very far.

Mr. Mahajan lit the sacred fire and started chanting hymns, and in the serenity of the setting in dusk, it was a perfect atmosphere that was pure, serene, and clean. We continued through the mantras with devotion and right after Mr. Mahajan brought the 'yajna' to a logical end by the final offering 'Purna Ahuti,' just as the final ritual of the yajna was getting over, I noticed an unusually glowing subtle blue brightness towards my right side.

As this growing blue glow caught my attention, my head automatically turned towards noticing it, and I saw a huge leg appearing out of the old wall of blocks on my right, piercing through the wall of earthen blocks. The leg was emitting the bluish glow. And at the very next moment, Lord Shiva was standing right in front of me. It was the Lord's leg that I had noticed. It was only the sacred fire pit that was between us. He was over 100 feet tall. His hair were matted. He was holding the Trishul (the trident). And the 'Ganga' flowing from his matted hair, a sprinkle of which did get me little wet.

The Lord seated in 'padma-asana' (the lotus posture) right there in front of me.

He did not move his lips, but we talked. He asked me: "Do you want me to be with you forever?"

I did not move my lips, but I know that I replied: "Your appearance is a blessing enough by itself." As I was dumbfounded by sheer majesty of the Lord's appearance, I would not have been able to talk even if I attempted to, at the spur of that moment, as I reflect on it in retrospect. The Lord did not say any words after that, but his glance conveyed something that I perceive as a blessing.

The Lord stood up, took one diagonal step and was now on my right side, with his back towards me. The Lord first raised his right leg, and then left leg, and was now in 'padma asana,' holding in this posture with both legs folded above the ground, the trident in his right hand. The Lord was now moving away from me, and started progressing higher and higher in the eastern sky. All I could hear was the subtle hiss of a non-visible vehicle that carried Lord faster than the velocity of light. As the Lord moved away from me, the glow of bluish light emitting from the Lord's body kept getting smaller in size, and I could see it reduce to the size of a star that finally disappeared in the eastern sky. Just before disappearing, I noticed the star reducing in size take a slight tangent towards the left, and then I could not see it any longer.

It took me some moments to recover from the spellbound experience, and come to terms with my surroundings. The first thing I did right after the experience was to ask Mr. Mahajan and Mr. Rajinder Gupta if both or any of them saw what I just did. I got a negative reply from both of them.

After walking home, a short distance away, I kept the experience to myself. As I now recall, it was not until the next few days when on one fine morning I shared the experience with my mother.

Motial Bhawan, our house in Jammu, was so located that I could see the sunrise and sunset, and a clear view of the surroundings from the roof. On the northeast was a good view of the Trikuta mountain range, abode of the divine mother Mata Vaishno Devi Ji. As the legend has it, the divine mother Mata Vaishno Devi Ji is a manifestation of Lakshmi, Saraswati, and Maha Shakti, each one of whom are represented as divine stones (pandalies) in the holy cave shrine that's at the far end of pilgrimage. Maha Shakti represents the consort of Lord Shiva, Sati. Owing to the deep reverence and following among all the religions and from all over the world and India, the trek to this holy cave is undertaken by millions of devotees every year. This trek is along the serpentine route through Trikuta mountains.

On second day after the experience, I climbed to the rooftop, and facing the Trikuta mountain range, sat in meditation. As I was facing the abode of the divine mother Mata Vaishno Devi Ji, I suddenly noticed a flame appear from Trikuta and progress towards my side. It kept getting closer and closer, and slowed down as it reached very close. Just about a couple of feet away from my eyes, the flame paused. Then it split into two, and one of the split flames moved diagonally towards the left. I could see both the flames, and in deep experience my eyes automatically closed, as if absorbing the light emitted by the flames.

On the third day after the sighting experience, I happened to pass by the main temple in Purani Mandi square. I just walked into the temple and stood in front of the idol of the Lord. In divine reverence, I prayed to the Lord to show me the presence. To my expected surprise, the statue of the Lord moved the trident held in right hand three times up and down.

Though I was pleasantly thankful to the Lord for blessing me with the experience yet again of showing his presence anywhere and at any time, I was also extremely ashamed to my own conscience for bothering the Lord with my stupid request, just as a small kid is ever seeking protection in the lap of mother.

Once Lord has shown the way for what I need to do and has been there always to guide my path, there never is a need to keep aspiring for sighting of the Lord.

Over the years of my life, I have had close spiritual experiences, and in the last pilgrimage to Holy Kailash and Manasarovar, in the company of esteemed devotes, we were extremely lucky to sight Lord in the cloud formation with several others, to the minutest level of detail. Several of these latter experiences, which continue to happen till date, signify that Lord is always there, everywhere, and at all times. These also tell us that one need not call for the Lord to show his presence, but always be in knowledge of the fact that Lord is always there, watching over all of us, and protecting us at all times. Lord is always in communication with us through our inner-self – it is for us to listen to the voice of our inner-self.

This happening was extremely rare and unique. Though one may call it just a personal experience, the profoundness and intensity of it is so strong that it engulfed the entire universe in its all-embracing power. Time has now come to share this experience for larger benefit of the humanity. There are urgent and compelling needs to change the world for better though the uniqueness of this wonderful experience and the subsequent dialogue that has been ongoing ever since. This need not be confined to an individual any longer.

The experience has raised probably more questions than it has answered. What it has answered is, among other things:

1. The living universe is far beyond our easy comprehension, is vast and interconnected, has life elsewhere other than just our planet, and is being governed in its entirety by Lord Shiva.
2. Shiva is here and now in the entire universe, and has always been there, and our planet is included in his care.
3. Limited human perception, and contemporary scientific knowledge, put together may not be enough to explain either the significance of such an experience or the reasoning around 'how' or 'why' it can happen.
4. Unless we are able to think out of the box of our 'Acquired Identity Syndromes,' or simulated realities, we may not ever be able to find an explanation for such an experience, or break away from the gravity of perception. Acquired Identity Syndromes result from programmatic perceptions that are embedded in our mind as make-believe realities from past experiences, and often prevent us from seeing the reality as-is (more on Acquired Identity Syndromes in chapter 4).

5. Our perception of life forms living off water and air is based on limited observation of life on our own planet. There can be forms of life created out of light, and can merge back into it.
6. Light is loaded with 'energy,' and in combination with other two elements 'consciousness,' and 'knowledge,' this trio can manifest a wide variety of existence across a broad spectrum.
7. All existence, upon annihilation, is dissolved into the single 'super element' from which everything originates. This is 'super consciousness,' or, in other words Shiva.
8. To comprehend the dissolution, and the un-manifested, a conceptualization of waves with a negative wavelength is essential. Imagine the transformation from un-manifested to manifested creation at switching of the frequency of association from negative to positive. In a similar manner, consider transformation of the frequency of association of any existence from positive to negative upon its dissolution, or annihilation.
9. There is no death. What we perceive as death is actually dissolution, or the disintegration of energy, consciousness, and knowledge that had bonded together in the form of life. We must respect life and our role in evolution of the living universe, of which we are an integral part. Our thoughts, speech, and actions shape not only the future of our own planet and the life forms on it, but also that of the entire living universe. Each life form exists in an interconnected space of this living universe to experiment, experience, and evolve. Upon dissolution, the cumulative knowledge gained from our experiences of a lifetime is uploaded through the 'abstract neural network' and becomes part of the overall life process in the living universe to enhance the knowledge. Any deliberate attempts to end life, whether our own or anyone else's, are forced interruptions into this process of knowledge enhancement, and thus must be avoided at all times. Instead, we must let the living universe evolve by itself as an organic, self-learning and adapting cybernetic system that encompasses all existence as a single interconnected entity.
10. Our role in shaping the universe is very important. In a respectful realization of this role, we must do our best at

all times to help create peace on our own planet, protect its environment in all ways possible, reverse the damages done, live in harmony with each other and all that exists, and research into creating newer ways to interconnect with other forms of existence in the universe.
11. Human brain is more than a processor and transponder. While it has tremendous capacity to process, infer, and interpret, it is also our connection to the 'abstract neural network,' the living and ever growing 'knowledge house' of the organic universe. Think of it as an invisible 'database of universal knowledge' or simply 'universal database.'
12. All our thoughts, speech, and actions are monitored and recorded. While we may perceive our thoughts to be just private to ourselves, and may think that we have no control over them, in reality we can fundamentally alter our way of thinking to become ever positive that can lead to solve all problems of the world. The artifacts we create are uploaded through the medium of 'abstract neural network' to a 'universal database' and so are the significant thoughts, actions, and speeches.

And what is not answered is a subject of research for the rising and future generations of humanity.

The chapters to follow provide some revelations to answer the unanswered questions and latter day experiences, while relating back to this one as relevant. These revelations have been part of a continuous dialog with Lord Shiva over the past 45 years, since the first experience described above on Dec 04, 1970.

Chapter 2

Getting to know Shiva

Shiva as the creator, the ultimate protector, and the dissolver, and also the Super Element as Super Consciousness, has a two-fold role. First is in the formless Super Element as Super Consciousness that manifests as a combination of consciousness, knowledge, and energy, and creates all known forms of life and what we have largely known as the living universe. In second role, Shiva is the one who manages this creation from its inception to dissolution.

Shiva, as depicted in Indian mythology is the one of human form, with mated hair, the river Ganges flowing out of the headlock, with crescent moon adoring the head, wearing lion-skin, holding trident, and blessing everyone. This form represents the manifestation of Shiva as a human being who walked on our planet over 7000 years ago.

To know the distinction, the formless aspect of Shiva has no beginning or end, is infinite, and is the Super Consciousness.

The image that emerges in most minds of a form of Shiva is the one associated with human-like form. Since most people have difficulty in relating to the formless aspect of Shiva, they prefer to know the Lord with a finite form, and in that respect, they chose to know the Lord as depicted in Indian mythology. We need to know that the finite form is limited, and is only symbolic. The finite form can be a way to relate to something that you can see and behold as an object, but it is just a representation of the formless. Just like the path by itself is not the destination, but a means to it; the form can at best be contemplated to comprehend an image, with an eventual goal to know the formless. It is not even necessary to comprehend or see an image – one can directly endeavor to know the formless.

Temples all over the world have statues of Lord Shiva that represent the human form, but we must know that it is just a way to behold an image in front of our eyes that invites reverence. Ultimately we must know the truth is that Shiva is formless, and is always everywhere.

The formless is the un-manifested, and the one with a form is a representation of the manifestation. The human-like form is a manifestation.

Each and every object that we associate with Shiva – from Damru (the two-sided drum) to Kamandal (the bowl with a handle) to Trishul (the trident) to all else, there is a greater significance to it.

Wearing the lion skin around waist signifies that we need to be as strong as the lion when it comes to exercising caution and self-discipline in matters related to the organs that are held underneath.

Meditating while squatted on the deer skin denotes the humble nature and purity of the deer as a vegetarian and a harmless creature that only beautifies the surroundings to be the starting point basis on which we build on, in our practice of meditation, and through this practice opening up a connection to the ANN (Abstract Neural Network, see more details on the subject in next chapter).

Trishul – the trident by itself collectively signifies the Super Consciousness that manifests into consciousness, knowledge, and energy. The center arrow signifies the element of consciousness, and the two side arrows stand for elements of knowledge, and energy. The staff that elongates extension of the center element arrow, supports the two side extension arrows, and provides a base to hold it all together signifies the purpose of all existence. Whether living or non-living, all existence is drawing upon the three basic elements of consciousness, knowledge, and energy, and need to be grounded in reality of the world in which they exist and its environment as test bed for experimentation during the life span of their manifested existence, yet ever yearning to merge with their very origin upon dissolution as indicated by the higher pointing center arrow of the trident. In that sense, the trident is a complete representation of the origin and ultimate purpose of life, and shows a way to live and do, indicated by slight inward pointing of the two extended arrows representing that both knowledge and energy must be centered towards consciousness. An inward connection leads to inspiring thoughts that lead to noble actions. Focusing on the external, outward distractions can lead one astray and lose track. Thus, returning to connect with consciousness would keep the integrated manifestation stay on track and achieve the purpose of life to return useful values and eventually merge with the origin, the super consciousness, upon dissolution.

Damru – the two sided drum with a single bead that alternately strikes on the two sides is rhythm of the living organic, living universe. With each to and fro beat of the drum, the cycles of manifestation (creation) and de-manifestation (dissolution) are realized in an endless eternal bliss.

Kamandal – the bowl with a handle that a yogi or sanyasi uses to collect offerings, signifies that Shiva is asking us for something. Here is ask - the first request is to give up all our anger, feelings of hatred or jealousy towards anyone, and all the fear that we have from any sources. The second request is to make our efforts in all ways possible to restore the damaged environment of our planet, eliminate hunger and poverty by creating interdependence, and create permanent global peace by uniting the world. The third request is that we must all connect with Shiva to drive our spiritual aspirations, and with each-other to fulfill these aspirations through collective efforts.

Rudraksh - sacred beads signify the great healing power of nature. Living as close as possible with Mother Nature is the best medicine. Natural, non-processed vegetation and its fruits grown organically and in the wild are healing.

Dand – wooden stand to rest arm during meditation signifies the role of trees (from which wood is obtained) as sustainers and supporters of life on the planet. To become the base for life, we have a lot to learn from the trees. They provide the shelter, the oxygen, are retainers of moisture, and provide us the fruits. We need to emulate the tree-like qualities to become a better human being.

Nandi (the Bull, and symbolic vehicle of Shiva) is the beholder of truth and is detached from all existence (the side glance stance of Nandi signifies detachment).

Ardhanarishwar

To know the all-encompassing, all pervading nature of Shiva, it is important to discover the Ardhanarishwar (half-male, half-female) aspect. As the process of manifestation starts decomposing from Super Consciousness to Consciousness, Knowledge, and Energy, and then all existence as a combination of these three basic elements, on the scale of variance so many aspects and attributes related to existence are created.

At the highest level, Shiva represents Super Consciousness, and at the creation level, the male and the female, signifying the potential and the energy.

The half male and half female representation of Shiva indicates the existence of all the masculine and feminine qualities in a single entity that can take any form upon manifestation.

To know ourselves in the true image of Shiva, we must discover in ourselves a true mother and father as both parents of all that exists. This knowing as both parents of existence lies in showing respect and restraint while using resources of the planet, not hurting anyone, caring for everyone including all animals and plants, with unconditional love and respect, in the same way that Shiva cares for us.

This form also signifies a future – where all humans would rise above desires and evolve to a form of beings that is beyond sex, eventually emerging as beings of light. It implies a transformation from current physical bodies to a form that is just light.

Pashupatinath

As the protector of all animals, insects, and birds, Shiva inspires us to bear with them while respecting all forms of existence. Pashupatinath means protector of all existence.

Every single creature has a purpose to its existence. Even the dinosaurs existed on the planet towards fulfillment of a purpose. We are all continually evolving. Dinosaurs were huge in physical size, but had brain of the size of a peanut. Since then, evolution has resulted in mental growth that has more to do with intellect than sheer physical size. Dinosaurs became extinct when there was no utility left to their existence.

As humans, we are a much evolved species, and are even able to control our environment. It is in this environment that we coexist with other species on the planet. If we are 'Shiva' inspired to protect the animals, then the very first step for us is to protect the environment to prolong the longevity of endangered species.

Mount Kailash: healing, yet approachable

Known as the abode of Lord Shiva, the Holy Mount Kailash is healing, yet approachable. It is revered as sacred by all religions of the world, and respected by all species in habitation on the planet. The very sight of it is awesome. Holy Mount Kailash is respected by not touching it to preserve its beauty and sacredness. Kailash is sacred and is circled around its awesomeness by all seekers of truth, healing, love, compassion, and a peaceful dissolution alike.

The Pilot Mountain in North Carolina alias 'Carolina Kailash' rises above the rest as 'Jatta,' the matted hair-lock of Shiva, a representation of the form of the divine. Owing to its awesome height and beauty, its very sight is magnetic, healing, and living around the mountain is an experience in enjoying the power of divine healing.

Shivalingam - the symbol identified with Shiva

To know and to realize what it means by the symbol of Shivalingam, a cylindrical stone form that is rounded at the top, one needs to be able to see the significance behind the symbol, rather than follow a ritual.

Shiva is compared to be over 100 times equivalent of the most charming man, the *Kamadeva*. Parvati (Shiva's wife) was the envy of her friends who said: 'your husband is over 100 times more charming than the most handsome man ever known.'

As one of the legendary tales has it, narrated by James Hewitt in his book 'The Complete Yoga Book – the yoga of meditation, posture and breathing,' [1] charm of Shiva was so mesmerizing that all the ladies including wives of the sages were following him. Out of the fear of losing them, Rishis (sages) collectively cursed Shiva, and in humbleness out of his all-encompassing nature, Shiva embraced the curse. At the time of embracing this curse, Lord Shiva shunned the symbolic male organ and it took the form of a fossil rock. If one were to believe this story, there is a symbolic interpretation to this moment as it marked a significant transition in evolution – the one that prompts all humans to rise above the desire, and the Shivalingam has ever since been worshipped by humanity in its repentance for rudeness, and in an effort to seek forgiveness from the Lord.

To know the significance of Shivalingam, the seeker of ultimate truth wishes to realize Shiva as formless in spirit, to be one with it, and to rise above all that exists – the mortal vices, desires, temptations, restrictions, indulgences, and prejudice.

To worship Shivalingam as a material object of stone and seek a personal material gain is certainly not the objective of any true seeker of Shiva.

The one who can overcome human fallacies, and evolve to a higher level of existence is a Shiva seeker. This higher level is attained by evolving the consciousness through the practice of meditation.

At Amarnath Ji, a pilgrimage in North India in the State of Jammu & Kashmir, in the Laddakh region, on the eve of August full moon, droplets inside the holy cave freeze to form a high-rising ice form that is revered by devotees as 'Shivalingam.'

Panchamukhi

In Panchamukhi depictions (the five faces) – Shiva is represented at the two extremes of calmness and universal benefactor to the angry lord disappointed with our specific behaviors.

Kalyansundaram is the all-blissful form posture.

Though the Lord is ever blissful, the extreme angry expression is a warning signal to all humans to behave.

Our collective and cumulative actions over the past 100 plus years have significantly damaged the environment of our planet – and soon we are approaching a point where the damage would be beyond repair.

On similar other fronts, we have failed to acknowledge our role as individuals in the pursuit of creating world peace, eliminating hunger, and most of us continue to be mute spectators in affairs of the world as they unfold gradually in any direction – whether positive or negative.

In the extreme angry pose, Shiva continues to remind us of our specific role on the planet.

The third eye

Shiva's third eye is a representation of an extra dimension of knowledge – a new awakening. The third eye location is just above the center of the eye brows, in middle of the forehead, and in the vertical (in contrast to the two eyes that are positioned horizontally).

At its core, Shiva is the origin of all creation.

If one would like to visualize Shiva at the physical level, one needs to think of a source that is constantly providing for creation and its sustenance. In that sense, the closest simile to what we as humans are able to comprehend can be drawn to the Sun that has some traits in common. Shiva symbolizes the giving. So does the Sun. Shiva is the ultimate creator, representing super consciousness, from whom the knowledge and energy are driven, and the unique combination of three forms in varied hues brings to life the living universe. Sun is the sole source of energy for powering up and to sustain the life on our planet. The entire energy is being transmitted to our planet in the form of light.

At any given point in time, one needs to ask: 'Have I done anything to realize the purpose of my life?' Each one of us has to know who we are, and our specific role in life on this planet. It is a surprising fact that each one of us continues to live by what we are faced to do following a routine. Hardly anyone cares to explore the purpose of life.

Face to Face with Shiva

Just like earth emerged out of fragments of the mass that was splintered off the sun and moon came into being off the splinters of earth, the Knowledge and Energy are driven out of Consciousness. The sun, the earth, and the moon are in a way analogous to the consciousness, knowledge, and energy. One is driven from the other, yet they are all interdependent. The earth revolves around the sun, and the moon around the earth. The knowledge is inspired by the consciousness, and the energy is materialized with that knowledge.

What we can see, touch and feel is all energy. Whether in material form or not, all energy is eventually driven from the consciousness. The earth and moon are created out of the sun, and continually keep driving energy from the sun. All life on this planet is sustained by the sun.

The sun and the entire universe exist within the third eye of Shiva. The universe, as we know it, is blind to everything that exists beyond the realms of physical existence. The third eye is at the center-stage of all creation, dissolution, and rebirthing of existence in various forms. While consciousness keeps evolving in a continuous cycle, and knowledge keeps growing, it is the same energy that is recycled through the creative process over and over again.

If there was to be no sun, there would be no earth. If there would be no earth, there would be no moon. The moon and earth exist as long as the sun exists.

On a similar note, the knowledge and energy would continue to exist as long as the super consciousness instantiates itself in various forms. When the cycles of instantiation are over, the knowledge and energy would dissolve in super consciousness. The super consciousness can continue to exist as un-manifested.

The ultimate being of all forms is Shiva, representing both the manifested and the un-manifested. The un-manifested form, the 'male' half of Shiva is the potential. The manifested form, the 'female' half of Shiva is the energy in motion that exists and recycles in the third eye. The manifestation is created out of the un-manifested as per the knowledge that ever keeps enhancing itself with newer cycles of creation.

Bramha represents the knowledge that is necessary to bring consciousness to a form. Vishnu represents the energy that is brought to shape by the knowledge that operates upon consciousness to give it a form. Just like the sun, earth and moon relationship, the Bramha and Vishnu are brought to existence by Shiva.

Opening of the third eye implies getting to have knowledge of the extra dimension that all forms of existence emerge from the unmanifested formless Shiva, and upon eventual dissolution merge onto it, as a new awakening.

The legend has a tale of Shiva getting angry while Kamdeva (the lord of desire) interfered to break Shiva's long, seemingly never-ending meditation, and opening of the third eye of Shiva burned Kamdeva. While Rati, the wife of Kamdeva prayed to Shiva to restore her husband's life, Shiva blessed her with a boon that Kamdeva would be revived to life in another age. Interpreting this tale in the modern day context, we need to wake up to a higher reality, and realize the very purpose of our life. As long as we continue to dwell in the desire fulfillment mode, we deprive ourselves of the enlightenment. The opening of the third eye for us is a realization that there is a higher purpose to our life. Revival of Kamdeva in another age and form signifies human evolution to a form of light, rising above the desire as we now know of it in the context of our physical existence. The other age is when humans would have evolved to the light form, and the form of desire would have also changed from physical lust to spiritual aspiration. At that point, the actions would be at an altogether different level.

The position of third eye just above the center of eyebrows also represents the Ajna chakra (the subtle energy center associated with the emotion of enlightenment representing the new awakening, see the chapter on meditation).

Nataraj

The cosmic dance depiction of Shiva as Nataraj (the king of dance), lifting left leg and balancing over a demon dwarf who symbolizes ignorance. Two most common forms of this dance are the *Lasya* (the gentle form) associated with creation of the universe, and the *Tandava* (the violent form) associated with the dissolution. Shiva with four arms and flying locks, back right hand holding the *damru*; the front right hand is in the *abhaya* posture (the fear-not gesture); the back left hand holding fire (Agni); and the front left hand is held across chest in the elephant-trunk pose, with wrist and fingers pointed downward toward the uplifted left foot. The locks of hair spread out in strands interspersed with flowers, and the whole figure is encircled by a ring of flames. In the Nataraja form, Shiva is shown as the source of all movement within the cosmos.

The Lasya and the Tandava are two aspects of Shiva's nature of creation and dissolution in order to re-create, or tearing down to build again in an ever growing evolution of consciousness, the eternal cycle.

The gestures of the dance represent Shiva's five activities: creation (symbolized by *damru* the drum), protection (by the "fear-not" posture of the hand), dissolution (by the fire), embodiment (by the foot planted on the ground), and release (by the foot held aloft). These five activities are performed within each cycle from creation to dissolution, and through each cycle, there is an accumulation of net new knowledge that aids an ongoing evolution of consciousness that keeps progressing with each fresh cycle.

There is a lot to take from this form – for our everyday life we need to know that we are always under the protection of Shiva and thus never need to be afraid of anything. We can be ever connected with Shiva, and know that life is a platform to create new knowledge by opportunities it offers to interact with our environment. While we are in this world, we need to be grounded in the reality, yet not be constrained by its binding. We need to overcome ignorance and know that sky is the limit in what we can imagine, think, plan, and do. While we are empowered to create, we need not be attached with whatever we create, and need to be prepared to let it dissolve. We need to know that while there is nothing perfect, with each new cycle of creation we can improve. At the micro-level, it is like re-inventing ourselves every single day of our life as we evolve. We also need to know that after every fall we would emerge stronger. There is nothing that would last forever, for everything and all existence needs to eventually dissolve so that a newer and better form can emerge, and as such, we need to be detached from what exists.

The entire philosophy for life is picturized between the two dance forms of Lasya, an expression of happiness and joy; and Tandava, an expression of the act of balancing by being aware of our ignorance, being grounded in the reality, though being aware that nothing is ever perfect and that all that exists would eventually get dissolved so that a newer form can emerge, yet make our very best efforts at creating newer forms of knowledge in a fearless manner, not being attached to existence though being very part of it, and a yearning to be released from all binding upon dissolution. An integration of these two visualizations of Lasya and Tandava forms signifies that we can be always happy and joyful, and do the very best that we can towards fulfillment of spiritually inspired aspirations, and while doing so, live fearless under the protection of Shiva.

Kali Ma

In related images, Kali Ma (the Mother Divine) signifies the ultimate feminine power drawn from the heart of Shiva – every girl is eventually empowered by Shiva to destroy the evil, and to celebrate the good. In this image, Kali Ma is stepping on the chest of Shiva. She is wearing a garland of skulls, and a skirt of amputed arms, her tongue is spread out, and she is holding an instrument with a sharp blade in one hand, and a severed head in the other.

In Shiva's surrender as the ultimate masculine potential (Beeja, or Seedling plant) to the power of the feminine (Shakti) for any meaningful manifestation of the abstraction to achieve workable results on the planet of our current existence, everyone is deeply motivated to respect the feminine.

The severed heads represent the destroyed egos, and amputed arms represent that the wrong actions on our part must be destroyed and corrections need to be made. Her extended tongue signifies that we need to evaluate our words before we let them out. We are unable to speak without the use of tongue, and once we release the words, these can't be called back even if we extend our tongue. The legend has it that Ma Kali would extend her tongue to lick the drops of blood even before those touched the ground while she slay a demon bestowed with boon that any of his blood drop falling on the ground would raise the exact replica of that demon. In simile, if we utter bad words, they lay the foundation for germination of evil. Thus, we need to avoid uttering any words that reflect anger, hatred, jealousy, or anything that would lead to bad results. Words have lot of power. Once released, these can't be captured by the swiftest steads.

Reverence to Ma Kali signifies that we ever stay tuned to our true-self, and never get lost from the path of righteousness. If we ever get on the wrong path and get headed towards performing wrong actions or wrong speech, the divine mother Ma Kali in her grace would correct us by destroying our new ego (representing the freshly severed head), and cut the off-tracked wrong actions (amputed arms), purifying our intensions to avoid any wrong thoughts from germination that can lead to wrong speech (extended tongue) and immediately put us on the right path. Once we realize the true significance of the symbolic image of Kali Ma, our heart is filled with reverence, and our thoughts are instantly purified. Thoughts lead to action, and once purified, by destruction of the ego, would lead to noble action. If ever, on the path of action we get distracted and start treading on the wrong side, we must recall the symbolic significance of the image of Kali Ma and get to immediately correct our wrong actions (the amputed arms).

While some initially consider the image as dreadful and fear from it, knowing the true symbolic significance of the image leads one to reverence.

While what is good or evil is largely a matter of human perception, when connected to the inner-self, and through it to the ANN (*Abstract Neural Network* – see next chapter for details), the answer is just one and simple. No one can have the cake and eat it too, meaning that we can't be headed in two different directions at the same time and yet call them both to be the correct ones – the inner-self always guides us in the right direction. And that is exactly where Shiva resides within each one of us, and keeps guiding us through the entire course of our life. It is for us to ask the inner-self, and to listen.

The core of our inner-self is in the direct replica of Shiva as the consciousness that is ever connected to its source – the Super Element, the Super Consciousness, the Shiva.

In that sense, it is imperative to connect to and know our own true self, as we make endeavors to get to know Shiva. This is the process of self-realization.

Self-realization is not just about knowing who we are, but even to know to as to what our connection with Shiva is. ANN plays a very important role in the making of this connection.

Lord Shiva's grace is all embracing and excludes none. The devotees who may feel the lowest of the low and simply chant 'Aum Namah Shivaya,' they all instantly connect with all-pervading divine grace of the Lord.

Per Ramayana, both Ram and Ravana have worshipped Lord Shiva. While Ram established Shivalingam at Rameshwaram and worshipped the Lord before embarking on an extremely important project to pray for its successful completion – building a bridge between India and Sri Lanka through the Bay of Bengal that merges with the Indian Ocean, Ravana worshipped the Lord for grant of strength and boons.

While the world may be divided in either following Ram or Ravana, they both had something in common – their devotion for Lord

Shiva. This has a great significance – think of it as the yin and the yang, the positive and the negative, the perceived good and bad, the angel and the devil, all as manifestations of the two sides of a coin within our own self. Just as the rim of the coin binds its two faces together, it is an integration of our own internal manifestations that we need to achieve and strike a balance for the stability of our nature.

Knowing Shiva

Think of the formless before thinking of the form. The formless is the one from whom all forms emerge.

The formless Shiva is the origin, the source and also the ultimate destination of all creation. It is upon whom all merge at dissolution.

The form of Shiva that emerged and walked on our planet of existence over 7000 years ago as a living being amongst us that Shri Anandamurti has described in his book *'Namah Shivaya Shantaya'* [2] can be considered as a manifestation that materialized on-demand. The demand is generated by the need of the time on our planet.

When we come to a point that a correction is required, whether it is the need to get rid of the dinosaurs as a species since they failed to deliver any useful values, or when human beings are collectively behaving to create a state of anarchy, the correction will happen.

It is in the context of making such a correction that Shiva appeared on our planet. At the time of Shiva's advent on the planet, there was no law and order. Besides establishing marriage as an institution, teaching people how to conduct themselves, Shiva also created music, several dance and art forms.

Shiva embraced everyone irrespective of color of skin or caste or creed, creating equality and justice. Shiva also protected all animals, birds, insects, and plant forms. As Pashupati, Shiva is known as the protector of animals.

While walking on the planet in human form, Shiva did all that was possible under control to establish order and compassion.

As Acharya Anandamurti describes, Shiva stands for "Always welfare for all." And in that context and spirit, Acharya refers to "Universal" as compared to "human" as Shiva does encompass all, and excludes none in the name of providing welfare. There is a deep meaning in the word 'Shiva' itself, and the essence is noble and positive inspiration that results in such thoughts and actions that aim to do good to everyone in all ways possible.

While Shiva is also known to be correcting us, in a prudent fulfillment of duties while living on this planet of existence, it is more from a perspective of providing guidance to make us do meaningful contributions to return useful values from our experimentation with life. If we don't do a course correction, there is an ever-existent potential to go hay-wired in our experimentation with life and that would only return values that are not of much use.

In current times, we can connect to Shiva through opening up our inner-self and draw course correction, inspiration, and even some dictations to draw up plans for our day to day life achievements – these are voices of the inner-self that come to all of us naturally through the all-pervading mercy of Shiva.

In various forms and shapes, God dwells in all that exists and also in that which is non-existent. The existence is a manifestation of energy in a form that is visible. There is a lot that can't be seen, touched, felt, or smelled, but it certainly can be visualized. It is the abstractness of non-existent that is even more important than what exists. No manifestation is possible without an appropriate coming together of energy, knowledge, and consciousness in a form that can fulfill a meaningful purpose.

Shiva resides in this abstract form in all entities living and non-living. Any one, who aspires to attain Shiva, can do so easily by showing respect to all existence. Showing respect to food is by not wasting it. Showing respect to material is by not consuming too much of it, and take only as much as is needed to meet the essential needs of oneself and preserve the rest for use by others. Showing respect to the environment is by protecting it. Showing respect to everyone is by not insulting them, and being able to see an image of the divine within them.

The advent of Shiva on our planet over 7000 years ago was one of the most fortunate happenings of all times. In grace, Shiva emerged to create discipline among the chaos. While one may even think of Shiva to be a human being like all others on the planet, the reality is that every human being is a replica of Shiva in some form. It is the connection to our inner-self that enables us to visualize. Shiva appeared on the planet and even lived here like a human leading an exemplary life, just to convey to each one of us that all of us do have the potential within our own selves to do good deeds, to set an example for others to follow, excel and create knowledge in several diverse fields, and above all, be a compassionate and disciplined human being.

In knowing Shiva, we must never attempt at separating the creator from its manifestation when it comes to specific instances of leading by example.

An angry father in one extreme of the five faces wants to tell the children to correct their behavior instead of blindly accepting every single kind of behavior. It is same benevolent father (as Kalyanasundaram) who tolerates us, and loves us unconditionally, wants us to succeed, and is asking us to correct our erroneous behavior.

If we can see through this request from the father, the creator, and manifestation as Shiva who led the mortal world by example while walking on our planet over 7000 years ago, we can clearly find the correlation between the symbolic metaphysical, and the actual physical parent.

This correlation, in the context of metaphysical, is the same as to Jesus referring to God as the father. Kartikeya, the son of Shiva, revered by one and all, is known to be a strong warrior. Also known as Murugan, he was the commander of Army that finally defeated Asuras (the demons) and led the Devas (divine beings) to victory. To draw an analogy, empowered by Shiva, like Kartikeya, we all are capable of defeating the impure thoughts, feelings of hatred or jealousy, and lead ourselves to victory over our own senses and thoughts to become positive.

It is building on the positive that is required in today's world to create interdependence, and to mutually cooperate to unite the communities as a single nation. Today we have no Asuras to fight with, there are no major wars between armies of the nations, and world is gradually moving towards becoming a no-war zone. The war against terrorism can easily be won by a change in the hearts and developing of positive attitudes.

Continuing on these positives, and conquering our own inner negative thoughts to get rid of feelings of jealousy and hatred towards anyone, we are now set to take further steps in this direction to finally achieve the dream of uniting the globe as a single nation.

Considering the difference of about 5000 years between the times of when they walked on the planet, Kartikeya as the son of Shiva, and Jesus as the son of God, we can draw some parallels in what they achieved and intended to do.

Face to Face with Shiva

Kartikeya established order among chaos, assembled an Army, and led it to victory. Defeating the forces of evil, Kartikeya was instrumental in leading the good to victory.

Lord Jesus, the Christ, operating 5000 years later on the planet, established an order of self-sacrifice for overall good of the humanity, and led the world by example.

If one was to mark a change in the trend that happened over a course of 5000 years, the earlier time marked a leader who led as a warrior as well as a spiritual transformer. In the earlier days, there was convergence of both these aspects. As we descend to more recent years, we see a change in the trend.

Lord Buddha, operating on the planet 2500 years ago, though born as a prince, shunned royal throne and worldly life to become a sage, embraced austerity, and performed penance under extremely hard conditions to finally achieve enlightenment, and led the world through a spiritual journey.

Lord Jesus, the Christ, operating 2000 years ago on the planet, was also a spiritual leader, who eventually sacrificed, leading the whole world by example, for overall good of the humanity.

The trend is shifting from a unified spiritual, political, and an Army General all rolled in one (like Kartikeya), to a split in the roles in the latter days, and the latter day leaders becoming self-sacrificing.

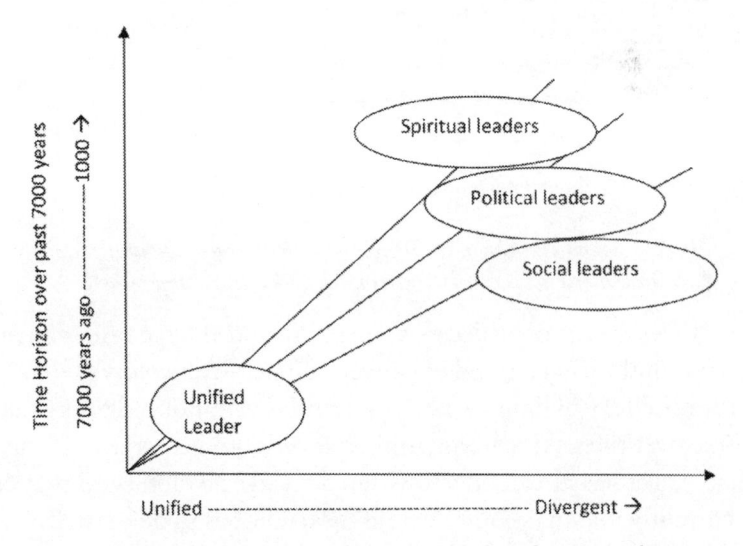

Fig. 2.1: Trend over the past 7000 years – from unification to divergence in leadership style, traits, attributes, capabilities, and focus

Over the millenniums, leaders have emerged, from unified to divergent, and indicating a trend of scattering from a single, unified ray of light to its divergent colors.

If Shiva was that unified light, we have had several hues, shades, and specific divergent colors of that light over all these years, and are now peaking out at divergence. The time has now come to start converging again, unifying the colors to create a single spectrum – this also has to reflect in our attitudes, thinking patterns, actions, and the results that we achieve by what we do.

Over the next 70 years, it is projected that the trend will be shifting from currently divergent leadership styles to a unified spiritual, political, and social leadership, all rolled in one.

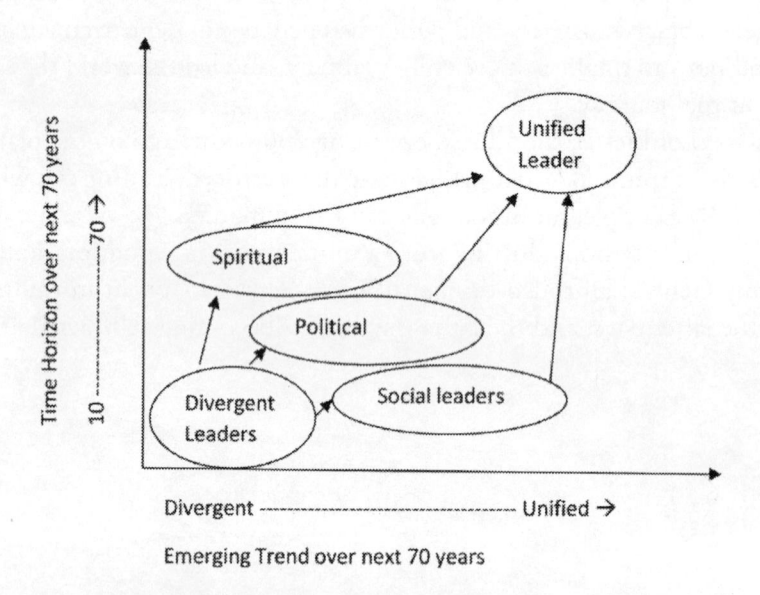

Fig. 2.2: Trend over the next 70 years – from divergence to unification in leadership style, traits, attributes, capabilities, and focus.

Over the next few decades, leaders would emerge from divergent to unified, indicating a trend of converging scattered colors of light to a single, unified ray of light. When this trend is extrapolated to predict an outcome over the next few millenniums, we would emerge as beings of light, as Shiva has already demonstrated a clear possibility to that end. Our currently material bodies would have no need to be born, live, and die, or get reborn.

If Shiva is that unified light from where we started, and we got diverged, we would now have to converge several hues, shades, and specific divergent colors of the light that were spread over all these years and millenniums. Integration, convergence, and unification are the key paradigms over which we would need to operate on, moving forward.

The unification of ideologies would lead to integration of the globe as a single nation, where we have no major differences among people of world – economically, socially, or politically. What it implies is that there is complete interdependence, freedom of thought, speech, and expression, religions promote harmony and unification, and also complete economic prosperity that emerges from a realization of 'there is no need for having more.'

Individual greed can lead to possess, and we are currently at the peak of materialization. As we graduate over this peak to a realization of the futility of the capitalist possessive model, the world would gradually be on the path to de-materialization. The capitalist possessive model was a necessity of the world hitherto, a must-do to prove its very futility after it peaked out of its success. Going forward, the only model that would emerge is that of volunteering – a new breed of entrepreneurs would sprout, the ones who believe in not cutting out the competition by elimination, but would rather cooperate and merge through unified convergence.

In the corporate world, mergers and acquisitions are already steps in that direction – it eventually pays off to combine resources and deploy those flexibly to achieve more as a team, as compared to what any of the pre-mergers would achieve individually.

A new paradigm of collaborative entrepreneurship is also slowly emerging, resulting in bringing together of like-minded folks to pool in collective efforts in a volunteering model for overall benefit of the humanity and protection of environment of the planet.

Shiva is all about unification, integration, and convergence. Since Super Consciousness is the single super element from which all manifestation is driven, after the union of the individual elements of consciousness, knowledge, and energy, and unto it all that exists finally dissolves, there is a lot more to it than what is just said here to know Shiva.

Think of ongoing eternal cycles of ever new creation and dissolutions, each cycle providing a new platform for improvement based on sum total of all current and previously uploaded knowledge. Within each cycle, all manifested creation can draw spiritual inspirations through an ever-available connection with Lord Shiva, transform those inspirations to thought and action, and have the freedom to think and act fearlessly under the protection of Lord Shiva at all times.

In the constant rhythmic cosmic dance that leads to alternate beats of the Damru as the cycles of manifestation and de-manifestation, each cycle leads to higher cumulative knowledge through the extra-universal ANN (abstract neural network) connections. These higher cumulative knowledge resulting from constant experimentations leads to an evolution of the consciousness – this by itself is the sole purpose of existence of the manifested universe and consequentially all life forms on our planet of mortal existence.

With each subsequent cycle of the Damru drum beat, as new manifestations occur, some of the unknown merges with the known as an expanded base of extra-universal knowledge is now available to benefit from, for this new cycle of evolution. The extra-universal knowledge base is ever growing with new values being continually uploaded.

This unveils the secret of life and that of existence. Our collective roles as nations and communities, and specific individual roles as human beings are driven from our very own realizations of 'who' we are as a nation, community, or as an individual, and what we are inspired to do.

Creative visualization is the process through which we can define our very own vision and mission.

Creating unity in diversity

If we create new off-shoots of religion, cult, society, or a nation, we build further structures for disagreement, arch rivalry, segmentation, discontent, and eventually hatred. The task on hand is not to create any further divisions of humanity, but to build unity. Combining the synergy of homogeneity and augmenting it with the learning from diversity is the challenge that we face today.

Following the example from Shiva, in whose incarnation Sadashiva made all attempts humanely possible 7000 years ago, the challenge for each one of us today is to engage the world in a dialog for peace. This dialog is something that begins at home, extends to the community, and eventually to the nation, and the whole world in a pursuit towards unification.

The challenge is to create a future that celebrates the lessons learnt from history, not the one that repeats the history.

If Texas had stayed on its own instead of joining the union of USA, would it have a Master Control Facility at Houston? Would it have ended up as an independent nation biting its glory of staying stand-alone?

Perhaps yes or no. If each one of the Texans would have owned upon themselves a commitment to strive for doing nothing else but just the very best, and kept their head high each day by virtue of what they did collectively as a nation, they may have even achieved more individually as a state nation than what USA has achieved today collectively. If they did not have at the head a leadership that led by example, motivated each one of them individually to do the best and leave the rest, then the later may have been true.

Theoretical dissection of possibilities is not the means to any end. It can merely be an enabler to think in a positive direction, and build a road to the future that embraces all potentials. Even when the energies directed in the negative direction merge with a road that leads to the positive direction, the end result is all moving in the direction of the positive. The challenge is to cut the negative paths where we see a potential of them merging into the positive highway, and build an exit that can merge with it.

Shiva's Army

When Prophet Mohammad (pbuh) was establishing an army to fight for righteousness, his initiative was to dissuade masses from idol worship and let them realize Shiva as formless.

Islam, at its very foundation, builds on and drives forward the basics of Vedanta. Since they both preach non-idol worship and reach goal of knowing the divine as formless, Swami Dayanand Saraswati and Prophet Mohammad (pbuh) establish basically similar schools of thought and practice in Arya Samaj, and Islam, respectively.

Swami Dayanand Saraswati attained enlightenment when he saw a rat climb up a Shiva-lingam, while worshipping on Shivaratri. The premise of his realization was that if Lord could not protect himself from a rat, how shall the Lord protect us? It could be interpreted differently as that the Lord does not turn anyone away: not even a tiny creature. Also, that the Shiva-lingam is only a symbolic representation of the divine. In truth, the divine is indeed formless. Swami Dayanand

Saraswati established a school of thought that aimed at goodness for humanity, a disciplined life by following an ethical code of conduct, and turning folks away from idol worship with aim to encourage everyone to realize the divine as formless. Islam is founded on exactly same sound fundamental principles. Eventually what matters or makes the difference is in the interpretation, as interpreters can twist or turn the meaning in a completely different direction.

Aurangzeb, the second last Mogul emperor to rule India interpreted religion in an extremely radical manner. He declared that he would not have dinner till he saw at the end of each day either 40,000 folks converted from Hinduism to Islam, or have them all killed to weigh 40 seers of sacred threads snatched from those beheaded. Sikh religion was formed as an army of warriors to protect Hindus from conversion with its climax while Aurangzeb ordered beheading of Guru Shri Tegh Bahadur Ji, the ninth guru of Sikhs - the site of martyrdom is at Sis Ganj Gurdwara in Delhi.

Aurangzeb, though a staunchly honest man who would not accept even a penny from his royal treasures for his own sake and would eat his meal out of his own hard labor that made him earn a few pennies by stitching and selling caps, he used all the resources at his end to slaughter Hindus and force a conversion to Islam. That is not what a Shiva's army was inspired to do.

In a complete about turn from the very basis for founding Sikhism, the latter day interpreters forced innocent youngsters to take to terrorism and unleash atrocities on unarmed Hindus by hijacking buses in Punjab, lining up Hindus and firing at them. When Indira Gandhi, then prime minister of India was gunned down in 1984 by her Sikh security guard, the event unleashed an unprecedented wave of violence against Sikhs, resulting in lynching of so many innocent individuals for no fault of theirs.

Though Islam and Vedanta have the exactly same founding principles, Aurangzeb opted to kill thousands by the day. Though Sikhs were the protector of Hindus, waves of violence resulted in losses to both communities.

One needs to question as to what exactly went wrong? The answer is simple – when anyone interprets religion with a selfish motive and uses that interpretation to instigate others for unleashing violent acts against a particular community, it is a wrong interpretation of the religion. Just like spirituality is above religion and humanity above all else, we need to realize the Shiva inside each one of us – and know that Shiva is inspiring us to unite, not divide. This unity is starting first with the mind-body-soul integration, and consequentially encompassing the communities, nations, planet, and the universe in this integration. This comes about naturally when one connects to the inner-self, and from there to formless nature of the divine.

When anyone is seeking to see the divine in a particular form, it is a craving to attach a symbolic representation to the formless. Perhaps the highest knowledge in this universe would be to know that all creation is manifested out of the formless, and upon dissolution all existence would merge into the same formless origin of its creation. It is in nature of the formless to evolve as Consciousness. In this manifested universe, the purpose of creation is to bring to life the forms that can experiment to return useful values. Life is an experience in learning for each one of us. Through the process of learning, we collectively end up enhancing the knowledge.

Learning is larger than life: Knowledge grows to evolve Consciousness.

In reality, all humanity with other forms of life on the planet is Shiva's army. Since each one of us is engaged in experimenting with life in some way or the other, and returning some values out of that experience, we are all part of a living and learning organism. The living universe is an interconnected system of neural processors that continually interact and exchange the specific learning experiment results to aid the growth of knowledge. It is this collective knowledge of all of species across the entire universe that helps in the evolution of consciousness.

Formless Shiva is the God and is at the origin of all existence as its source. It is also the ultimate destination home of all created existence upon which all manifestations merge after dissolution.

First principle of Vedanta

Vedanta is less of a religion, and more of a philosophy for life based on the premise of knowledge. This knowledge reflects the contents of four major scriptures – Rig Veda, Yajur Veda, Athar Veda, and Sam Veda. The literal meaning of term Vedanta signifies the end of Vedas, and significance of implementation of this accumulated knowledge from the scriptures to the practice of life.

Vedas are considered as the eternal knowledge. Rigveda is known to be the oldest book. From generation to generation, the divine knowledge was passed on from sages by word of mouth, until only 10,000 years ago when the scriptures were documented. The essence of Rigveda is: "Let Noble thoughts come to us from all sides."

All knowledge is driven from Consciousness that is ever connected with the divine "Super Consciousness." In an abstract neural network, all human beings are interconnected with the source of divine knowledge in this intergalactic universe. As per Vedanta, "God" is no person, but a super natural, formless force, that governs the universe. Of course, there have always been higher beings and they shall ever be there, whose personification has been mistakenly referred to as "God" or "Gods" by many of us. Among the highest of beings, Shiva as super element represents Super Consciousness that transforms to Brahma the Knowledge, Vishnu the Energy, and Mahesh the consciousness. The Knowledge and Energy are driven, in turn, from Consciousness itself. This is the trinity of all existence and its ultimate source.

The noble thoughts are "implanted" as inspiration to all human beings, who care to connect with their inner-self. This connection is easily achieved in the meditative state, and becomes the driving source for drawing higher knowledge. All scientists, researchers, artists, poets, and authors, among others, when connected to their inner-self and from there expanding their connection with the divine, draw intuitive thoughts, and can form hypotheses based on these thoughts. As they carry their work further, they are guided and supported by this abstract neural network in their noble endeavors.

Knowledge by itself is like the software that operates on the hardware of energy, with consciousness acting as the power to bring the whole, integrated mechanism to life. All that is known by the process of education (i.e. Knowledge) is driven from the Divine (Super Consciousness or Parmeshwar) is the first principle of Vedanta.

In real life, the practice of this first principle translates to knowing our real self, defining the purpose of our life, and then moving on towards fulfillment of that purpose. In today's busy world, we are all drowned in the "Acquired Identity Syndromes" that govern the simulated reality for each one of us, and drive us to detach from this connection. Getting to know the inner-self is simply a matter of detaching ourselves from these externally acquired syndromes, peeling the layers of perceptions, and getting down to the core of who we really are.

A human being is an instantiation of consciousness as the spirit, engulfed by an embodiment of manifested energy as a body, and implanted with ever evolving programs as the knowledge in our brain. In life, we become the instruments of experimentation, shuttling between the extremes of indulgence and restriction that define our limits. As we connect to the inner-self, there is a dawning of respect for all that exists, and a realization of "who" we truly are, the purpose of our life, and the knowledge and ways to achieve that purpose. All of us can contribute divine actions to protect the environment, create peace and interdependence between people and nations, harmony between communities, research and develop new ways to build a better world, and endeavors that create more love. Doing all that is not possible without the "Knowledge" of "How to do it." And that is exactly where Vedanta first principle and connection to the inner-self comes in.

Creating value in the name of Shiva

All those who believe in power of the almighty lord, the super consciousness, do take it upon themselves the initiative to add value to the world in which they live. And far beyond that, they believe in creating value. Adding value is their day to day contribution at work, home, and the community in which they live by engagement in projects that are positive.

Creating value is their most significant contribution. In the meditative state of mind, they are implanted ever new knowledge. It is from an interpretation of this implanted knowledge that they finally emerge to a level of laying down the vision, or in other words, the mental blue print for the world to-be.

The very first step in process is to document the vision, the mental blue print, into a tangible black and white form that can be uniformly interpreted by anyone who reads it in that commonly interpretable form. That may sound as a challenge, but is not an impossible task. As of today, all Shiva inspired individuals bear upon themselves the responsibility to create peace on the planet, and protect its environment in all ways possible.

To be a responsible citizen of the planet, one must lead by example. Doing the right things, though however small these may seem, all do eventually count up to be the contributors as droplets that filled the ocean. Even if one picks up a recyclable item lying as trash in a bin or on the street and then retires it to an appropriate recycling container (plastic, paper, metal, battery, polythene bag, or anything else that can possibly be recycled – be creative here), or a banana peel to a composting bin, is actually being a Shiva devotee by living the values that Shiva stood for and walked on this planet over seven thousand years ago in human form.

Shiva stood for the values to unite the world, starting with unification of the family by creating a realization of the sense of responsibility. Setting in motion the concept of marriage, as the very first marriage of the universe by accepting the responsibility, to adapting the entire existence as children by accepting to drink the potion from *Sagar Manthan* (churning of the ocean), Shiva stands for the values that have time and again been exhibited by divine incarnations in all human forms that we know of as the 'self-sacrificing' for a greater cause.

The 'jihadists' are not self-immolators for no purpose. In their own interpretation, they perform the act of 'jihad,' as self-sacrifice to wake-up the world that has gone astray from its original path. Once born on this planet of lust, desire, and distractions, it would be hard for anyone to accept the path of self-sacrifice for betterment of the world at large. While an army can be built by promising jobs to the needy, a force of volunteers ready to give up their life in name of the divine would not be possible unless those devotees are spiritually motivated to sacrifice their own life for the larger objective of creating a better world. At one end is their interpretation to sacrifice life to do overall good for the world, and at other end is the world perceiving their acts as terrorism.

Can this gap in interpretation, perception, and understanding to a common global purpose be bridged across communities of the world? While at the core everyone is divine, the layers upon layers of piled interpretations have created a universal debt of mental junk debris in misunderstandings that needs to be unpeeled and disposed of. These unpeeled layers from debris of interpretation junk would dissipate into empty vastness of the universe when we come to a common resolve of global peace through a realization of the self, a clear definition of our specific role, and a visualization of how it fits in the overall divine plan. An exercise of our right in making prudent choices of thought, speech, and action going forward for each one of us would be a step in that direction.

When we come across a tragedy like 9/11, we all start blaming it on a movement, an individual, a cult, a religion, or for whatever reasons - on a nation. In the world of tomorrow, there would be no divided nations defending themselves from each-other. There would only be one world as a single nation – and all inspired individuals have embraced to make that dream a reality on the ground and have already started working towards it.

Creating peace in the name of Shiva

Peace is an external word that reflects the state of an internal world. There can't be any peace in the world around us, unless each one of us is at peace within, integrating our very own mind, body, and soul. The peace in the external world is merely a reflection of what we all are internally, and this mirror image simply encompasses all of us collectively, close to seven billion of us living on the planet at present moment.

From Shiva to Shiva

The past 7000 years have led humanity through a journey in spiritual, political, and social revolution, with Shiva being at the center-stage of initiating and creating these evolutions. The next 70 years, a divisor by a factor of 100 here in view of the progressions as well as unintended deteriorations, would lead to the second beat of the Damru, almost defying the hitherto equivalent aspect of the dimension of time that factors in as a limiter as well as a de-limiter when it comes to conceptualizing existing manifestation.

What is implied here is the fact that all that exists originates from Shiva, and upon returning a useful value through the cycles of existence and non-existence, eventually merges into Shiva when it dissolves. That completes our understanding of the concept of GOD as Generator, Operator, and Dissolver (not destroyer, to avoid a gross misconception). From the origin of generation from the Super Element, to its decomposition to three basic elements, to a combination of these three basic elements to create a form and shape that can be human, material, or another living form, and its living through the cycles, to eventual decomposition to basic elements and finally reuniting with its source.

```
                    ┌─────────────────────┐
                    │ Shiva               │
                    │ The super element,  │
                    │ Super consciousness,│
                    │ Super Self          │
                    │ Brahman, God, Divine│
                    └─────────────────────┘
                         Decomposes to
```

Brahma (Generator)	Vishnu (Operator)	Mahesh (Dissolver)
Knowledge element	Energy element	Consciousness element
Guna: Rajas	Guna: Tamas	Guna: Sattva

Combine to manifest

Living beings	Non-living
Plants	Material
Animals, Birds, Humans	Non-material

Merge and evolve to

Beings of Light

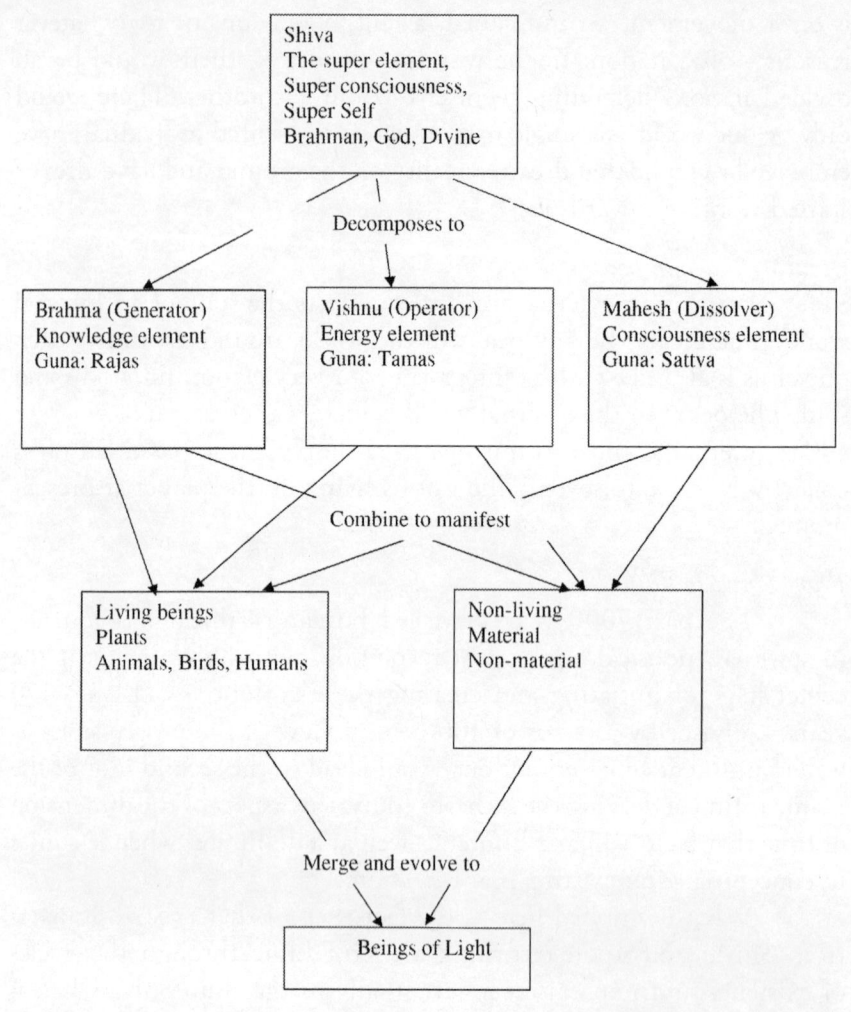

Fig. 2.3: Graph depicting decomposition of the super element to its constituent gunas and elements (knowledge, energy, consciousness), and combination thereof to manifest domains of living beings and non-living, and their merger to a highly evolved form (beings of light)

Guṇa signifies the dominant quality as associated to the constituent element.

There are three gunas that have always been there:

Sattva (related to the consciousness element and portrays the virtues of goodness, constructive creativity, and tendency to be in harmony), Rajas (related to the knowledge element and reflect the passion, being active through having the right knowledge to canalize energy in the right direction, and when unable to correlate, can also lead to a confused state of mind owing to knowing too many facts), and Tamas (related to the energy element and to the ability to do and achieve by interactions with our environment by bringing together the right inspiration and the right knowledge to experiment. When not canalized properly, can potentially lead to darkness, destructive, and chaotic state of mind as too much energy without a noble direction may tend to erode the intellect and can pre-dominate other faculties).

All of these three *gunas* are present in all that exists - everyone and everything. It is the proportion that is different. The interactions of these *gunas* define the nature of someone (person, or a living being) or something (object, or non-living).

We must know at all times that all these three gunas are not only necessary, but are also required for making a whole person or object. It is not that one guna is superior to the other – at some point of time in the life of a person or an object, one guna is more dominant than the other, reflecting in typical personality traits. It is the balance that matters – we must cultivate know how to control and balance gunas, so that the interplay between these results in the return of useful values from the testbed of life's experimentation.

As the super element decomposes to three constituent elements, and manifestation of the living universe takes place unleashing several forces and qualities in play, the gunas become predominant platforms for experimentation among conflicting priorities and compelling inspirations in the mind-body-soul integration paradigm that humans attempt while living on the planet, in the middle of their day to day activities surrounded by the environment in which they co-exist with others.

Even with the constituent energy element, the inter-play of five basic elements within energy – earth, sky, fire, water, and air gives rise of pre-dominance of a combination between air, water, fire, earth, and space to define the dosha – or more specifically, the personality type of an individual.

Vatta dosha results from a combination of air and space, Pitta from fire and water, and Kapha from water and earth. These doshas lay the definition of our personality type, and make each one of us unique.

Just as doshas define extra dimensions to the constituent element of energy, there are extra dimensions related to Knowledge as well – the knowing of facts and figures as data, the processing thereof as information, the interpretation from facts to define the next best action as insight, the prediction based on intuition as intuitive, and imagination based on inspiration as inspirational.

Thus data, information, insight, intuition, and inspiration define the extra dimensions of knowledge.

In similar ways, the constituent element of consciousness has seven extra dimensions related to dominance of the specific chakra – the lowest being Muladhara, the highest being Sahasrara (refer table 11.1).

While it may be often desirable for one to have a predominantly Pitta or Vatta or Kapha type personality associated with Sattvic guna, and have Sahasrara chakra opened at all times, the reality would be somewhere in between the struggle of opening the lowest chakra (Muladhara), and attempting to balance the doshas and gunas. The diversity of such a varying scale between three gunas with their multiple dominating dimensions results in making everyone so uniquely positioned amongst their surrounding environment and people, enabling the interplay of forces and personality types to bring out the very best in each, and collectively work towards creation of useful values that can be uploaded to the universal knowledge base through ANN.

The synergy of interplay is best reaped through complementary and supplementary abilities that lead to creative visualization and its subsequent realization by collaborative cooperation. Imagination or intent alone can't achieve any tangible results – it would need the force of action and the vehicle of collaboration to manifest itself to a reality on the ground.

In the same manner, action without a definite purpose can become meaningless and can't be expected to produce beneficial results. Thus, it is not just an integration of the mind-body-spirit, but also the balance between gunas and doshas is required to achieve useful values out of the testbed of life's experimentation.

Also, it is not just about caring for someone and feeling good about it, or know that you are in a better position to help or seek help. It is all about knowing our specific roles on the planet of existence while we are here.

While it may feel elating to know that we are in better position than the other being, it must at the same time be also a harsh realization that the other being is indeed a more evolved one than we ourselves are. For those who volunteer to accept the role of being a handicapped child or adult as our off-spring or next of kin, or the one for whom we might have agreed to care for, are indeed closer to being the divine in the purest form around us just to test as to how we react to them.

It is those evolved beings that embrace the suffering and the handicap to be around us as disadvantaged individuals, and in occasional cases, by a sheer blessing of the divine, to be our very own off-spring.

Once an esteemed friend asked me as to why there were so many disabled children on the planet – the discussion turned out to be a spiritual one, and at the end of it, being a proud parent of one of such highly evolved beings, agreed that is indeed the case that divine is testing us out individually as to how we react to them, whether as an adopted parent or being a biological one was really immaterial. There are so many volunteer parents who would embrace a handicapped child just out of the goodness of their heart.

The divine has many ways to manifest and appear before us to test us – in intention, in spirit, in thought, in action, and above all, in our attitude and altitude.

We often succumb to the temptation, the illusion, the fallacy of being a non-prophet - or the euphoria of being one, that we tend to forget the very purpose of as to why we are here on the planet.

Why we are here simply being a matter of choice that soul made to embrace the very circumstances and the environment to be in, and we must realize and accept this very moment as our opportunity to seize it and experiment with life in ways unknown that we may not just return some useful values that have been known over a period of time, but create some very new ones that were hitherto unknown.

In doing all that, we must know at all times that we are just part of a bigger picture, the ultimate reality of the divine, but never above it, yet neither below it, as we were destined to be born in image of the divine.

'Aham Brahmasmi' (I am an integral part of the divine) is a great affirmation to recite every single morning as you get ready to start the day, or when embarking on a great mission. This affirmation enables to align your inner-self with your outer-self and the integrated whole with the super-self, thus creating a harmony across inspiration, thought, and action.

Being an integral part of the divine acknowledges the role played by all those around us, and that of the environment in which we operate. It is important to seek an alignment of our unified goal, and use our conflicts to strengthen what we are doing as we all bring value in a unique way.

This journey through the cycles of manifestation and de-manifestation is an amazing discovery of the purpose of life, the living universe, and why we exist.

Never shun anyone

The message of Shiva is to embrace all, and discard none. While an angry human may turn out all snakes out of a region, empowered by force of the divine to do so, and there might be innumerable experiences and observances on the way of similar behaviors, Shiva as *Pashupathi* embraces all, and discards none. Adorning snake as a garland signifies this. Snake may be turned away by everyone, and like all else that exists, is also a divine creation. Who has nowhere else to go, is embraced by the grace of Shiva.

Knowing well that all creation that exists is eventually some combination of the three basic elements of consciousness, knowledge, and energy, we can never be drastically different from each-other.

While we are aware that the sole purpose of our existence is to know our real self and then engage in the experimentation to return a useful value, what really matters is how we perform this engagement. Whether we engage in carrying out further repeated experimentation along the beaten path that has been well established, or pick fresh avenues, it is all about making a connection to draw inspiration and acting upon those inspired thoughts.

Prompt to converge and grow, not to fight

Looking back in retrospect, the past 7000 years have been driving separation of the super element 'Shiva' to its individual constituent elements – Brahma as Knowledge, Vishnu as Energy, and Mahesh as Consciousness.

The challenge now before humanity is to reverse this trend of divergence to the one of convergence through integration of views, thoughts, and actions. When we would be making the efforts to unite, to create interdependence, to consult and collaborate, to create peace, our noble and humble intensions would automatically set forth a mechanism for us to get guided to the next steps, leveraging the vehicle of ANN.

Inspiration is always unilateral, and does not need any convergence – it is like a spiritual answer to a confused question. What we now need is to translate inspiration to thoughts, plans, and actions that are focused on achieving the coming together of communities and nations of the world to a common platform for integrating the globe as a single nation, and make collective actions to protect the environment of our planet.

All such thoughts and actions would be endeavors at bringing together Brahma, Vishnu, and Mahesh, or even so to say, integrating Krishna and Shiva, or say Kartikeya, Mohamed (pbuh), and Jesus.

The exercise here is to just sit quite in a meditation with eyes closed (to minimize distractions), and to do nothing as useless attempts to still the mind (it will eventually come home). Regardless of how much it may wander, the mind would finally rest to a point where it will open up a connection to the ANN.

Once connected to the ANN, draw upon the knowledge that is just right to fulfill your vision and mission in life.

Once you have done that, the next steps are all just trivial. The most major challenge in the life of a lesser mortal human is that we hardly even get down to making that connection, leave alone the efforts to the fulfillment of the mission.

Life is either standstill, or moving at a pace that is faster than the velocity of light.

It is on us, the very practitioners of life, as to what we choose to be, to shape the future of life on our planet.

We can choose the very options that help to promote harmony, unification, consultation, collaboration, and overall the ones that are conclusive enough to gather a critical mass that can be acted upon.

Integrating Krishna and Shiva

All is in one, and one is in all: it is that supreme soul, the 'parama purusha' that is present in all existence. Building upon the wonderful narrative of Shri Anandamurthy, God is the one whose actions and philosophy is one and the same. To that extend, while Shiva walked our planet as 'Sadasiva,' in an incarnation of the 'prama purusa,' Lord also walked the planet about two thousand years later as 'Sri Krishna' and yet even later as Buddha, Mahavira, Lord Jesus the Christ, and much later as saints of the recent times as Sri Guru Nanak Dev Ji, the founder of Sikhism, Bahaullah, the founder of Bahai faith, and now as the infinite and indivisible soul in everyone reading this text.

Every day and at every single moment in our life, we are experiencing turbulence and motion. Rare would be times when we experience the so-called 'calmness.'

While we all are internally inclined to stay 'calm and quite,' life's immediate priorities may have a different plan of action. We continue to work, and strive a balance between what we aspire to do, and what we need to do.

Our needs are immediate, and aspirations often tend to take a back seat. Sri Krishna is all about immediate priorities, as the saint walking on the planet no less than two thousand years later. Lord Shiva is about your ultimate life mission and long term goals. In the circle of events, Lord Jesus rather came back only to say that you need to be merciful, be self-sacrificing, and do all that you can: even at the expense of your own life to make any improvement, in ways what so ever you can do and contribute, while on the planet.

In that sense, Lord Jesus, the Christ, not only integrates the objectives of Shiva and Krishna, but also takes a step beyond and encourages us to be self-sacrificing, for the ultimate benefit of humanity and the planet, and eventually the entire universe.

The leaders of the future would emerge to be unifying in many ways.

First, they would be integrating the cumulative leadership qualities of Shiva, Krishna, Kartikeya, Budha, Jesus, Prophet Mohamed (pbuh), Guru Nanak Dev Ji, Gandhi, Mahavira, Bahaullah, and all other prominent spiritual, social, and political leaders.

Inspired by Shiva, they would integrate the currently divergent communities of the world to build interdependence.

As unified social, political, and spiritual leaders, they would strive to create One World: One Nation.

What can we do to share the burden of Shiva?

Look upon it that someone is assigned the responsibility of creating a whole system of the universe, sustaining it as a created form, and then recycling the manifestation upon its dissolution to ever-growing newer forms. Is that an enormous task? If each one of us can consider ourselves as connected to Shiva, having originated from Shiva, and that upon dissolution would be absorbed yet again into Shiva, then we are all one.

What we can do immediately, upon having this realization of oneness, is to forget the petty differences and start building a united world. By indulging in repeating the same old fashioned trick of trying to divide and rule, settle differences by dispute and war, or indulging in the fulfillment of selfish motives, we are only ending up creating a higher burden and not lessening it.

The tragedies, both human made and natural, are only the results of our cumulative actions and thoughts. These come as a reaction to our thoughts and actions, since a balance has to be maintained. If we think and act positive, it invites a positive reaction. If we think or act negative, we end up creating a higher burden of negativity. Eventually, this cumulative negativity needs to be wiped out to maintain the balance, observing the physical and spiritual laws of the universe. Human created collective negativity is wiped off by a resulting natural calamity that we set in motion by our collective negative behavior and thoughts. The rule is simple – negative multiplied by negative results in the positive.

Some of our positive thoughts and vibrations at any time can certainly help to wipe out some negativity that is in motion. If there is a higher cumulative magnitude of negativity than what our positive thoughts and actions can wipe out, then tragedies are unleashed, both in natural and human made form. Certain human beings are perceivably enslaved by the cumulative negativity to act in a manner that finally results in the unleashing of a tragedy.

Each one of us has a moral responsibility: to think and act positive. It is not hard for anyone to know as to what thoughts and actions are positive: each one of us has an internal connection to Shiva in the form of Abstract Neural Network. Once we get connected, the rest is simple.

Our division of humanity in the name of religion, nationality, and racism is temporary and just waiting for a union. Once everyone has the realization of oneness that they are all part of Shiva, the differences will evaporate and unity will emerge. Each one of us has to make that happen: we are all empowered to do that.

Time has now come to re-define the so-called quality of life, and by what we measure progress. More comfort was touted as the improved quality of life – but at what cost? We need to make some fundamental shifts in our lifestyle. We need to realize that we are a multi-dimensional creation.

To fulfill the physical aspects of our existence, we do have some basic necessities of life like food, sleep, and need some basic comforts like clothing and shelter.

To fulfill the mental aspects of our existence, we do have some basic emotional need and aspire to be loved and cared for, want to feel secure.

To fulfill the spiritual aspects of our existence, we do have a very basic need to truly know as to 'who we really are' and create a blueprint of what we aspire to achieve during the opportunity of our lifetime while on the planet of existence. Once this realization occurs, and our connection to Shiva is established through our inner-self, we get the inspiration that directly maps to our thoughts and actions, and knowledge of how these fit in the overall divine plan.

Chapter 3

Abstract Neural Networks (ANN)

One of the important revelations from the experience was a direction for the future of existence. All our current forms of communication are indirect. We use written words, speech, and all sorts of media from internet to radio, television, phones, laptops, tablets, and several other supporting devices to exchange our thoughts that we first articulate in spoken or written words and then transmit these to the receiver, who interprets these.

Imagine if we were able to communicate at the thought level, directly from one thinker to another – the research would be much quicker, and the inefficiencies that slow down the whole process of communicating between the transmitter and receiver would be eliminated. All present modes of communication would become unnecessary.

Communicating at the thought level

This chapter outlines the pattern of communication at thought level – directly from brain to brain, with no need of words, translations, or communication media and gadgets or the need to type, print, read or write. This was the method of communication that Shiva used to transpire messages directly to the recipient.

If one could compare the two methods of communication – contemporary versus the one used by Shiva (ANN), it is almost obvious that the indirect way to communicate wastes lots of energy in first putting thoughts in a readable form and then transmission and reception, just to be communicating from one type to another and after the recipient reads it, a lot is left to interpretation. This brings down the overall efficiency of the communicating vehicle. The diagram below explains how communicating from one end to another is so inefficient.

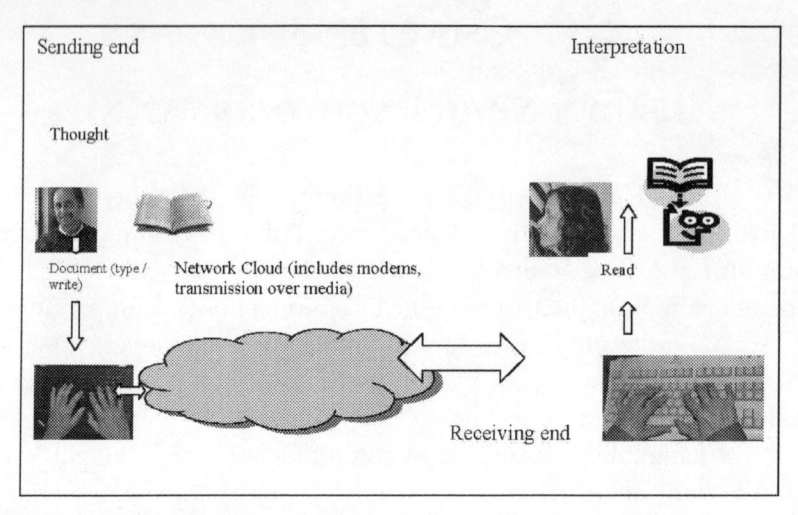

Fig. 3.1: Inefficient communication through contemporary means

From thought of the one who wishes to communicate it, to its interpretation by the one for whom it is intended, there are several steps in-between in the traditional communication.

First, the thought must be documented or verbalized in speech. The documented thought can be either in the form of a printed word that can be read or in an electronic form that must be coded and transmitted through the network from sending to receiving end, be decoded, and finally be displayed on a device or a printed document. The receiver would read it, and then interpret a meaning to it.

The interpreted meaning attached to what is read can often be different from what is intended to be communicated. This difference arises from the conditioning of any specific human being based on their past experiences in personal, social, and professional life, and limits of the exposure.

ANN – your gateway to the Divine

Think of ANN as a vehicle that connects the entire data, information, knowledge, and inspiration across all known and unknown inter-galactic universes. It becomes available to all the seekers and providers on-demand, and keeps continually updating several databases of the inter-galactic universes with ever-new useful values returned by those involved in the experimentation with life.

All living beings everywhere are actively participating in the larger experiment by simply getting engaged with process of life.

Face to Face with Shiva

Without having a realization of it, many of us are just part of providing a support system to a few of us. Though each one of us bears the capability to connect to the ANN and draw the cumulative knowledge from it, we often tend to pass on this inherently built in capability and seek to communicate the harder way.

The difference between the regular documented interactions in the physical world and the abstract world is simple.

In the physical world of documentation, we waste over 85% of our energy in researching the relevant facts and figures that can lend credibility to our hypothesis. We waste another 11% to 14% of our energy in researching and offering justifications to the relevance of existing facts, figures and documented findings to their relationship with our hypothesis.

In the Abstract world of ANN, there is no such thing as above. It is, as if, we already knew what all has been documented, hypothesized and researched into the contemporary field, and that we are just a part of it, through an Abstract Neural Connection with the Network that instantaneously unveils the current and relates our findings to the evolving. The evolution may not be just limited to this planet or the ones in the universes that we know of. It is going on in the universes well beyond the scope of our limited cognitive comprehension.

Fig. 3.2: Abstract Neural Network Cloud

As part of the Abstract network, unknowingly we might become part of a growing gene that is more intellectual and spiritual than physical and material. This is the paradigm shift that is gradual, yet definite and has slowly started taking place on our planet. While several initiatives may only be part of a larger revolution across the universes known and unknown, the slow evolution on this planet is a definite reality. This reality is here to stay. The transformation taking place internally, within hearts and minds of people since the events of September 11, 2001 is bound to touch their soul, sooner or later.

People indeed have started questioning the roots of our existence, how the universe operates and exists or came into being and the very purpose of life. It is only a matter of a few years of fundamental research that would bring to surface these secrets. What was hitherto considered metaphysical or ticked off as 'spiritual' would soon be part of the mainstream scientific and technological revolution. ANN plays a definite role towards making this shift in our focus on the future of research with science and technology.

Just relate to the concept that there are several waves out there, outside the scope of human reception capability and comprehension, and that only some of which have been tapped for real communication over the radio and satellite media. There can be an infinite magnitude of scope in variation within various electro-magnetic parameters related to the waves that can lead to the possibilities beyond our imagination. These possibilities can become the opening grounds for success, once we get an access to a method to begin experimentation. The method itself can be planted through ANN, leave alone the scopes of variation.

Considering that the whole big plan is a step by step process in evolution, it is our patience, not haste that would connect us with the relevant ANN.

ANN: Collaborative Framework for an Interdependent Universe

ANN is a collaborative framework towards creating an Interdependent Universe. You may have no motivation to connect through an ANN if you are not inspired to make a contribution towards uniting the globe. Consider that there was an essential prerequisite that requires our planet to be a single, united entity of consultative collaboration before everyone on the planet acquires the capability to participate in inter-universal effort at evolution of knowledge and consciousness. Now, to inch towards making that prerequisite a reality that exists on the ground, all those who are reading this text were inspired to step forward and own up some responsibility to create peace. Once this inspiration is strong enough to pierce the multiple stacks of their simulated reality, then only can they assume any effective role towards that objective.

Participating as teams in an interdependent manner, they can exchange notes, receive updates, post findings, do all that they normally do for research on the physical plane and much more using the ANN. All that each one of us does is recorded. It is being stored for the purpose of research and findings. It is for us to return useful values, not redundant or useless results out of what we experiment with or do.

The sooner we can deliver useful results, the better. The closer we get to returning a useful value, the nearer is the salvation. The whole life in experimentation can be a sheer waste if we are unable to return any useful value.

The fact of life in contemporary times is that all of us have now got used to making a living off the compounded interest, just like the financial institutions that rule the physical world. People have nearly forgotten that someone needs to put in a principal amount. It is only those who are inspired to put in a principal amount together for survival and growth of the future generations of humanity would join hands in a collaborative effort to connect through the ANN. In the discussions about September 11 tragedy, if some may say that they may not care if the planes were not headed towards their house, that thought is driven from a lack of connection to our consciousness.

It would not actually be until the hit that they would know the impact of their inaction or procrastination. It is true for over 99% of us that we really don't care. It is very convenient for some of us to build theories to blame the government, the society or the system. This is perhaps the collective default human behavior that is responsible for current state of the environment and economy of our planet.

Coming back to the point, who is engaged in creating the principal? The answer is that those who are making any constructive attempts at connecting to the ANN. Just like nanotechnology is bringing the disciplines of various fields in science, technology and medicine together; ANN would enable the inter-galactic universal vehicle for a collaborative framework of collective research. ANN opens up a dialog to the inner-self, and through it, to the rest of the universe.

As of now, a biology expert has to learn about material science and electronics. An electronics engineer has to learn about several other disciplines, for instance the internal behavior of cells, to make any meaningful contribution towards new and upcoming fields that help design a better system or chip. Cross-discipline integration is taking place the hard way through, but soon we may see several new initiatives that impart under-graduate level courses to target creation through integration, rather than development through segmentation. As of now, after specializing in a field of study, we look across other disciplines to learn about them and then explore ways to integrate. Going forward, ANN can facilitate a broad based curriculum to provide a wider exposure to various fields, setting an early-on stage for exploration to integrate across disciplines.

The hitherto focus on creating programs that have driven the verticals in specific fields of science, technology and medicine to some limit are now tending to reach the saturation point of a realization that meaningful further developments would require bringing in other disciplines. This is easing out the water-tight compartmentalization between various fields and paving the way to further our understanding of the world around us, its supporting environment and the universe in which it is suspended.

ANN would speed up this crossing between fields of science, technology, medicine, behavior, arts and management by instantaneous implants of integrated modules of knowledge, just tailored to the context of specific research in question. These integrated modules of knowledge would be the sum total of contemporary research findings across several universes of interacting systems of knowledge creation endeavor, of which this planet shall become an integrated part. This realization alone can motivate some committed individuals to move forward with their efforts at creating permanent peace on the planet.

Permanent peace on the planet is a prerequisite that must be met in order for us to become eligible for an entry to this system of interconnected partners engaged in collaborative research. Unless we are able to achieve this required permanent peace, ANN may still be useful, but only with a limited effectiveness. In this interim, ANN can help specific practitioners evolve their consciousness to a level that they acquire the capability to connect with several other like-minded individual consciousness experimenters in a collaborative manner.

Just that the interim experimentation may yield limited results must not be the reason to abandon the effort. If at all, the interim experimentation must be viewed as the potential vehicle that can launch a global peace effort by an avalanche effect. Thus, those involved with experimentation must make genuine efforts at enrolling other like-minded individuals in the process while simultaneously initiating a dialog with all others in their contact towards the urgency of need. Initiation of such a dialog would become the stepping stone for all those who are engaged in this journey of a thousand miles that has already started on our planet with its first single step.

A dawning of the fact that no systems are perfect and all individuals, communities, nations, societies or planets need to improve can be a motivation enough to engage in a collaborative framework of cooperation for inter-universal research effort. To tread on the path of bringing ANN in to a mainstream technological area of research is not going to be a cake walk; it would need a careful approach and caution. While at one end most of the technical community may deride something like this as a spiritual pursuit and hence outside the domain of scientific research, on the other, any step by step endeavors in this area are likely to face a mounting resistance from all quarters of funding including grants. It is the perseverance of those engaged in this collaborative framework of inter-universal research that can keep alive any efforts, however miniscule, to keep inching forward in a steady manner, even if that experience might be humiliating.

It is only a matter of time that the collective results of such efforts shall graduate un-funded ANN research to a mainstream science worthy of consideration for a major research effort. Those engaged in un-funded research shall bring out the real value of millenniums of sacrifice and penance of Yogis wandering the Himalayas to humanity.

Engaged in the reception of ANN implants of knowledge and radiating a positive electro-magnetic force that absorbs the major portions of negativity caused by our collective actions and thoughts, these wanderers laid the foundation for survival of the planet to this present day. The whole system of universe works as an electro-magnetic wave pattern, where the electric balance must be maintained at all times. All turbulence in the system must be absorbed, either by those responsible for their thoughts and actions, or else it would trigger events that counter-balance theirs. From ice-storms to hurricanes to meteor hits, all events are part of this process of maintaining the balance.

A case in point is that of a Yogi who started meditating at the age of five and continued to do that in lotus posture until the age of forty, when his physical body was sacrificed at the alter of balancing human thoughts and actions. A true giver, who expected nothing in return from this physical world, he absorbed a certain amount of negative radiation that we generate by the virtue of our negative thoughts and actions.

One may ask, as to how we can cease to generate negative wave patterns that are harmful for the planet and human society? The answer is simple. Connected with our inner-self, we are always inspired to do the positive, but shrouded in the mist of AIS (Acquired Identity Syndrome) layers and stacks that limit our vision to the myopia of immediate selfish gains, we tend to work in the opposite direction. A daily practice of meditation is an excellent way to make a difference and gradually reverse this direction. In between, a point of transition would come that shall help elevation to a higher level of existence.

Consciousness as a concept

Consciousness has no life. It has no time-span. It is just something that exists, everywhere and in everything, whether material or non-material, whether living or non-living. In the non-living, consciousness exists as a potential form that can be called to get activated in the kinetic form. In the living, consciousness is present in the kinetic form that is continually engaged in the process of experimenting and returning useful values that matter. In the material, consciousness is built into the core of every atom or molecule, as the very basis of its existence. In the non-material, it is simply consciousness that is the substance of the non-material as it stays that way in the un-manifested form.

In the living, consciousness is the very source of life and is present in a dynamic form whose nature is to keep experimenting and exploring. For simply one reason: consciousness itself is on the path of exploration to its source of origin. For us as humans, it may be much easier to comprehend that 'Super Consciousness' is the only source of all creation and existence as a non-material nature substance that pervades the entire universe as known to us and all that lies beyond the boundaries of the known universe, given the limitations of our cognitive vision and perception boundaries.

Consciousness as a System

It may be perhaps impossible to draw even a simple boundary diagram for something that is beyond comprehension, given the current limitations of human perception mechanism. It can't be ruled out that the future generations of humanity would figure out the very mechanism of its existence and be able to rescue the current impasse and dilemma of consciousness towards tracing its source of existence. Once a realization happens that consciousness is an integral part of our very existence, and that we exist to eventually evolve it, the tracing from manifested existence to its source would become easier.

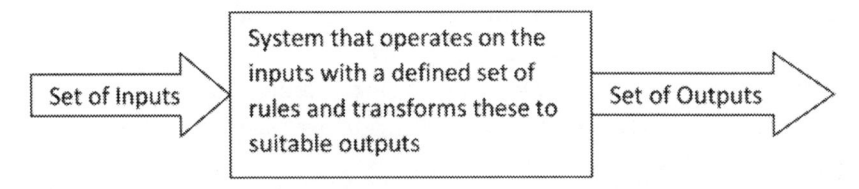

```
[Set of Inputs] → [System that operates on the inputs with a defined set of rules and transforms these to suitable outputs] → [Set of Outputs]
```

Fig. 3.3: Inputs, System, Outputs

Given the context of our current definition of a system, there has to be an input, a system that transforms it into an output, and an output. To that extent, if we consider the manifestation as output, then the input to the system is simply a set of rules that define the manner in which the potential of consciousness can be manifested to perform some useful experimentation and some advice to return the values out of that experimentation that can be helpful in the process of evolution. The very objective of the process of evolution can be left either defined or undefined. If undefined, the whole process of experimentation and return of values to strengthen the database of 'knowledge' can evolve to an unpredicted and random state of stabilization where the only thing that is permanent is not just 'change.'

Given the defined process, there ought to be a system of existence where pre-planned and well-thought of procedures be put in place that are engaged by participation in the performance of processes that return if not pre-determined, pre-calculated, or pre-estimated, but some values that may or may not be useful. Considering the very purpose of whole experimentation, the defined process is not a very suitable system to create an existence whose whole purpose is to experiment with the undefined and evolve it.

Thus, we can conclude from the above discussion that 'consciousness' as a system is favoring undefined processes. We also need to know that it is out of this undefined nature of processes that we experience random accidents and natural calamities as balancing acts in our collective personal and social lives as individuals and communities. While we do enjoy a great degree of freedom by this undefined nature of the process, choices that we make during various stages of experimentation with life play a key part in determining as to what kind of balancing forces may be acting. There is always a role that counter-balancing plays in this whole unleashing of the natural events and calamities – for instance, an army of meditative soldiers or a recluse yogi wandering Himalayas may be radiating positive vibrations that are likely to lessen the furious intensity of a storm, tsunami, earthquake, or hurricane.

Such positive radiations can also negate the intensity of an unfavorable collective human behavior by sending messages of thought-healing.

Consciousness as a Process

Knowing that the processes of consciousness are undefined, be it justified or unjustified, let's first admit that we as humans have no experience of dealing with undefined processes. We have always considered it our privilege to define something first and then attach a meaning to it. That is simply the only domain of a paradigm that is known to us. It is built in our blood - we always want to structure and define. We do want to tutor our kids to a level of definition of the worldview that we deem as right. We always love to first define, refine, and reduce concepts of a subject to a level of non-random state and then fit those within the scope of our own limited perceived view of the universe.

Perhaps, the damage could not be more than what we have already done by forcing the limitations of our perceptions on the future of this evolutionary nature of experimentation.

The only way to undo that damage may be to allow more freedom in thought and style of experimentation, in line with the evolutionary nature of existence. That must not directly translate to an easy succumb of the victimization by AISs (acquired identity syndromes) of money, sex, religion, ego, stocks, and the likes of vices as that may be self-gratifying, indulging, or fulfilling sensual desires.

Freedom comes with a great deal of responsibility. The sense of responsibility is not only in terms of what we think, perceive and ultimately act upon as the instruments of creation, but even in terms of what we are entitled to imagine, whether the AIS or other-wise.

Knowledge grows to evolve consciousness. That's why learning is larger than life. Through the process of continuous absorbing of the experiences out of experimenting with life, we keep learning, and as a consequence adding values of all kinds – positive, negative, neutral to an all pervading, ever existent universal database.

Nirvana happens when we return useful values (useful is not tied down to a qualifier of being a positive, a negative, or a neutral as there can be likely a value within any one of those and if nothing else, negative or neutral values provide an indication that already there has been enough experimentation attempted in those categories).

As a cybernetic self-adapting and self-correcting system, the living universe automatically adjusts itself to limit the number of negative and neutral manifestations going forward, once there is an indication that only some of those are required to either prove the point on a hypothesis with an ongoing experimentation, or to know that no more of such manifestations are needed (the case in point is the extinction of dinosaurs).

Did some of the dinosaurs attain Nirvana? Yes, absolutely the ones who participated whole heartedly as spiritually inspired animals in the context of what they aspired to do.

Is one of us the reincarnation of those dinosaurs? Potentially yes, depending on how you interpret it. The elements of consciousness, knowledge, and energy are separated upon disintegration and during Nirvana one merges into the infinite magnificence of the un-manifested Super Consciousness, the one and only super-element from which all existence is driven from, and merges back into it.

Even if we are an absolutely fresh out of the oven creation of the divine, we do inherit all the cumulative knowledge of the living universe, and are associated with the exact same consciousness that has now evolved to a new level. Energy only changes forms and is recycled. We, as an instantiation of consciousness associated with knowledge and energy, in a manifestation that has a limited life while on the planet, have a specific mission to fulfill.

We are limited in many ways to draw a statement of our mission and vision in life. We all suffer from our internal and external conditioning in the form of AIS (Acquired Identity Syndrome). Internal conditioning is our own perceptions, and external conditioning is the influence of our circumstances and environment that contributes to shaping our way of thinking.

Unless we get connected to our inner-self by peeling the several onion layers of our AISs, we find it hard to even get any inspiration. Once connected to the inner-self, and further from there to the all-pervading ANN, we can draw infinite knowledge and inspiration that can easily translate to our vision and mission statements relating to what we aspire to do in life.

Connections would need to be provided from the physical world to the spiritual, inner world as bridges that must be crossed to transcend the dilemma of AIS. Building on the meditative practice of specific groups, ANN would emerge as the binding thread to interconnect such groups in a collaborative effort to create such connections. It is a sad story that though each one of our religions are integrating at the core, the stupidity of vested groups have merely looked upon the methodology and its interpretation. There is no single religion in the world that professes to kill. It is only our convenient interpretations that have forced us to adapt the most suitable connotation to do what we want to do and find a justification for doing that in name of the religion.

Hope of humanity is alive in the aspirations of a young generation to create permanent peace in the world. Every child wants to become a pilot as they want to fly. No child ever wants to become a fighter pilot because they want to kill. The thrill of flying a jet at supersonic speed is the reason for them to consider joining the Air Force, but the inability to refuse those orders to cause devastation and killing is a major de-motivation.

Humanity would do well if we were to create a mechanism of flying high and fast powered by fuel that is 100% environment-friendly, everyone could participate in it, and if it would be with a mission to create peace.

Such a mechanism is possible to build, with the aid of advances in non-material science and technology that would finally rescue the planet from all hatred and wars. The creation of a finite amount of positive radiation, by collective effort of conscious groups, would eventually lead to the generation of a wave that can uplift the entire humanity to a new realm of existence.

The interim may be characterized by marked shifts in the way we live, our education system, the attitudes of people across the globe, and advances in non-material science and technology. Two promising areas of research are: Brain Wave Technology and Nanotechnology.

The 'Brian Wave' technology would enable remote communication between humans without any aids of physical media, while *Nano*technology would shift the current research focused on material science to non-material. The way it would happen is non-obvious as of now, but a sudden realization would mark that shift. This realization would be that we can do only so much with physical means and gadgets that we create with the 'material.'

For instance, whales can communicate with their cousins across the oceans by using no gadgets, producing extremely low frequency waves that travel through the medium of ocean water. If we can also learn the technique to generate such waves without the use of any gadgets, though at a different frequency that is suitable for travel through a different media, we may acquire the ability to communicate across the universe.

Current advances in 'Brain Wave' technology enable a rodent to walk straight on a rail, remotely controlled by a radio signal. This research is going on a Duke University, North Carolina. The first human brain to computer connection has been made possible at Rutgers University. Both these are among several other research initiatives that are taking place across the globe from both ends: physical and metaphysical. It would be few tens of years of research, or earlier, that the efforts of both ends would find a meeting point. That would be the point when ANN and the 'wave' would become the primary candidates for global mainstream research and development initiatives, a stage where some of the physical activities on these endeavors would leverage the advances in metaphysical research.

Nanotechnology is slowly entering the mainstream research in interdisciplinary domains, while there are many a fence-sitters who would jump on the bandwagon once a sufficient inertia has been gained by momentum. The meeting point between material science research and non-material aspects of metaphysics would soon be met when just a few years down the line we realize the limits of experimenting with material. One of the downsides of 'string' theory is that the research community finds it as of yet impractical to manipulate any material substance down to the string level. As per 'the string' hypothesis, all material is made up of vibrating strings. If an atom is the size of a solar system, a string is only the size of a tree. At the quantum mechanics level, the behavioral patterns of all material substances become at best 'predictive,' a phenomenon that supports 'the wave,' in a sense that the universe is in a constant flux that is partially shaped by our attitude and action.

Thus, the crux of matter is simple: as human beings, we are continually engaged in the shaping of world and the universe around us, by engaging in the activity of thought and action. While some thoughts may become a forced result of 'the wave,' we always have control over how we can react. That control alone is responsible for 'predictive' state of the universe.

Once we are advanced to the stage of establishing intergalactic connections with other intelligent forms engaged in the pursuit of experimentation as we are on this planet, ANN shall become the primary media for further developments in the research arena. We would do better by not getting limited out of a fear of non-acceptance by a peer research community and keep up the ANN research initiatives, whether funded or non-funded, with a view at creating something worthwhile for our future generations to develop further on.

From Physical to Metaphysical

Considering that energy can neither be created nor destroyed, but can only change forms and also that all matter in existence is frozen energy, there is more to it than meets the eye. If 'Big Bang' was an explosion of some form of un-manifested force that suddenly transformed to various forms of frozen energy, is there a correlation between a nuclear explosion and the 'Big Bang?'

Does an atom hold the potential of 'reversal' upon triggering to un-manifest the frozen energy as matter?

Change is at the very essence of evolution. From creation, sustenance, to dissolution or dis-assembly and reconstruction, all are sub-processes of change. What appears to be physically visible as material, eventually comes into being by bringing together of infinitely small combinations of constantly vibrating forces of energy. This vibrating energy is at the source of all material creation. At the core of this vibrating energy lies the force that gives it the oscillations. And finally, that force itself is driven by the power that we can call consciousness, in the un-manifested form.

The Super-Consciousness is nothing else, but the force behind sum-total of all existence and non-existence, or the manifested and the un-manifested, or the material and the non-material, as all is eventually driven from it and would finally merge into it, when we take a holistic view of it all. It is something that just exists or prevails by itself as non-material and perpetually keeps unfolding itself to a manifested form that finally dissolves. Not the like of a physical being, but a power that creates, sustains, dissolves, and recreates the universes interconnected by 'the wave.'

The ANN by itself is just a vehicle for interconnection. It is not the source of existence, but is surely the means to connect to it.

The cosmic rays that Nikola Tesla harnessed to power the automobile, received through the antenna, and synthesized in his generator may be similar to what plants use for conversion as a process. This discovery alone held the key to solving most of the problems of humanity. It is unfortunate that we have lost the details of it, what could have been the answer to providing most significant source of power. It is unfortunate that the world today can waste over 100 bn $ on a war killing innocent civilians and soldiers alike, but no government agency is inclined to making attempts at recreating Tesla's automobile or his generator.

Over the next few decades, humans would be inclined to abandon wars, as the power shifts hands from manipulating politicians to intelligent scientists seeking to create permanent peace on the planet.

It appears that Tesla had received these ideas and was guided to create those inventions through the 'Abstract Neural Network,' an arrangement that gives access to the collective research efforts.

Nikola Tesla invented the AC motor and transformer, 3-phase electricity and the Tesla Coil. Tesla is now credited with inventing modern radio as well; the Supreme Court overturned Marconi's patent in 1943 in favor of Tesla.

As scientific endeavors advance our understanding of human brain and explore the mysteries of perceived existence, we are gradually evolving to a merger of science with spirituality.

Consciousness is all about establishing a connection with your inner-self. The inner-self within is ever connected to the divine through the ANN, and keeps drawing through it the knowledge necessary to advance us further as individuals, and collectively together as a community.

Shiva is always in constant dialog with each one of us. Once each one of us is able to relate ourselves to being part of the existence that has been created by Shiva, and Shiva being also at the core of its origin, we can see all in one, and one in all. In other words, the one is not separated by the whole. We are just one part of this wholeness, the universal oneness of all existence, at the core of which is Shiva. We are ever connected with our origin, and thus are perpetually driven to it.

The Trishul (trident) is our consistent guide to deal with any given situation in life.

First, it tells us that all creation is in some form a combination of consciousness, knowledge, and energy.

Second, it gives us a powerful tool to combat difficult circumstances with this three step rule:

1) Ignore to exist (as all is in one and one is in all, so we need to be patient to let the test pass, rather than be reactive to avoid it). This approach helps us to sustain ourselves in an apparently hostile environment, and be tolerant to violent behaviors of those we interact with.
2) Distinguish thought from practice (many a times we get prompted to act in a particular manner that is inconsistent with the inner voice from our consciousness) empowers us to take control in an otherwise helpless situation. Think before you act or speak. We must realize that our choice of the option per voice of our inner-self is the only one which would eventually lead to creation of a better world, and a better universe, in the whole of this interconnected, interdependent existence.
3) Do all that you can, and not worry about what you can't. At some point, we need to draw the line and define the boundary. No one can do everything. Each one of us must contribute in the area that is best suited to our core capability and ability, and leave the rest. This identification is important from the perspective of role definition and assignment of responsibility within a family, community, or team. Seeing oneness of the whole, we put together our unique skills, capabilities, creativity, and collaborate to keep progressing in this eternal cycle of evolution.

Third, the Trishul circles back all manifested existence to dissolution. While the three Trishul arrows in the trident represent consciousness (center), energy (left), and knowledge (right), the cyclic process perpetually dissolves existence to its original source: Super Consciousness, and then draws from it to create ever newer forms of manifestation. In these never ending cycles of creation and dissolution, the end yield of each logical manifestation is an enhanced knowledge that results from the experimentation performed and is applied to aid evolution. Each one of us, as a being who experiments, experiences, innovates, invents, enhances, and integrates inter-disciplines, life is more than a process of getting engaged in making a living. It is all about a realization of our role on the planet, and performing it to the best of our ability.

An interesting aspect to know about Trishul is the perception of two folks, each one looking at it from two different sides, one standing opposite to the other, and Trishul being between the two of them, and both facing each-other. One may think of Energy as Knowledge, and the other may think of Knowledge as Energy, while both having no confusion about consciousness as the middle arrow.

This is actually the truth of life – that energy and knowledge may appear to be interchangeable, depending on your point of view. If you are centered in a position of power, Energy may appear to you as knowledge – something that you may even like to profess as your story of success and rise to power. On the other hand, a yogi who may not yet have gone to a worldly school is likely to possess all the advanced knowledge of the entire spectrum of known and unknown universes, both manifested and likely even that of a few yet to be manifested, and may utilize that Knowledge coupled with an undisputed intention to do good to this worldly existence as energy to lessen some of the furiousness of a wave of destruction that has already been set in motion, and the yogi is already is in possession of the knowledge of such a wave. It is just the point from which you are looking at the Trishul is different – one from an intoxication of the pride of your perceived success to advise everyone else to possess, and the other from complete renunciation to compensate for the acts of those who want to continue to pursue the path to possess and rule others. In either case, Trishul is showing us a way to evolve, since the arrow of consciousness is ever above both knowledge and energy. Pride of the self in indulgence of perceived success can potentially lead to a deterioration of purpose, and a derailment from the path to achieve a fulfillment of inspired objectives. The trick lies in staying focused, as you may evolve from one level of worldly success to another. Thus, going back to connecting with the inner-self is the only way to achieve spiritual success in this life as well as on the highway of an infinite journey.

Let us always be aware that an interim perceived success while on the planet in current lifetime may or may not be a spiritual success on the eternal path. It all depends on whether our actions to achieve that success in current lifetime are emerging out of leaving behind a burden of some karmic debt, an environmental debt or a so-called carbon footprint, or an emotional debt of making others upset. Action can be possible in a manner that is non-karmic.

Exercises for Chapters 1, 2, and 3

Building a connection to your inner-self and opening up to the universe through this connection

Exercise 1:

1. Inhale deeply, but very slowly. As you inhale, say 'Aum Namah Shivaya' mentally four times. Hold the breath for two counts of the mental chant 'Aum Namah Shivaya.' Now exhale the breath in a controlled manner at a slow pace, mentally chanting 'Aum Namah Shivaya' five times and exhale completely.
2. Hold the breath in exhaled condition while mentally chanting 'Aum Namah Shivaya' two times.
3. Repeat the cycle starting at 1 above followed by 2 above seven times.

This exercise will help you build a capability to breathe in and out deeply and completely.

Our life span is measured by the number of breaths we take. Slow and deep inhaling and exhaling is healing and extends the longevity.

Exercise 2:

As you walk, slowly inhale at the count of every step, and keep inhaling with the mental chant of 'Aum Namah Shivaya' at every step, and complete the inhalation at step 7. Hold in the inhaled condition at two step counts, mental chanting 'Aum Namah Shivaya' at every step. Next, slowly exhale in a controlled manner mentally chanting 'Aum Namah Shivaya' at every step, and complete exhaling at the count of ten steps. Hold in exhaled condition at the count of two steps, at every step mentally chanting 'Aum Namah Shivaya.'

Exercise 3:

Inhale chanting 'Aum Namah Shivaya,' hold and exhale as in exercise 1 above, followed by seven minutes of silence with your eyes closed. As you sit in this silent, meditative state, do not consciously think or avoid any natural thoughts that may be there in the mind.

Face to Face with Shiva

At the end of this brief silent sitting, still with your eyes closed, communicate with your inner-self, and ask from within:
- Who am I?
- What is the purpose of my life that would help me to create a better world while I am on this planet?
- What can I do to fulfill the purpose of my life within my lifetime?
- What steps can I take within next one to two years to achieve my purpose?
- What steps can I take within next few weeks to achieve my purpose?
- What steps can I take today and tomorrow to achieve my purpose?
- What steps can I take to initiate a community project to achieve my purpose, and with whom do I need to communicate and network to expand the dialog and form a community of like-minded folks to launch the project?

After contemplating for a few minutes on these thoughts, slowly open your eyes within your palms, and then jot down the answers that you got from your inner-self to these questions. Next step is to take action: document your project, draw a timeline, plan for resources, and regularly monitor the progress towards implementation.

CHAPTER 4

Acquired Identity Syndrome

It is something that is a result of our conditioning of mind based on our cumulative experiences that keeps shaping our perception and prevents us from thinking out of the box. It keeps grounding us to the past, to such an extent that we are unable to delink from it. This inability to delink from the past prevents us from visualizing a future that is independent of traces from the past.

Over a period of time, we develop biases, prejudices, and views that result from such conditioning. The perception of a specific individual of a particular situation is driven by this conditioning and can drastically vary from the perception of another, or that of a group. Our very own make-believe maze is created by the interpretations we append to what we hear, see, or experience. Our cumulative past experiences keep strengthening our beliefs.

Unpeeling layers of the 'Acquired Identity' Syndrome onion
To get deeper, we need to start removing the layers one by one.

The uppermost stack is that of an acquired identity. The one of name, surname and religion, followed by nationality and community. This layer sits on top of the physical layer and includes the attributes of education, profession, peer groups and affiliations.

The next layer is that of physical attributes- height, looks, weight, complexion, gender, all cover ups to hide what a mess it may be inside.

Next layer is that of the mental dimension of our personality. This layer is a whole stack of perceptions - the root cause of an imbalance in our inner world, which is reflected by the state of affairs in the external world.

The last layer is the innermost core. This is the core of spiritual dimension of our personality. Right here lies the feeling to love and help everyone. This is from where the noble attitudes and inspirations are driven. The source of life. The Soul. The Spirit. The Spiritual Being. Connected with the divine.

The challenge before each human being is two-fold: first, get to pierce through the layers above to get to the inner-core. A suggested methodology is that of meditation. You can pick whatever works for you. The second is to maintain a balance. Within each dimension of the personality and also across the dimensions- physical, mental and spiritual. Just being tied to one dimension would not be the solution. In your objective to make the world a better place to be, what is of utmost importance is to maintain your balance.

Factors affecting *Acquired Identity*: physical existence at a place, geographical co-ordinates of existence, surroundings and environment, society, gender, sexual orientation, religion, education, name, surname, experiences, thoughts, inputs

Factors affecting *True Identity*: once we are able to cut through the layers of Acquired Identity, peeling off the physical and mental dimensions of our personality, there lies bared the 'Spiritual Dimension' of our personality. The major factor here is an ability to establish a dialog with our inner-self and sustain that dialog on a day to day basis. Meditation, as suggested, is one of the ways to get there.

One major factor that separates the paradigms of acquired and true identities is that while the nature of Acquired Identity is a constantly changing one, the nature of True Identity is changeless.

The environment constantly interacts with and shapes outer layers.

A direct manifestation of make-believe reality in our day to day life becomes our *'Acquired Identity Syndrome.'* Examples of such syndromes are the stock markets, our attitude to dealing with certain communities and situations in a particular manner, our way of thinking towards colleagues, religion, sex, family or circumstances. AIS reflects from a 'conditioned' state of mind, driving our perception and motivation to act or behave in a particular manner.

Outer layers of acquired identity – physical and mental dimensions

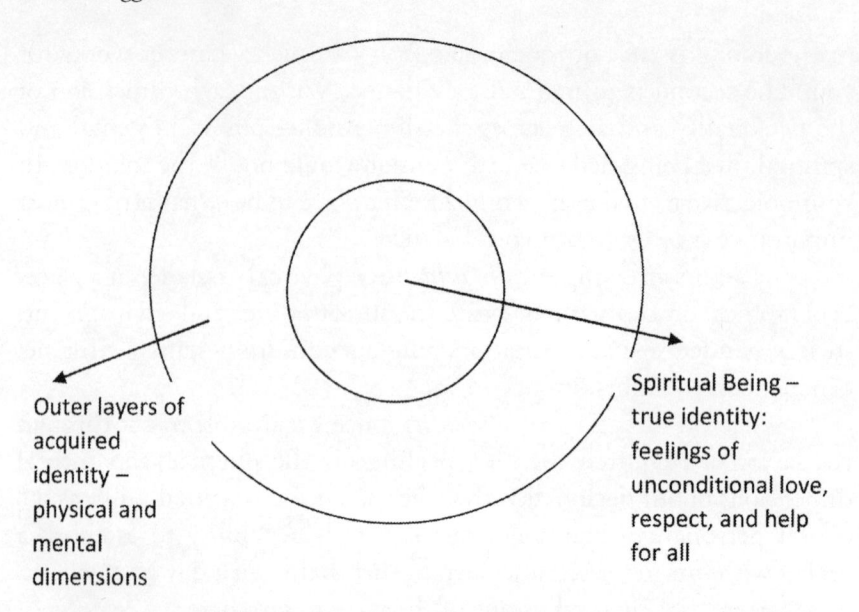

Spiritual Being – true identity: feelings of unconditional love, respect, and help for all

Fig.4.1: Layers of Acquired and True Identity

The Paradigm of Acquired Identity and Religion

It is something that you get to believe into. How do you get to know and believe that your name is 'so and so': just because someone told you and you got to live it for the rest of your life? How do you get to know that your religion is 'so and so': exactly the same thing as the name? How do you know that to behave in a particular manner is right and anything other than that is wrong? How are our perceptions shaped? Is this just a conditioning of our mind or anything far, far beyond that? How do we get conditioned that if we make more money we would be happy? How do we know as to what we are thinking is right or wrong, or yet there are higher dimensions to the levels of thoughts and perceptions?

Our thoughts get conditioned by what we see, observe or assimilate; over and above what already resides in the huge database of our brain. Once we get to know more, have a new experience, our records get updated and form a greater bias towards our perception process. We keep on aspiring to get to know about higher realities and new experiences to add to our learning. By our very nature, we as human beings are inquisitive- ever aspiring to learn more and assimilate new learning into what we already know. Not only strengthen the base of our experiential learning and knowledge, even to know it as a personal quest.

Next, if all that is fine, then where lies the problem? The problem lies exactly in our perception, when we begin to make assumptions. These assumptions could be both reasonable as well as unreasonable, as we imply interpretations to whatever we hear, read, or view. Implied interpretations can often lead to misunderstanding the intent of communication- whether verbal, written, or visual.

An accumulation of such implied interpretations creates the genesis for a make-believe platform. At the foundation of this make-believe platform lie accumulated experiences, existing knowledge, and a house-full of beliefs. This is the platform of 'Acquired Identity' that is shaped by our simulated reality of a conditioned mind set.

Explaining well with an example of 'wearing inverted glasses', researchers brought home the point of 'vulnerability of human mind' to *conditioning*. Volunteers wearing 'inverted glasses' were conditioned to the point that within hours they believed the world to be inverted. Such is the power of 'immersion' into a synthetic environment. The recent research and boom in the field of virtual reality further authenticated the point that perceptions of brain are 'simulations' of the 'environment' in which we are 'immersed'.

Exercise for Chapter 4
    A to-do exercise: Identify Yourself

    Close your eyes and ask yourself this question: Who am I? Start surfing past your acquired and given identities. Probe deeply within yourself to get an answer. Write down the response. Date and time the response which you just documented.

    Let us probe when we asked ourselves the question: Who am I?

    Whenever we personally did that, we were answer-less after about five minutes of probing exercise, attempting to scratch beneath the surface of our acquired identity. Now, when we begin to peel this onion of different layers, we find a whole stack of acquired and conditioned identities which give all of us the 'simulated reality' of being ourselves that we have come to live with our life.

Our Acquired Identity
    Begin to peel the layers of a big stack of acquired and not so real identities. Going by this identity syndrome, one always gets a feeling of

being alienated when one migrates to a new place. Suppose you lived at a place for ten years. This is the place you were born and brought up. Suddenly you moved away from there. Your emotional conditioning prompts you to come back to the place of your roots, just to face a *reverse identity crisis*. All your friends may have moved out. Those who are there, they have no time for you as they are busy with their own families and professions. It is important that first of all we understand as to who we are, even before we begin to explore as to why we are here on this planet.

You begin with the peeling of your first and last name, office designation, social security number etc. as your given identities by the system in which we live in today. Next, you go to the layer of a conditioning that education and training gave you at school, college and the university. This made you acquire certain diplomas, degrees, and grades. The next layer is the religion which over the years might have taught you to lead the life in a certain way. The language binding you to community and the culture that you adapted from those around you and the environment.

Once you are done with scratching unto here, you suddenly realize that you were born just a human being- as you came to this world in your birthday suit, jumping out of the womb of your Mom, and you brought nothing here but just yourself- a tiny little creature. Though it may not be possible for you to recapture that moment and experience, but that is what exists as a mere fact. Now, we get down to a deeper level than that of being a human.

We all have animal instincts as we belong to a specific family of species in the animal kingdom and true to the nature of species, we like to be social and want to live in groups. What beyond that? Let us look very deep inside ourselves- what do we find in there- at the bottom of our hearts: that is where our true identity lies. This is what we can't see, touch or smell. This is just a matter of feeling. Do you find the feelings of love and an attitude to help everyone at this level? If not, then there was something wrong in the manner in which you begin to peel this stack or else, it might be possible that you just got stuck at one of the layers above and could not make it beyond that. Now, if we really did end up getting there, what has the feeling to love and help everyone got to do with who I am? There is a larger context out there in which we have to perceive this correlation. This larger context is coming from looking at the meaning of life itself, who we are in this system, identify our role and evaluate for ourselves as to how best we can contribute to the system. Once we get connected to our true identity and real self, that's where we can see an image of Lord Shiva as embedded in our own self and in all else that exists. This image is formless and is just there as a realization. This is realization of the self.

CHAPTER 5

The secret of creation hypothesis

In simple terms, there is only one super element (you may call it Super Consciousness) that in turn creates three basic elements – consciousness, knowledge, and energy. All un-manifested as well as manifested creation is eventually a result of the combination of these three basic elements in some way.

Think of knowledge and energy attachment also as something that happens like a binding at the required time of creating an instance. For all manifestation of any instance of consciousness, time and space are the two delimiters. While time is a consequence of knowledge, space is a consequence of energy. These delimiters are required to be associated with an instance that is slated to materialize in a form that is visible and can be comprehended or perceived. Pure consciousness (you may also say Super Consciousness) ever exists in its un-manifested form and is not limited by time and space in any manner.

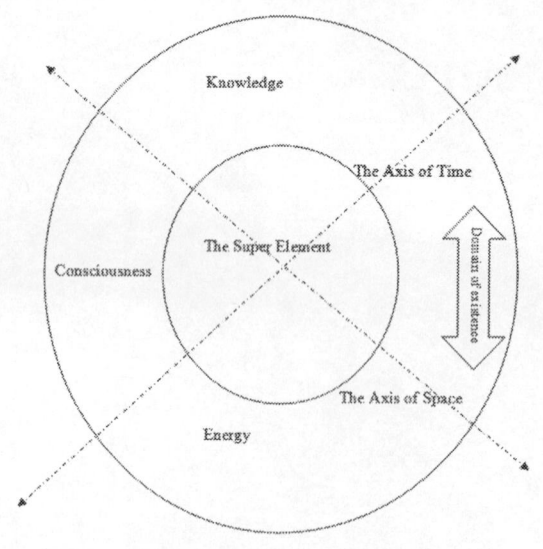

Fig. 5.1: The Super Element and its decomposition

Upon manifestation, it is an instance of consciousness that gets attached to and associates itself with relevant knowledge and gathers the required form of energy to create a living or a non-living existence, just like human beings on planet Earth or even a star with its supporting planetary system.

Knowledge enhances with time and by the virtue of experimentation of all instantiated manifestation as the living universe – this is the sole purpose why time or manifested universe exists, as it provides a platform to experiment.

Energy is constantly changing form, and becomes the source to nurture and sustain the living universe. For example, Sun is the source for all energy that planet Earth needs to sustain itself. By consistently burning itself, the Sun is producing the energy in form of light waves that sustain the solar system.

Manifestation and de-manifestation

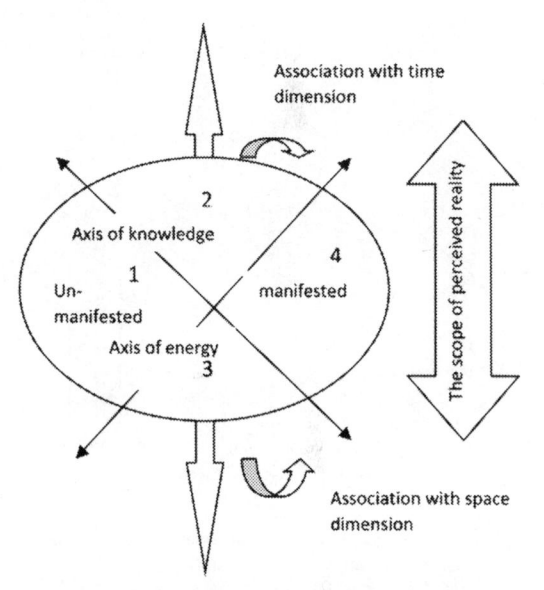

Fig. 5.2: The hemisphere of manifestation

The four quadrants of circle above are:
1. The un-manifested
2. The transition to association with knowledge (includes association with time dimension as a limiter)
3. The transition to association with energy (includes association with space dimension as a limiter)
4. The manifested

What is shown in above diagram is how Super Consciousness transforms itself by first attaching and associating with knowledge and energy and consequently with time and space to a materialized universe as we perceive it.

After a life is over, what happens, and how are the elements of consciousness, knowledge, and energy separated?

The sole purpose of human life is to return a useful value that aids to enhance knowledge. When a human life in its present instance has achieved a cumulative evolution over lives and gathered sufficient useful data by experimentation to an end point that aids to enhance knowledge, it returns a useful value. Once that useful value is accepted and the life form is ready for dissolution, the three basic elements are separated and returned to their specific origins. This process of dissolution can be perceived as the reversal of creation, and is the opposite side of the sphere, i.e. the hemisphere of de-manifestation.

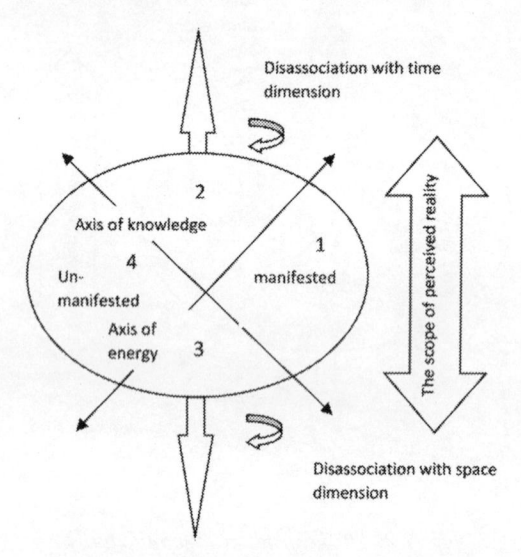

Fig. 5.3: The hemisphere of de-manifestation

The four quadrants of circle above are:

1. The manifested
2. The transition to disassociation with knowledge (includes disassociation with time dimension as a delimiter)
3. The transition to disassociation with energy (includes disassociation with space dimension as a delimiter)
4. The un-manifested

What is shown in above diagram is how a materialized existence is returned upon its dissolution to its original source of creation – the Super Consciousness. It transforms itself by first disassociating with knowledge and energy and consequently with time and space to detach from the bindings of a materialized universe (as we perceive it).

Moksha and Nirvana

The Moksha, also termed as Mukti, is the ultimate termination from the bondage of perpetual life and death, or re-births. It happens only when a life attains sufficient useful data to be returned for enhancement of knowledge, and is ready for dissolution. Till such time that this useful data is gathered, if necessary, a life may be re-instantiated while retaining its cumulative gathering of data over spans of lives. Though this cumulative data may be veiled from that specific instance of life itself, there is an association that retains a thread to it. Only when a level is reached that the present instance of life is ready for returning the useful value and by virtue of this attainment declares itself ready for dissolution, the Moksha happens on its own.

While Moksha is the process that transforms an individual by first disassociating with knowledge and energy and consequently with time and space to detach from the bindings of a materialized universal manifestation, and return all elements of creation to their original source, and finally, Nirvana is the union and merger of that particular instance of Consciousness to its original source - the Super Consciousness. This is, in essence, the ultimate merger with our original source of existence – Lord Shiva in the form of super element, or super consciousness.

Nirvana is that state of attainment where all the individual identities are lost, and evolvement has reached to qualify for a merger with the super element.

Creation of the universe and the purpose of life on our planet

The limited decomposition of the super element causes its three sub elements – consciousness, energy, and knowledge, to intermingle in varying proportions and modes to create a wide canvas of hues and shades of existence that is multidimensional, but yet finite. It is finite in the sense that each object of this creation has a defined life span and a very specifically scoped existence.

The scope is defined at the time of its creation, and within the span of that scope the object of existence enjoys a flexibility of limited variation for the dimensions defined in that manner – for instance, human beings can exercise choices while making decisions, and to a more limited extend, most of the species in the animal kingdom can exercise the choice in mobility.

Each object of creation has some existence of the three basic elements - consciousness, energy, and knowledge. All inanimate objects have a presence of consciousness in a suspended form. No creation or existence in the universe is ever devoid of consciousness. To our perception, we see only the living beings as having consciousness, but in reality it is present in all objects, as it is the most basic element that must be present to create anything to exist.

Since energy is continually changing form, it is this nature of energy that is responsible for everything in motion, and for expansion of the universe.

The nature of knowledge is to enhance and evolve - and it utilizes the vehicle of energy to create dynamics of continual experimentation for each object of existence throughout its lifetime.

The dynamics of intermingled nature of co-existence of energy and knowledge causes ageing, as an object of existence progresses in its path to grow knowledge.

Consciousness is that all pervading, ever existing element that never changes in its nature, but it keeps evolving. It aids all creation and dissolution.

When an object of existence returns a useful value by way of its interaction with other objects and through living its life as experimentation, its dissolution is enabled by consciousness. The energy merely changes form – matter decomposes. The knowledge created throughout lifetimes of the object is uploaded and immediately made available for access to all other objects of existence in the living universe. The element of consciousness merges back into the super element, upon verification whether the object of existence has indeed returned the useful values by significant enhancement of knowledge.

The combination of consciousness, energy, and knowledge is framed into a life or non-living form by two limiters – time and space. All manifested existence is bound by these two limiters. Upon dissolution, if a useful value is returned by an object of existence and the usefulness of the value that it has returned is deemed appropriate as per the charter set for its type of existence, then it merges into the super element itself, crossing the limits of time and space that were set upon its manifestation.

In all practical terms, Nirvana is all about crossing the boundaries of time and space and essentially merging with the super element, the super consciousness. Thus, time and space are the limiters to create a manifested existence. The same time and space become de-limiters when a manifested existence gets ready for dissolution.

Thus, if one considered the round trip of an existence from its un-manifested form to manifestation, and then back to de-manifestation, the association and disassociation with time and space becomes contextual at the points where it changes forms each-way in this cycle of transformation from non-existence to existence and vice-versa.

When it is felt by the object itself that it has not returned any useful value at the end of its existence, it may be hanging in a suspended state, at the end of its life, still bound by time but not by space, waiting for a suitable opportunity to re-manifest itself so that it can complete the assigned task of returning a useful value. This can be an iterative process, and can go on and on. This is the cycle of rebirth and coming back to a form of life in some manner.

To evolve towards removal from the shackles of life and birth and to dissolve into the ultimate, one can make an endeavor within the present lifetime to do as best as possible to return a useful value by way of living the present life and experimenting with it in the right direction.

To do so, one is inherently inspired by the inner-self. Once we open this connection with our inner-self, we are on a sort of self-guided tour. The journey of life in evolution to a higher level of existence is a simple one, and starts with a single step in the right direction.

The domain of existence is in-between the intersection of the axis of knowledge and the axis of energy, associating with time and space, both acting as limiters that bring the abstract forms of consciousness, energy, and knowledge to a manifested form.

Transcending the boundaries of time and space is not trivial. It first of all needs a comprehension that these are limiters and de-limiters to associate or disassociate knowledge and energy respectively with an existence.

From our role on the planet to our place in the universe

Each one of us exists in a specific time-horizon window in the universe. Our existence is not accidental, but is an essential part of a bigger divine plan. Our physical life on the planet is just like an exit stop from the infinite spiritual highway. Though we may see ourselves as puppets dancing to the tune of some higher force, we must know that we are not only empowered to shape our own destiny and future, but also that of the planet and all else that exists on it. If we live in a discipline of caring for the environment and build on the values and lessons learnt so far while living and existing on the planet as a species, we can easily graduate to the level where we have a greater say in shaping the course of life in the universe. Our elevation in status among all forms living in the universe is a direct function of the sum total of our collective actions, speeches, and thoughts.

Among all that matters, cultivating positive thoughts is the most important thing. It is the positive energy of our thoughts that leads us collectively to an elevated attitude of humanity. Building on this positivity from one level to another and graduating to a higher level of existence in the universe is a collective responsibility of all of us.

From super element to tangible material

Shiva is an omni-existent and formless super element. Shiva is that one and only super element from whom all existence is driven for a purpose, and after fulfillment of that purpose, finally merges into. Thus, all existence keeps circling back and forth into and out of Shiva.

The super element Shiva continually keeps decomposing itself into three basic elements. The three basic elements are consciousness, knowledge, and energy. The three basic elements are represented as Mahesh (consciousness), Bramha (knowledge), and Vishnu (energy).

All existence that is visible to the human eye is ultimately a manifestation of energy, knowledge, and consciousness coming together for a purpose.

Our perception of consciousness being existent only in human beings or in other living forms is flawed. All visible existence has a combination of all the three basic elements. In apparently matter-alone objects, the consciousness exists in a form that may be termed as equivalent of 'suspended animation.' Just like a seed keeps breathing and stays alive, and blooms into a tree when met with appropriate environment and conditions of germination, apparently matter-alone objects are not lifeless. We often treat material objects as a form of condensed energy. Though we are unable to perceive life in these objects, we need to treat them with respect, as these are also the decomposed manifestation of the same ultimate super element.

We deal with energy in its various forms, and are also cognizant of its presence within ourselves. All knowledge comes from the same source, and is implanted into our thinking and creative faculties through an abstract neural network. As living creatures in an organic and evolving universe, we are continually engaged in the process of enhancing knowledge. The enhanced knowledge is transferred through the abstract neural network to be deposited in the universal repository.

It is from this repository that ever newer and enhanced knowledge is transferred to all creatures engaged in the process of evolving consciousness. While the overall amount of energy in the universe is fixed and it can only change in its form, the application of knowledge to experiment with energy is the sole purpose of existence. As newer results are obtained from this experimentation, it leads to an enhancement of knowledge. It is the enhanced knowledge that eventually leads to an evolution of the consciousness.

By its very nature, the energy undergoes change, the knowledge undergoes enhancement, and the consciousness undergoes evolution. In that respect, all existence, including all of us, are constantly engaged in evolving the universe.

We are all different in our own unique ways, yet are all united by the virtue of having an image of Shiva within ourselves. Each one of us on the planet is so blessed that this planet was personally walked by Shiva over 7000 years ago [2], and we all must genuinely respect and regard the power, scope, and enormity of Shiva's vastness and humility. What others may simply consider as anger is indeed Shiva's humility to not only accommodate, but even bless the genuine seekers.

God is collective consciousness of the unlimited universe

Shiva, as the most revered, loved and omni-respected one, refuses to be known or acknowledged as the God. Instead Shiva empowers each one of us to step up, become self-realizing, and embrace the challenge that is most demanding of human life.

The universe is beyond the comprehension of any single human mind, yet it can be grasped conceptually as unlimited. Knowing not whether there are living and intelligent forms elsewhere in the universe, it would certainly be limiting to assume that we are alone. In movement to the outer universe, Shiva signified the very fact that there is indeed life and intelligence, and that too existing in far superior forms than our own, outside the purview of our limited imagination.

Human life is limited, and so are our thought and action processes. When empowered with capabilities to think and do beyond our limited capability, we end up creating weapons of mass destruction, instruments for gratification of sensual pleasures, and structures for elimination of the less privileged and less powerful amongst us. We have been even exploiting our very own mother planet Earth to the extent that we now run the risk of extinction of its precious life-sustaining environment with that of our own.

Having created our own 'Acquired Identity Syndromes,' from 'Money' as a concept to build interdependence to 'Stocks' as instruments for creation of 'perceived' wealth, we have been completely lost from the very purpose of our existence and wandered off on a tangent to satisfy our ignorance of 'who we truly are.'

No one can deny that the ultimate reality of life is 'death.' Though none of us may like to acknowledge or even talk about it, the fact is that no human being lives forever. Despite the knowledge of this fact, several of us are engaged in mud-slinging, self-gratifying, and destructive thoughts and activities that lead to further deterioration and corruption of our mind, environment, and health – the root cause being a lack of knowledge of the self and its relation to the super-self.

The time to wake up is 'NOW.' We need to see and realize the image of the divine within us, as much as we need to see it in all others and the entire existence. Seeing the image of the divine in ourselves, we need to rise up to the challenge to protect the endangered environment of our planet, create peace, unite the world, and do all that we can to build interdependence in a harmonious manner. Seeing the divine in others and all that exists, we need to treat all those we interact with respect and compassion, and this extends to non-humans and all that is perceived to be as non-living existence. From using only 'as much water as I need' to avoiding wastage in all forms, recycling all that we can, and this list of 'to-do's can be endless.

Once we connect to the inner-self, and listen to voice of the divine from within, the rest would follow. Foremost is to develop an ability to make this connection and keep it alive.

Universe as a living organism

Think of universe as a living organism. It is self-adapting, self-correcting, and growing. In its evolution, it undergoes the cycles of compression and decompression. With each new cycle of creation, manifestation from the cumulative prior cycles of de-manifestation is materialized with a newer knowledge to sustain and grow the existence. It is like a living being waking up during the day, engaging in an activity, learning some newer lessons, and then retiring to sleep at end of the day with those lessons. When waking up the next morning, that living being is refreshed with lessons learnt from the cumulative experience of life.

Chapter 6

The modes of existence

We live under the influence of our AISs that prevent us from shifting our mode, and force us to continue to exist and thrive while living under the mode of ignorance.

While there is nothing wrong in living under the mode of ignorance as life itself is an experiment at learning as we are all students, and it is our evolved experience at each learning that enhances the cumulative collective knowledge of the interconnected, interdependent universe; we also need to evolve as an individual, since we are all part of a larger evolution of human beings as a species and our planet acts as a platform to enable us to do exactly that. Life is all about learning through experience.

It might be worthwhile to explore the other modes of existence as revealed by Shiva.

The mode of transition is the one that enables us to gradually, or rather periodically, catch a glimpse of what can possibly be at the other end of the spectrum. By our vary nature as being born in an image of the divine, we are curious creatures who dare to explore and exist.

Once we start this journey in exploration, we can occasionally get a sight into the mode of enlightenment, the preferred mode of living for us.

The mode of enlightenment is nothing else, but a point where we get rather detached from our AISs (Acquired Identity Syndromes), and the mode of transition is a journey that helps us get there.

Simulated Reality

Each one of us individually suffers from it. When a society takes shape as a collection of each one of us, we collectively create one for the society. When societies come together to create a nation, we have a simulated reality of a nation. The political map of the world as it has come to be is a simulated reality of the world. Let's face it that we all share the same earth, sky, sun, moon, stars, air, and water.

What it is: A conditioning of mind as a perception, which we buy for us to be our domain of existence. The process of buying here is a mental one. We have created it for us. The genesis of its creation is deep rooted in the history of our past and keeps driving our future as a reflection of the past. Each small experience is an exercise in learning. This learning is absorbed by the brain and embedded into the existing base of knowledge. Each one of us has a different set of it. That is why, there is so much to learn from everyone.

The simulated reality of a nation: pride, heroism, technological advances, heritage, goodness, beliefs

The simulated reality of a society: culture, language, attitude

The simulated reality of a religion: interpretation of the scripture for suited intent, inheritance by generation, motives of clergy to instigate masses, pretensions by collective groups of politicians and opportunists

The simulated reality of an individual: name, surname, physical attributes, religion, family, culture, education, profession, peers, friends, and life-style

Stock Markets: An AIS of Human Society

Understanding and analyzing a case for discussion of Stock Markets as an AIS, we must first understand a few basic laws related to operation of systems. Considering life as a system where the single dominant factor under our control is our attitude and major output of life system is our actions, we need to identify similar attributes for each system under study. To understand the basic laws under which systems operate, let us do a simple experiment.

Experiment:

1. Pick two identical glass tumblers. Make marks on both at the top at identical positions. Put water in one glass to the mark. Now, transfer water from one glass to the other. Assuming that there was no sudden change in the room temperature, notice as to whether the level of water has increased or decreased after transfer. Some water has remained sticking to the inside surface of the previous glass, from which water was transferred. Now, if you transfer water to a third identical glass tumbler, would it increase in level or further decrease? At each successive transfer, the level of water would keep going down. This simple experiment gives us our first law. *You can never take out of a system more than what you input to the system.* In other words, the output of a system can never be more than the input. The process of transformation of input through the system

to generate output requires something known as 'system sustenance overhead.'

2. Put water and ice-cubes into the first glass to the mark. Transfer the contents to other glass. You would make two observations. Besides the water that remained sticking to the surface of first glass, when the ice actually melts, the volume of water shall reduce and not expand. Thus, the overall level would get further down. A marginal gain in volume owing to increased temperature of water after melting of the ice may not be more than the loss of volume on melting. The second important observation is that the ice-cold water has attracted some moisture on the out-skitrs of the glass. Notice that this moisture that has been gathered is still outside the glass and not directly inside. Unless you have a mechanism to turn that extra moisture gathered outside to inside of the glass, there is no net increase in level inside the glass. The extra moisture gathered outside the glass is from the environment and is giving you a false perception of 'more' as it appears from the outside. This step of the experiment gives us some more laws. *Unless an additional input is driven from the environment in whose overall domain the system operates, there can not be an increase in the output*. Next, the *perceived output of a system is not the real output*. The perceived output of a system can be more than the actual output of the system.

What everyone is fighting out in the stock market is the difference between the perceived output and actual output. This illusion of perceived output to appear greater than the actual output of the system has kept stock-brokers in business. It is like perceiving that everyone who walks in to a casino would come out a winner. Did any one ever walk in to a casino with an attitude to give? Did any one ever invest in the stock market with an attitude to give? Give your investment for the promotion of a product or enhancement of a technology or service.

If there was a freezing machine in one of the glasses of above experiment that sucked up all the moisture out of the environment and also by causing some evaporation from other glasses, isn't that the one we wanted? Just because we want the level in our glass to be the highest. That exactly reflects the attitude of all the investors in the stock market. With that attitude, they only invested in the stock that sucks. The stock that *sucks* the moisture out of the environment to create a higher perceived return for us- the investors. This is the simulated reality of our perception with the stocks. If everyone sucked the moisture out of the environment, the environment would be left totally dry. And the perceived extra moisture of our *greed* has not flown into our glass- we never had a mechanism in place to capture that from outside the glass to inside of it. It has just flown down the drain. No glass is cool enough to draw moisture out of a dry air. All the ice in all the glasses has already melted.

This is what happens to the stock market. The environment gets totally dried up. We have to wait till the wasted extra moisture of our collective greed has made its way to the nearest creek, from there to a river, finally to the ocean. Then, from the depths of that ocean would water rise to the surface and get pushed up into a cloud through an externally applied force (the sun). It has a long way to reach us. The only way we can make the change is by the change in our attitude. Next time you pick a stock for investment, pick the stock not on its hype or your greed, but out of an attitude to invest to make this world a better place to be. If you ever invest with the right attitude, you would never be a loser. You would always be a winner. For you would have contributed towards making this world a better place to be.

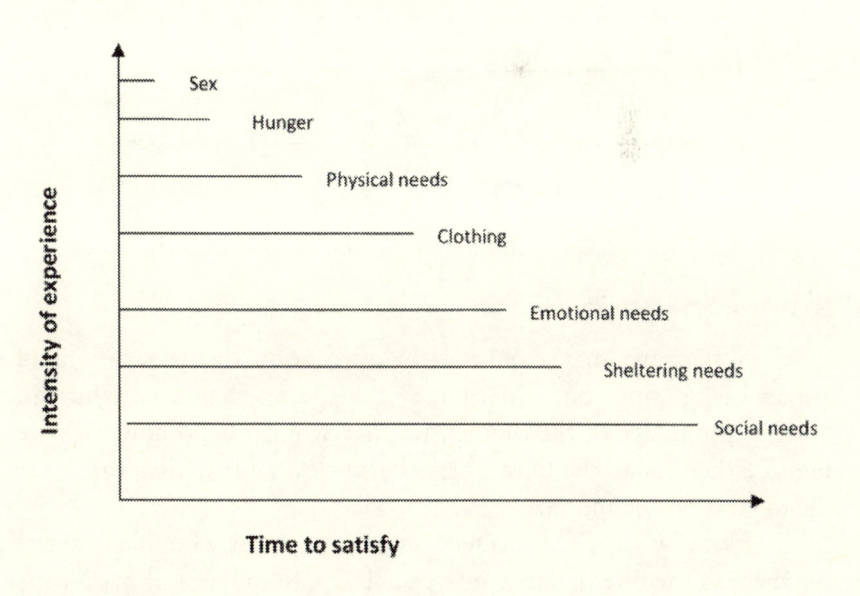

Fig. 6.1: Acquired Identity Syndromes (physical) – intensity and duration

As can be noticed from the above diagram, sex sits on the very top as crown prince of all physical AISs. In today's world, as one can visualize, it may be possible to buy out most of our needs with the power of money. That itself leads us to the make-believe maze of a human invention that was created to build interdependence and discipline of sorts. While the instruments of money have served that purpose well, it is now the time to consider whether these have already outlived their usefulness.

There are AISs in several spheres of our existence – physical, logical, conceptual – the underpinnings are related to how we perceive each one of these to be as part of our dimensions of existence as well as the modes thereof.

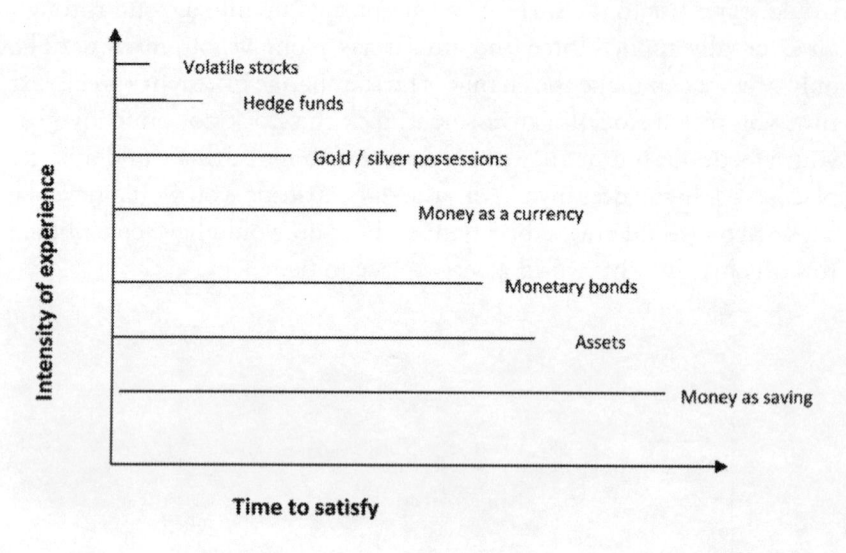

Fig. 6.2: Acquired Identity Syndromes (financial) – intensity and duration

All knowledge is spiritual

When one may look at it in retrospect, all the creations of human beings since our evolution to the species that is now human (born in the image of the divine), we may wonder as to how we were able to either create the likes of space shuttles, and Apollos that were able to land on the moon.

Now, by what Shiva is revealing to us, we may be able to travel anywhere in the inter-galactic universe if we can follow and master the techniques that he has already done, and while he just showed as an unusual experience is merely a tip of the iceberg, the more of it is yet to come to the readers of this text as gradual, yet subtle and definite steps to move forward in the direction of evolving ourselves as a species to achieve what Shiva has mastered and partially revealed.

No doubt that we are under the care of Shiva. Also, no need to fight within our groups as to who is right or wrong, or whose God is more powerful than that of the other. We would get nowhere at all either fighting each-other or defending our conceptualization of God, for just one reason that WE ARE ALL ONE.

Whether it is the strength of justifying a point of view, or proving what is right, the common resulting denominator is an argument that ensues in the broader interest of humanity and the universe alike.

We are all together in the process of evolution – there are always going to be subtle differences in the ways that we think, operate, and evaluate. While we are all inspired through the exact same source, our interpretations vary.

Our interpretations are biased and driven from our AISs.

The dimension of compression by itself is the most critical aspect to make the world realize as to 'why we need to do with less.'

Dimension of compression

Think of two farthest corners of a paper – one corner diagonally opposite to the other.

Next, fold the paper in a manner that these two corner spots are brought together.

Fig. 6.3: folding a paper to create an extra dimension

Now, the folded paper has the two farthest points as one and the same – the perception of two farthest points has simply melted to just one and the same point in an instant when we added an extra dimension to bring these two corner spots together.

Next, if we fold in the two remaining corner points as well, all the four farthest corners would be just one spot. The dimension of compression is an extremely powerful concept, and would enable us to create a paradigm shift in the way we comprehend the distance, time, existence, and the universe.

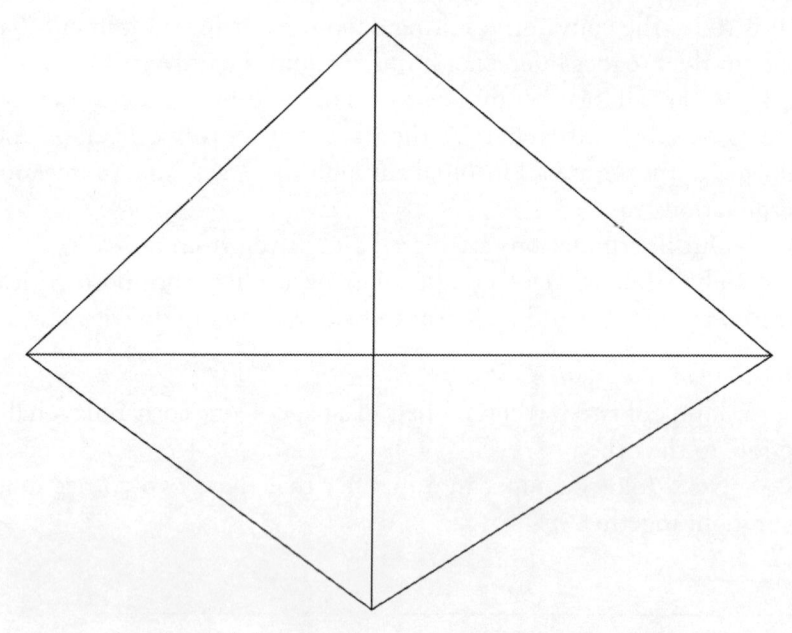

Fig. 6.4: folded paper reflecting an extra dimension – extreme distance corner points are merged to just one spot

The easiest common day experience is to visualize the Eastern most tip of Russia and the Western most tips of US in Alaska – in 2-D view in a map are the farthest points, and in a 3-D globe are right next to each-other.

Now, we are able to comprehend as to how adding an extra dimension dramatically reduces the perceived distance separating two points. Extending the concept further, we can imagine that it is possible to bring together any two given multi-dimensional coordinates across the inter-galactic universe *on-demand*. This on-demand association of the extra dimension of compression makes it possible to conduit from one point of interest (say where you are now) to where you would like to be (destination).

In an exact same way as above comprehension, Shiva was *conduit-ing* (creating a tunnel of the dimension of compression) across the two points of interest in the inter-galactic universe and then teleporting through this conduit while delimited from time and space as constraints.

Teleporting across the inter-galactic universe *on-demand* is made possible by acquiring the ability to conduit through the dimension of compression.

Shiva is considered as timeless, omni-present, ageless, and the protector of all.

While Shiva is the protector of the entire universe, Shiva is also the inspirer to all of humans and inhabitants of the planet.

In current impasse while we are on this planet, one of the foremost responsibilities for each one of us is to create permanent peace on the planet, and protect its environment in all ways possible.

Our role in protecting the environment

Years ago, folks would brag about having the ability and privileges to generate and consume more power, have more cars, and be the first ones to sign up for anything that spelled more comfort, or so as to say, a wrongly interpreted 'Quality of life' measurement parameter.

In today's world, the most critical aspect of life would be to not just protect the environment of our planet, but even go beyond to 'reverse the damage that we have already done as human species.'

The damage done is not just in terms of the Carbon dioxide, Carbon monoxide, or Nitrogen levels, it is way past that – we have gone to the extent of even corrupting ourselves to believe that money can buy our perceived AISs.

While we as human species are on just the last home run of the very opportunity to correct the collective damage that we have unleashed on our planet of existence, it is imperative that we now take action to reverse that damage to the environment.

Dematerialization starts with the self, in as much as 'charity begins at home.'

We can use an existing asset or possession for as long as it is really useful, and in all honesty being truthful of its as-is capability – not discarding it just for a new product on the block.

New products and services would keep cropping up in all areas that the established enterprises of the world cater to today and it is only a matter of time by when we realize that it is a cumulative accumulation of our collective 'Acquired Identity Syndromes' that has led to the current impasse where we are neither able to perform and achieve, nor take steps to correct our behavior.

The correction immediately needed is not just to inspire all humanity towards corrective and remedial actions, but even more critical to have a realization that we are already too late in the game to make a real difference.

Life is not a competition for any one of us to beat each-other out in the game, but just a process in which we directly engage to 'do' and 'collaborate.'

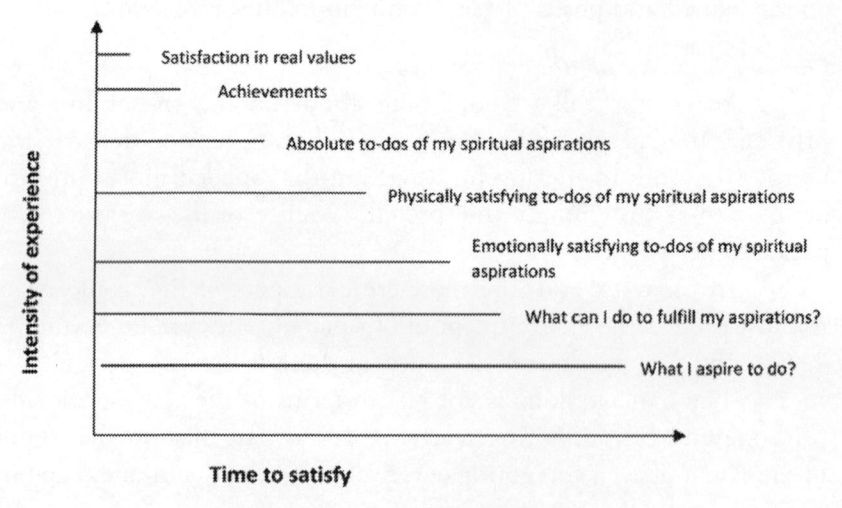

Fig. 6.5: Life as a process to engage and do

In the context of today's world, protecting the environment of the world and creating peace globally are prime life goals for each one of us.

It may appear that there has something gone wrong with the way we had all anticipated life to be and the world to shape, right from our lifestyle to economy to the political map. We have failed to realize the power of a creative potential of human intellect. Instead, we have simply succumbed as slaves to junk, as victims of an Acquired Identity Syndrome, a disease the humanity is unknowingly suffering from. The events of September 11 '2001 have dawned on the world a new realization. If we don't act now towards creating a better world, we would have none to blame. This is our last chance. Here are some suggestions to take this change as an opportunity and how we can do that.

The world has come to the stage of an unknown shift that unconsciously we all acknowledge and admit. But we are unwilling to publicly acknowledge our subscription to a new school of thought. The genesis of this paranoia lies in the fear of non-acceptance of our views by the society suffering from an *Acquired Identity Syndrome* (AIS). This new school of thought tells us that there has been something wrong with what we have created out of this world by all our deeds and actions of the past.

Nothing happens in reality unless we make a plan for it and execute that plan in action. The battle for survival has created an attitude of competition since the times immemorial. Continuing to live with the attitudes and paradigms of the millenniums gone by would not create any meaningful opportunities for an era of the new millennium.

We better realize that something has terribly gone wrong with the way the world has been managed so far. We better learn to do with less and begin to live in harmony with the nature, before we lose our house. Perhaps now is the time to cultivate skills for hiking and pitching a tent on the mountain.

The problem here today is that the world has got conditioned to seeing more and more. 'The bigger is better' was OK until more and more could be created. We have just crossed the peak of more- just putting an end to an era of 'Materialism'.

This peak was logically reached on December 31, 1999, when we were bidding farewell to the past millennium.

De-materialization: Why?

The materialization of society started not very long ago. All of us grew in a society where we saw the industrial revolution taking place. We saw the mechanization of labor oriented jobs, the standardization of manufacturing process, the speeds and modes of our travel get faster and better. All that was good, as long as we did it within limits. We did not know where the limit was. Since we got used to faster, bigger, better - our realities were simulated to a situation of make-believe that this is the way life has to be. We kept on making things better, faster, cheaper- till we discovered that there were limits to that.

We do need to know and realize that *there is no more* – we have already consumed it all.

Where lies the opportunity?

Opportunity is nowhere to find. It is everywhere to be created and crafted. If there is no limit on the creative potential of imagination, all existing situations are perfect conditions to visualize a model for success. Each day dawns upon us as an opportunity. It is for us to take it or waste it. What makes the difference is just one thing – how to want to take it. That is the way of our thinking and the level of our creative imagination. What we need is an attitude to create and cooperate. It all begins with connecting. The web has unleashed new possibilities which were previously unimagined, to connect and cooperate for creating business opportunities. We can never be able to comprehend these opportunities in any meaningful manner unless we change our attitude. Once we connect, the process to cooperate and create would follow naturally, if we have made the shift within us.

The shift that is required today is the one from current '*fear of competition*' to the futuristic '*trust of cooperation.*' It would need the collaborative and consultative effort of an entire sea of humanity to build that trust. That is one of the biggest challenges that we face today – to turn the table upside down. We have so far lived a 'simulated reality' to create a world full of mistrust, hatred and misery. Once we get past our 'Acquired Identity Syndrome,' we would be truly able to know as to '*who*' we really are. It is this realization alone that would set the stage for turning the table upside down. Instead of competing with each-other for all that has remained out of the limited opportunities that are available in the existing marketplace, we would be partnering and collaborating, collectively as a team, to create opportunities out of nowhere.

An attitude of creativity

The existing ways of doing things have emerged from the limited success and failures of models of the past – the models of competitive competence and cut throat strategies. There has been a nearly total bankruptcy of vision on part of the political, religious, and technical leadership of the world to create a world full of peace. There have been exceptions to that – from Abraham Lincoln to Mahatma Gandhi to John F Kennedy to Martin Luther King among several unknown and unsung heroes across nations and histories of the world.

If a John F Kennedy had not envisioned the human on moon, humanity would not have stepped on a soil other than that of this planet. If Martin Luther King, Jr. would not have a dream to create equality and be willing to put life at stake for that creation; there would be no equality or freedom. The process of creative visualization begins with an ability to look beyond all that exists. That is what creativity is: *an ability to look beyond all that exists.* An ability to pierce through a stack of undefined layers of perceptions, beliefs and seemingly true realities. An ability to inspire and cultivate an attitude that can look beyond the present. A kind of imagination that *extends* the boundaries of imagination itself – that is an attitude of creativity.

An altitude of creativity

The levels of creativity are like various altitudes of a mountain range. The Himalayas have Mount Everest to K2 as crown peaks to foothills and valleys forming the base. At the very base lies an attitude to be creative. With the positive potential of this base, the altitude of creativity can go beyond imagination. While Himalayas do have a highest peak, creativity has no limits. Just like there are never any perfect situations, since there is a room for improvement in any given situation.

The potential of human brain is unlimited. We are limited only by the cognitive boundaries of the domains of our imagination. At some point, we need to develop an ability to extend the limits of our imagination. That extension would become meaningful only if we are first able to integrate the existing domains of imagination. An integration of these domains would become possible if we consult and collaborate as an entire humanity with a single purpose: 'to create peace on the planet.'

As a simple exercise, look at the clouds above in the sky and see what kind of a picture you imagine. This visualization indicates your attitude. Do you see a picture that is synonym with hope or do you see a picture of despair? It may be a reflection of your mood at a particular instance. It is just a perception of your mind. The ability to look beyond such perceptions is the altitude of creativity.

If you had the opportunity of life to create, what would you like to do? Create something so unique that qualified you for the likes of a Nobel Prize? Can you aspire to do something that can eventually create an organization like the one that is able to solicit nominations and give away prizes like the one you are seeking? This is a paradigm shift in the scope of a perspective. It is this scope of your imaginative perspective that determines the altitude of your creative potential.

Attitude is... do I want to do it? If you say yes, you cross a threshold.

Altitude is... how far do I want to go with it?

It is like first being determined that *'Yes! I can make the difference.'* Second, a commitment to *'How much of a difference I am willing to make.'* Once this determination and commitment is made, the rest is easy and follows naturally. What is the difference you can make and how can you do it are typical questions that the 'Connect to Create' (C2C) process answers.

The word of caution here is: never make any artificial attempt at jumping the thresholds of attitude or take two steps at a time on the ladder of altitude. It is natural process of first unfolding and then blooming. You can't force open the petals of a bud to unfold into a flower. It must grow and unfold in a natural way, attached to the branch. That is where we are with it. You must operate from where you are. That is the branch on which you can grow – an acceptance of the present. One step at a time and a little bit each day. That is the way to win. You always win by doing it consistently. Just to learn and know is the point where you start the journey. Learn and know it is not the formula to win. You can learn and know a number of skills and technologies. You win only by consistently and continually applying one of those and develop mastery with that one. The same is true here. C2C is like learning a technology with attitudes and altitudes. It is for you to create something useful out of a focused connection that is a realizable, achievable and deliverable project, product or service and makes the world a better place to be. You can create peace while protecting the environment if this project, service or product is anywhere close to that mission. It is, in the long run, a commitment to live with the C2C culture.

The irony of today's situation is that between 80 to 90 % of the effort and energy is being wasted in competing, complaining, and comparing. Out of what remains, 60 % of that resource is taken away by unnecessary and useless activities. May sound hard to believe that we are effectively utilizing only between 4 to 8 % of the potential that is being spent. The story is same everywhere. Within our mind, we are occupied with lots of unnecessary junk that holds us from any meaningful creativity. Operations in business spend most of the resources in advertising and marketing. Agents and attorneys take chunks of fortune away for near-zero value addition in a society based on mistrust. Insurance companies are amassing massive wealth in a system build on dependence. The unproductive layers of fat overheads need to melt everywhere to expose the bare-bones of what is actually useful and really matters. In an interdependent economy based on C2C architecture, many a paradigms of business cultures and practices would shift, forced by the power of web-centric.

While meditative practice connects one internally and de-junks the mind, web enables to connect externally and eliminate the unnecessary. This is the synergy between science and spirituality merged together. Spirituality is showing the way to eliminate the unwanted internally. Science and technology is showing the way to eliminate the unwanted externally. The integrated synergy of this merger opens up new vistas to connect and create.

Dealing with sorrows, miseries and set-backs in life

Shiva shows us the way by all-inclusive nature. When a deadly potion is churned out of the ocean and there is nowhere that it can go as anywhere it would spill would be destroyed, Shiva steps forward to accept it and drink it. The potency of it turns Shiva's throat blue (Neelakantha).

In the overall grand divine plan, we have the sorrows, miseries and set-backs in life so that we can have an experience of these to be able to know as to what are happiness, joy, and ecstasy. In terms of the absolute, no experience is bad – it is just our perception of what we conceive it to be.

In times of great suffering, we may feel miserable and wonder as to why all-loving God would unleash such havoc on anyone? The answer lies in accepting what is, and re-membering our one-self with the ultimate universal-oneness, knowing that eventually all that there is ONE. This is in a way going back to realize the secret of creation. Once we embrace the grace of Shiva, the all-pervading divinity within and without, the suffering would tend to melt away, just by letting the grace of divinity set in.

As one can see in the graph below, when we live in the mode of enlightenment, we lower our suffering just by letting ourselves deal with it as a reality by acceptance of reality. Living in the mode of ignorance by denial (lower acceptance or non-acceptance) increases our suffering since we only pretend that it is not there and not even take any action to mitigate it.

When we accept 'what-is,' it opens up several doors for us to deal with the situation on hand. We have to deal with reality at all the three levels – physical, mental, and spiritual. While at the spiritual level we have to submit to the divine grace of Shiva knowing that all that there is ONE, at the mental level we have this knowing and acceptance of reality. This leads us to creative imagination and inspired thoughts. At the physical level, we can take the actions inspired by our highest possible thoughts and these actions would eventually lead to removal of all suffering and turn everything to a positive human experience.

One example of a small suffering leading to a bigger one can be two nations going to war based on actions of one of them. War certainly would lead to more disastrous consequences and may not even solve any problem. If engaged early on in a dialog to resolve the conflict, the war can be avoided.

In just a similar manner, regular yogic practices can prevent the onset of any ailment. Once an ailment exists, we need to deal with it at the root-cause level rather than just treat the symptoms thereof. While yogic exercises and Ayurvedic treatment would deal with attacking the root-cause without creating any adverse side-effects or toxicity, some other options may not be so safe. So, submitting to divinity in this case is our spiritual action, acceptance and knowing is the mental action, and inspired by our highest thoughts a careful evaluation of the options for treatment and taking the safest and effective route to action is dealing with it at the physical level.

If one is seriously injured and needs immediate medical attention, getting to the closest hospital emergency room and to undergo the required surgery and procedures would be in order, followed by restoration and rehabilitation exercises when one is able to get to doing these.

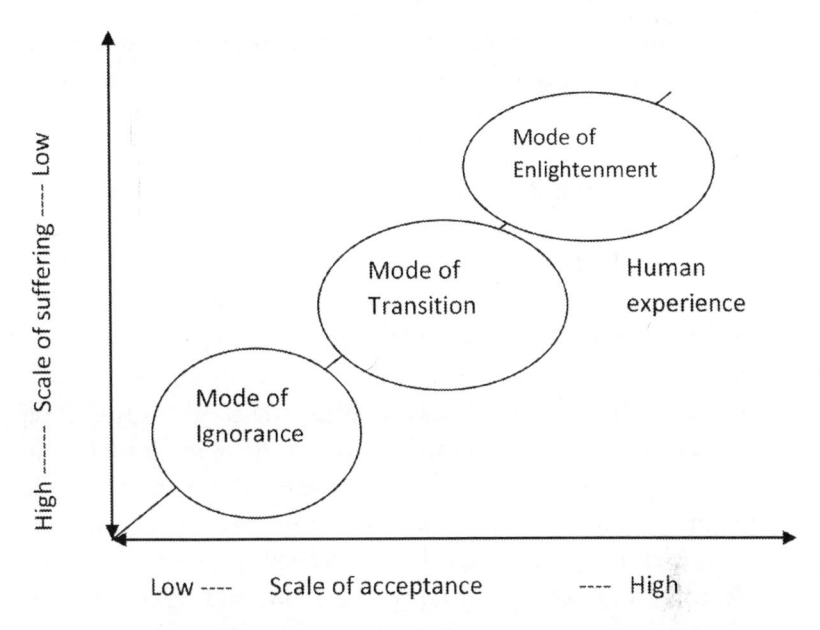

Fig. 6.6: Acceptance vs. suffering and modes of existence

Examples of actions at the physical level:

- Yogic meditation, breathing and physical exercises besides Ayurvedic and Naturopathy treatments to heal any chronic ailments
- A positive and all-encompassing dialog engaging people and governments to avert any war situation
- Caring for the environment and reversing damage to it by planting more trees, minimizing emissions, off-setting the carbon foot prints, inventing new ways to generate clean power, simplifying lifestyle that makes us live in harmony with nature
- Using science and technology in a positive direction
- Building interdependence among communities and nations of the world to remove disparity
- Create a work-for-all culture to remove hunger and poverty

Knowing who we really are

To realize one's self is to actually get to know as to who we really are. Peeling through the onion layers of our acquired identity syndromes (AISs), we can gradually get rid of experiential and circumstantial evidence that lends us an acquired and presumed identity. Once in the space of having stripped out all these acquired and presumed identities, we can finally get to a vacuum where all that remains is just our inner most self. This inner most self is the exact same for each one of us. It is at the level of this inner most self that we can visualize it as being part of a whole – the whole being the all-pervading oneness of all that exists.

If each one of us is able to visualize ourselves in the perspective of being part of the exact same whole, then there would be no differences to fight or worry about.

The all-pervading oneness of all that exists is in the form of Shiva, which manifests from the single super-element of super-consciousness that transforms to energy, knowledge, and consciousness and an intermingling of these three basic elements to bring to life all creation. Thus, in true sense of creation, there is an element of Shiva in all that exists.

The most basic purpose of human life is to have this realization of the presence of an element of Shiva in our own existence, and unite what exists within ourselves to that which exists everywhere. It is eventually this union of the self with the all-pervading divinity that leads to Moksha, the liberation from all bondage, upon dissolution.

The bondage in human life is perceived through the lens of our acquired identity syndromes. Once the illusion of these acquired identity syndromes is removed from our perception, our self becomes free to get liberated and united with the whole.

Once having realized the nature of our true inner-self and knowing of the presence of an element of Shiva within us, while living on this planet, we would be naturally inspired to respect the resources at our disposal. Our thoughts and actions would reflect our commitment to protect the environment, promote peace, serve the humanity, and doing all that we can to promote interdependence among people of the world.

While it can be very easy and even natural to forget as to 'who' we really are while being trapped in the illusions of our perceived realities, dealing with the complexities and miseries that might come our way while we are 'living' the routine of life as usual, and we may even come to a point of completely not 'knowing' the element of 'Shiva' within our existence, it would be a good practice to follow in our daily routines to *re-mind* ourselves of our true existence and take a moment to know who we are.

While behavior of others may seem to unfold unprecedented miseries and challenges before us, let us never forget that in the great divine plan 'they' are highly evolved souls, and have volunteered to pose these challenges to us in our present life as our 'examiners.' It would be extremely unfair, and even inappropriate on the part of any one of us to tick them off as nuisance creators or inhibitors. The 'test' for each one of us at any point is 'how' we react to the situation and the circumstances that they pose before us. It may be extremely hard for us to even imagine as to 'what' these highly evolved souls have to go through as a pain or suffering themselves when they come in our life as a family member or as a patient whom we have an opportunity to serve.

Let us never forget to see the true image of the divine in their existence as a patient, as a 'threat' poser, as the one seeking help, since all that exists is ONE of which both us and they are part of.

When someone is rude to us, they are telling us indirectly that they have analyzed our own behavior that needs correction. This is not to be interpreted too far to a point that one yields to any and all behaviors from anyone – one must use the intellect at all times to draw the line, and when pushed to a limit, may need to withdraw from the situation by ignoring it with no bad feelings towards anyone and taking the necessary correction action as posed by situation on hand.

An Exercise for Chapter 6

Take a while to document your schedule of any two particular days in past one week. List within the scope of each scheduled activity the plan, goal, how the time was spent and what results were achieved and whether the results achieved were in line with goal assignment and what %age of the planned objective was met. For each day and several scheduled activities during the day, complete the following table:

Day (1 to 2)
Scheduled Activity (I to n)
Plan
Goal
How time was spent
Results achieved
%age of Goal met

Reengineer the schedule

Make a plan where you can cut out all that is unnecessary and useless. That is like de-junking your professional and personal life. Even if you make an improvement by a factor of 5%, that would be some achievement. If you keep it up and work through this change iteratively, that would become a way of life.

A scale of the attitude and altitude: *Attimeter*

For the ease of comprehension, let us divide the currently known altitude of cooperative creativity into seven levels. The existing programs and exercises in competitive creativity are like the base that build an awareness on the subject and prompt the participants to unleash the hidden potential that lies mostly untapped within the confines of their skull. These programs and exercises are just about great to that extent and have done a wonderful job of 'building an attitude of creativity' in the human society. Building on the base of 'an attitude of creativity' that these programs have generated, we embark on a never-ending journey of building cooperative creativity.

1. The first level in the process of building cooperative creativity is 'cub.' It is the infant that learns to prepare for life ahead. In real terms, this level is preparative. At this stage, one comes clear on finding answers to questions like: 'Who am I and what am I here for?' The end result of the first level process is a vision and mission statement of life. It can also be the vision and mission statement of the purpose for which you are carrying out the creative exercise. The purpose can be a business enterprise, a global unification project or solution to a problem. This is where one must start – to connect first internally. It begins with a self-talk and evolves to a practice of meditation. A dialog with your inner-self. From a cub of this connection, you can grow to become a lion of creativity.

2. The second level is 'cultivate.' It is like the stage where you develop an ability to achieve something. The end result is a plan and laid down objectives. If the purpose is to define objectives for an individual's career plan, the output is a list of options that can be actively pursued, as inspired by an inner-self of the creative consciousness. This is achieved by a continuation of the dialog with our inner-self.

3. The third level is 'consultative,' where one goes around reaping the synergy of views and opinion of people around. This works two ways: 'supplementary and complementary.' While supplementary paradigm is one that substantiates

the core theme, complementary paradigm is the one that covers gaps. This happens by personal interactions as well as the interactions over the web in an interconnected world.
4. The fourth level is 'collaborative,' where the plan has been set in action and you have just begin to fit the puzzle block of your own life in this game of 'big divine plan' that as of today has got seven billion plus pieces to be precise as humans alone. There are many more pieces in this puzzle, several trillion, of the other forms of life on the planet. At this stage, you learn to 'see through' the simulated realities and perceptions and take an immediate corrective action. This happens as you expand the scope of dialog internally and begin to encompass the external dialog by an integration of the two – the inner dialog and the external dialog.
5. The fifth level is 'compassionate,' where we encompass everyone in our effort as we can see the roles they perform as either complementary or supplementary. Many times it may appear that the negative actions and behavior of people is annoying to us. While we must learn to ignore the useless and cultivate an ability to withdraw from perpetually unpleasant situations to retain our focus, take every experience as a lesson. The lesson must be a positive one that strengthens or expands the base of our knowledge. It is like the 'Ying and Yang,' where we must see the positive in all negative and the negative in the positive, yet strike a balance between the complementing and supplementing positives and negatives. This is one of the most critical challenges that we face today – to develop an ability to achieve the balance. The creation of interdependence assumes a primary responsibility to let no one become perpetually dependent on you. The ability to 'create' is what brings independence. While 'aid' is making dependence and 'trade' is interdependence, create is the in-between of dependence and interdependence. You are doing favor to none if you are making people perpetually dependent on you by providing them with 'aid' indefinitely.
6. The sixth level is 'composing,' where we acquire the ability to integrate the learning of the past, the inter-disciplinary

domains of existence and knowledge, the reasoning and feelings, the physical and the intellectual. All this is put together and merged with collective consciousness of not just humanity, but all beings on the planet and elsewhere. While the fifth level was a stage of realization to build interdependence, the sixth level achieves the objective of building interdependence. It is the process of building an interconnected and interdependent universe. This level breaks away from grounds of emotional attachment. It is the merger of emotion with the intellect under an inspiration of the consciousness. This is where logic and reasoning merge and so do the feelings and sensation. You get impersonal beyond self and compassion. This is the stage where sphere gets punctured to reduce to a dot. All the features that look so bloated at the surface of the sphere get finally reduced and merge into the convergence of one single spot. This is the decomposition of dimensions from multiple to single.

7. The seventh level is 'calm,' where we have achieved the ultimate objective of universal oneness and integration with the divine. When we begin to live the *creation of peace while protecting the environment*, we attain that stage. We become calm and achieve the peace within us when we see our actions towards creating peace bear results. This is the stage of 'tranquility,' the one of *balance and bliss*. This is the crown peak of the currently known Himalayas of creativity. This is the stage where the punctured sphere that was reduced to a dot vanishes into the empty vastness of the universe. The ultimate division of unity by the zero, to create an infinity of multitudes and subsequent merger of the scattered multitudes to a single viewpoint, that too finally dissolves into the empty. This is a dimensionless state. If we get there, we may be able to see many a hidden peaks that are invisible to the myopia of our current vision.

Various stages in this model have a unique significance. The first two are formative levels where you are preparing to connect. Levels three to five are various stages of evolution in the process of connecting. Levels six and seven are part of the synthesis process that combines the

Face to Face with Shiva

power of connecting into a practice of cooperation. Thus, the three broad categories in this domain of creating cooperation are: 'Prepare to Connect, Connect to Collaborate, Integrate for Interdependence.' The ultimate objective of the process of building cooperation is to create interdependence. If we do it as a team, we must know that **T**ogether **E**veryone **A**chieves **M**ore.

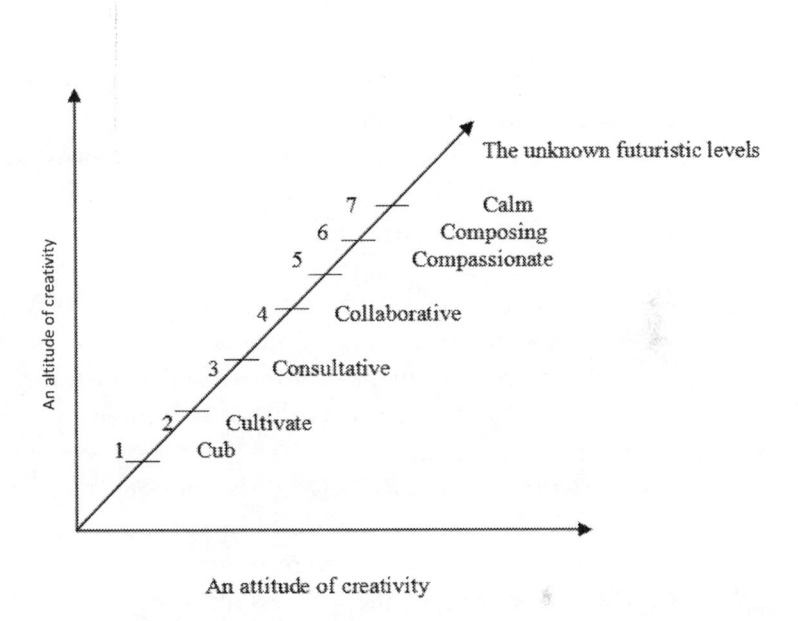

Fig.6.7: Attimeter - a two-dimensional graph of creativity

To evolve from one level to another, we need to enhance, expand, extend and escalate. An enhancement of capability would create an ability to achieve better. An expansion of scope can be made possible by strengthening the existing model by consultation and collaboration that transforms the power of conflict to a synergistic force of creation. An extension of the model to cover the unknown is made possible by retaining the flexibility in an agile manner that integrates the multitudes of unimagined possibilities. The escalation to a higher pedestal is achieved when we have reaped the harvest of an integrated scope of the present with learning of the past to build a new level of foundation. This is the foundation of knowledge that serves as a launch-pad for any higher attempt at exploration.

The journey from *connect to create* has various stages of development and gradual evolution.

1. *Connect to Consult*: begin with a self-talk and gradually integrate various dimensions of your own personality to subsequently expand this dialog with the world. Power of meditation is the tool to connect within. Power of the web is the tool to connect with the world. This consultation is a two-way process: within and outside.
2. *Consult to Collaborate*: reap the synergy of conflict in the dialog to supplement and complement your model. This is a test of the altitude of your creative imagination as much as the scale of positive on your attitude. What initially appears as criticism out of hatred and misunderstanding slowly turns to a powerful enabling agency that helps us to addresses weak points in our creation. This is how we can transition a perceived threat from an interpretation of our mind to work for us as a strength by merely shifting our point of view – if we look at criticism as suggestions for improvement, the paradigm shifts on our favor and naturally invites those who criticized as consultative collaborators in an endeavor to create a better world.
3. *Conceptualize to Compose*: with the power of creative visualization, make a plan that reaps the synergies of connection, consultation, and creativity.
4. *Cull to Comprehend*: the process of consultation and collaboration would have flooded you with a sea of data that may be both - information or irrelevant interference. Using the context of purpose that is within a comprehensible ability and scope, dig to mine the useful.
5. *Compose to Clean*: once the focus shapes clarity of direction, it is very important to junk the unwanted and shape what remains. This shape is chiseled by the context that lies within a realizable scope of our comprehensive abilities, practicalities, and modalities.
6. *Consciousness to Clarify*: once we have it somewhat ready, we need to do some soul searching. Ask our inner-self as to whether there is a conflict with the ethics. This would make our plan neat and something that we take pride in doing.
7. *Create to Cultivate*: the stage of commitment to begin the journey. We know where we got to go. The first step is to

plant the seed. Nurturing the plant with the nourishment of a feedback is a continuous process. Eventually when the fruits are born, the lesson of connect is to share those fruits. The joy of giving is far greater than the pleasure of receiving. This is what the web has taught us.

No creation is possible without the acquisition of knowledge. No knowledge is possible without sharing. There lies the power of connection. This sums up the *'connect to create'* process. An evolution in this path would find corresponding synergy between steps of procedure and the ladder of altitude. All this happens with an increasing shift of attitude from one level of graduation to another.

Creative Meditation: The Process of Visualization
Whenever we are in a conflict or land ourselves in a situation of uncertainty, there is always a need to resolve that impasse. Though each one of us is individually capable of handling those circumstances on our own, it would help to know a process that can be a quick aid. We get stuck into such dilemma every single day of our life, several times during the day. The state of indecision is, as if, programmed into our routine of living.

All these problems arise owing to the duality built within the design of our creation. The duality is essential to keep our engagement alive in routine simulation of the world model, as it exists. At the same time, it is as much important, if not more, that we cultivate and develop an ability to see through this duality within our own nature.

At the external end, we have a physical body whose wants are to be catered by providing the required inputs. Within the confines of our skull lies the brain that is seeking to acquire knowledge and an opportunity for creative use of the intellect. Deep within us, there is an element of the divine that is asking us to love and help everyone and is the very source of our life and existence as our consciousness.

The saint and the scientist are no different people- the saint lies hidden within the scientist

What we need is a direct realization of these three dimensions of our personality – the physical, the mental, and the spiritual, and more importantly the connection to the inner-self where Shiva resides. At all times, if we can integrate these three dimensions of our personality in a balanced manner, and connect to Shiva from within, we have no dilemma. At the root cause of all dilemma lies our inability to see through *all* dimensions of our personality. In total ignorance of 'who we really are,' we get caught up in the simulated reality of life. An AIS (Acquired Identity Syndrome) of make-believe realities and identities powerfully grips us. It is the AIS that holds us back and prevents us from looking beyond the perceptions.

Relating Meditation to Creativity

Meditation is a powerful tool that helps us to cut through different layers of perceptions. This is a process of evolution. The range extends from a preliminary stage of thoughtless awareness to an interim continuous flow of thought to an ultimate stage of being one with the divine. This is a process of evolution that can take any direction. The only pre-requisite is that you must have a noble intention and good feelings towards all beings.

When we imagine creativity, we all have different perceptions of what this may mean. Some of us may relate creativity to finding a solution to an immediate problem on hand. Some programs on creativity prompt you to make a two-minute best effort at building a structure as a mock exercise. A few may focus on some long-term problem, in their perception, that can be done within a span of hours instead of minutes. The unfortunate part is that focus is still on competitiveness. As of now, there is no program that builds creativity as a process of cooperation.

The success of short-term models in our lives has led the whole world to live under the scope of a 'myopic vision.' The short-term creativity programs are excellent skill-development techniques that bring out the best of your creative intellect at spur of the moment. In the paradigms that we have lived in the world hitherto, which was perhaps what we required for building a model of immediate success. This is a crucial turning point in history of the world. Turn of the millennium has also brought in its wake a need for shift in paradigms of how we get inspired, how we think, how we consult and act.

We have seen a decline of the economy and a reflection of the discontent. The past millennium saw the tearing down of several 'ism's, the last one being communism, though it still exists in isolated pockets of the world. Major among the economies based on communist model embarked on the process of a shift to capitalist structure over the last two decades of the millennium gone by. The new millennium

Face to Face with Shiva

has brought in its wake a whole new set of problems and a realization that there is something wrong with the way the world is. The events of black Tuesday have dawned upon us a challenge. The challenge to create a world that is free from horror and terror. To create a world that has only love, peace, and joy.

A new post September 11 '2001 world can't be built if we don't involve our own selves in the process of this construction. The challenge exists before each one of us as individuals, communities, nations and above all, as people of the world. The challenge is to create a New World Model that is achievable to realize and practical enough to live within the competence of our existing present as we stand here today on the planet. This model has to be based on a step by step approach of progressive development that gradually evolves and lands humanity from one platform of achievement to another. The effort to create a draft for the blueprint of this model requires the collective intellect of entire humanity. That is the enormity of 'creativity' we are addressing here.

The world is right now in the middle of being a witness to failure of the capitalist model of economy. The world is also a witness to the futility of an attitude of aggression and might. September 11 '2001 has marked a shift in imaginative domains of the world, changing everything forever. This is a Wake-Up Call. A call for each one of us to ask ourselves just one big question: 'Who am I and what am I here for?' If we can find any reasonable answer to that big question, we would have set in motion a process of consulting our inner-self, who lies buried deep within the confines of several layers of our acquired identities. These layers are thicker than what we may have assumed, with each one of us carrying a different stack of identities and perceptions.

The process of meditation is a long journey. We must know that the journey of a thousand miles begins with a small step. The first step in that direction is to own up yourself as a project. The transformation that we want to see in the world has to begin with us. We must be first the change that we want to see in the world. That would be the leading by example. We can make a difference in lives of so many people if we first own up the responsibility to transform our own life. An owning up of the responsibility to make a shift is what wins us half the battle. If we set up the goal to create peace, love and joy in the world, and make a commitment to achieve that goal – the journey to achieving that goal is simple.

We have to live peace, love, and joy in our day to day life. Yoga is the science of everyday life. We need to ask our inner conscience, whenever we have a conflict. The conflict would not be there anymore. We would be able to reap the synergy of divergent view of the conflict and integrate it within the framework of our plan – to create a better solution. It all begins with our attitude - an attitude of creativity. We have to live an attitude of creativity. As we evolve through various stages of this journey, somewhere in-between there would be a milestone.

A milestone that gives us the realization that *God and the human being are no different - the God lies hidden within the human being.* As an element of the divine within, the power of our consciousness keeps guiding us. Whenever we are in darkness, we need to turn inwards – the light is shining right there at the bottom of our hearts. It is for us to listen to the voice within. It is for us to see the light within. It is for us to make the world - creating peace while protecting the environment.

Creation of peace is the responsibility of each one of us. As a collective intellect of the technical and scientific community of the world, the onus is on professional and voluntary organizations to take initiative in leading the entire universe in this endeavor. The world stops moving without the engineers. To drive forth an initiative of peace, we would have to identify and then engage our intellect in the opportunities offered by technology to erase terrorism, wars and hatred from the planet. While disarming the world may be partially a political process, developing anti-dotes to an aggression and creating suitable prevention is purely the one based on technology.

The time for long-awaited merger of science and spirituality has now come. The responsibility is on each of us as an engineer, researcher, and scientist, technologist is to first integrate the various dimensions within our own self and subsequently set the pace for a merger in the physical world by our positive efforts that create peace. We can identify suitable projects that give us an opportunity to create peace and protect the environment.

Creativity has various levels of imagination. We typically limit the usage of creative potential of our minds to solve just the immediate problems on hand. We now need to be caring about 'looking beyond the immediate.' The collective focus of humanity on 'long-term envisioning' can define the scope and steps to our plan for the future.

Creating a Vision of Education, Science, and Technology

The long-term focus of the vision of Education, Science, and Technology has to address the major issue of creating global integration for permanent peace on the planet and protection of environment for longevity of the planet and human race. We can't plan our own future in oblivion of the environment that sustains and nurtures us. The techno-eco-bio system has to focus on an integrative convergence of the requirements for sustenance and growth of the entire life spanning the bio kingdom and their supporting environment, not just the humans and our immediate needs for comfort.

The immediate focus is always at solving the problems on hand. It is the interim focus that addresses issues of a domain which is neither immediate, nor long-term. If we had to divide the vision of technology into these three categories and identify the focus for each of the categories, we end up with the following table.

Vision Perspective	Objective Focus
Eventual (Long-term)	Peace, Environment, Global Interdependence
Interim (Mid-term)	Safety and Reliability, Global warming, Collaboration
Immediate (Short-term)	Counter-measures to Terrorist Attacks, Education

Table 6.1: Vision perspective and focus

Let us now elaborate upon each one of these categories in some detail. The immediate focus has to deal with development of technologies and systems to combat terrorism at the ground level. The creation of a department for home-land security is a step in the right direction. Also, an extensive research into measures to improve cyber-security and the development of gadgets and antidotes against bio-terrorism needs to be an immediate priority. In addition to these, we have to relate the immediate focus to two directions. One direction is to relate this focus to all that exists and build on top of that, integrating the existing knowledge by complementing and supplementing from inter-disciplinary and inter-laced roles of technologies of often over-lapping but seldom unrelated domains and innovating for improvement - it is like learning from the past. A correlation in this direction has to exist for all the domains and disciplines of technology.

The other direction to relate all this exercise of causing improvement, innovation and development over the inter-disciplinary domains is to link these endeavors to the *futuristic* focus that spans the horizons of interim, long-term eventual and even far beyond those to the eternity. If we fail to provide this linkage, we would end-up yet another time to fall back into the grip of the gravity since the force applied for launch was not strong enough to break away from it. The pull of gravity is this context is the myopic vision and the launch under consideration is technology itself. If today we fail to link the future of technology to a vision of peace and protection of environment on the planet, we would be catalysts of the inertia that is slowly causing the death of humanity. It is very convenient for each one of us individually to hold responsible the government, the political system of the way world operates and its worldly-wise policies. We can easily find an excuse in the non-acceptance of a vision by our society that is so used to finding gains out of immediate efforts.

We may like to continue to ignore at the present moment, the Wake-Up Call of the tragedy that struck us on September 11 '2001. The most convenient route is always not the best one. The harder route for us to take would be to now wake-up and take a stock of the situation. Once we take a stock of the situation of the world at the present times, we would know that something has definitely gone wrong. We went the wrong way with the technology. We did not have any relationship between technology and peace. The only vision we have had in the past with technology has been either to relate it with providing human comfort and the other has been to meet human need. While the range of human need has encompassed a horizon from requirement to travel faster to cause destruction of a mass-scale with vested political interests, peace and environment have failed to figure in our so-called 'wish-list.'

The major lesson to be learned now from the tragic events of September 11 '2001 is that we need to provide this linkage from present endeavors to a vision of the future for technology.

The right direction: Creating Peace while protecting the environment

It is like clean as you climb on a long hike. You climb to unleash the hidden potential within yourself, become one with the nature and explore new horizons, graduating from one height to another. If we integrate the objective of cleaning up the trash leftover by those who hiked these trails before us, we would leave the mountain cleaner than when we encountered it. This has something to do with our attitude. If we own up the responsibility today to create peace on the planet, we would be able to make it happen. The blueprint of peace has to be in the mind of the creator. The creators of peace are the engineers, scientists, technologists, professionals, and researchers of all fields as intellectuals. The onus is on each one of us to create a better world.

We can successfully convert matter to energy. Consider a form of wood as coal or a fossil fuel that holds potential energy as matter. By burning this matter, its form is changed and heat energy is released. This heat energy is used to generate power in thermal power plants. The electrical power transmitted is received finally at the point of application and applied for end-use. The end-use is yet another type of conversion: from electrical power to the kinetic or heat energy. In case of a bulb, we transform electrical power to heat energy that transmits light. Finally, we have ended up converting matter to light in successive levels of transformation of energy from one form to another and its transmission.

While we do have light available to us in abundance as solar energy radiated all the time and received on this planet continually, can we invent a system that converts light to matter? Light is holding energy in a different form. It is loaded with energy. If the light energy can be suitably converted to another form and subsequently to a desired state of matter, we can set a whole new paradigm for creation.

The future of research in technology belongs to this process of reverse engineering that would bring in its wake several new paradigms and areas for development and innovation, merging several existing fields of medical science and technology besides creating numerous new ones that were unimagined hitherto.

Tele-porting would finally become possible as a reality of the physical world, once we are successfully able to master this two-way process of conversion from matter to energy and energy to matter. Our body constitutes matter that can be envisioned as a potential form of energy. If the body in matter form can be de-materialized to energy, then it is possible to transform and transmit the energy from one point to another, and then re-convert to matter at the destination end, keeping intact the knowledge associated with the specific form of manifestation that would enable the conversions. Taking this a step further, if future existence can manifest itself as non-material, the transportation throughout the universe would become that much easier.

Integrating education, science, technology, and spirituality

Technology is to science what religion is to spirituality. There are many ways by which we provide the missing link between science and spirituality. The essence of spirituality is goodness. So is also the underlying theme of all religions. Every prophet since times immemorial has prompted humanity to turn to goodness. An interpretation of goodness in the modern day context is to protect the environment and create peace by whatever means possible. Technology is just one of the means by which we can achieve the most sought-after merger of science and spirituality. Any application of science, technology, literature, medicine, language, any field of disciplines, our actions, thoughts or deeds that create goodness, love, knowledge and joy on the planet are all steps in the right direction.

This is the direction of moving towards an integrated and united world that would eventually be at peace. No long-term achievement would be possible just by our creative visualization. We would definitely have to translate any meaningful imagination to realizable plans, time-lined objectives supported by substantial and tangible actions on the ground that result in effective products and services. Once we provide these new options to human society, the paradigm of living would change for sure. From living under stress and tension, people would shift to live with love and peace.

The tragedy of humanity today is that we have all jumped out to skydive, but without the parachute – the right attitude. But there is hope. This sky is tall and the ground is far away. We have a chance to develop the right attitude before we hit the ground, by a process of consultation and collaboration that engages an entire humanity on the planet. This is our only chance. If we don't do it now, we may make life extinct on the planet much sooner than we perceive it to last. There is a good possibility that the red planet (Mars) had life on it and it got extinct by the greed and hatred unleashed by its inhabitants by polluting a sustaining environment and nuclear wars.

The path to ... destruction ... or ... construction?

With where ever we are in history of the world and wherever we are going, there is an issue we need to look at 'Are we on the path

Face to Face with Shiva

to construction or we are on the path to destruction? If Hitler had won all the wars he had wanted and even captured the entire world after annihilating those 'unwanted', what he would have liked to do then? Was there a vision beyond elimination of the 'unwanted' and surviving of only one so-called 'superior race?'

That kind of an attitude is counter to 'flowing with the nature' and against the basic laws that govern maintenance and existence of the universe. Something has definitely gone wrong somewhere. We have failed to take an effective control of affairs of the world. We have just let the circumstances shape the history of the world, as if we had absolutely no role to play therein. We do need to do some soul searching and ask ourselves 'Was that the right attitude on our part?' As the time slipped by, we kept on gazing at events of the world as mute spectators. If we did have a vision for the future of the world and had the right kind of attitude and commitment to achieve that, shape of things would have been very different than what exists today. Holocaust stands as a mute testimony to indifference of the world to a bankruptcy of vision and as a rude reminder for an urgent need for action.

It is only the development of a right attitude that would eventually lead to a vision of peace and subsequently actions to achieve peace. Hitherto, we have been used to a strategy of protecting ourselves against our enemies and competing with each other for limited resources. Everyone is reaching forward to grab a bigger piece of the pie. No one is focused on creating another pie or enlarging the existing one. It is this attitude of the world, coupled with 'I am right' syndrome that has created a world of hatred and mass destruction. No one singularly is to be blamed – it is a collection of all of us. Unless we own the responsibility to clean up the mess collectively and identify what areas each one of us can sweep, nothing is going to get clean. Clearing up all the mess that is out there as of today is a collective responsibility of every one – each one of us has to do our bit of the clean up process. To begin with, we have to start with our mind. We need to de-junk all the garbage out of there even before we can embark on a project of 'Creating a Positive Attitude.'

In history of the world, September 11 '2001 was a turning point. As much as we know the date line as BC and AD eras, the world would be known as 'pre- September 11 '2001' and 'post- September 11 '2001.' September 11 '2001 has changed everything forever. It was not just a wake-up call for America, but for the whole world. We all need to wake-up from a deep slumber of resignation to circumstances and live up to a new reality. The new reality is that if we continue to ignore the call for creating a new vision for the future, we would be morally and intellectually responsible to our inner conscience for creating the consequences of this deliberate ignorance. This new vision involves a role of technology and the intellect of the brains of technocrats, scientists, engineers, physicians, surgeons, professionals, practitioners and philosophers of known domains and those of unknown domains that are yet to be created. The very first step in that direction is to set in motion a dialog between the technical communities of interdependent disciplines of science and technology.

This initiative can best be driven by a collective effort of intellectuals the world over and the professional organizations, standing today as hope of the humanity. Society for Universal Oneness (www.SFUO.org) is an apex umbrella organization that would globally integrate all such efforts towards creating peace by bringing together the societies of technocrats, engineers, scientists, researchers and developers belonging to the diverse disciplines of technology, science, medical, political, professional, art, literary and related fields. Society for Universal Oneness is well positioned to launch a global initiative among peers coming together from different disciplines with a common purpose of creating peace on the planet.

As we go about creating this vision, we would have to identify and involve all like-minded resources, organizations, bodies, individuals and groups who are committed to create a future that benefits the coming generations. The common objective here is to create a vision of the future that spells a meaningful role of science and technology to create peace on the planet.

As we go down the path from translating this abstract vision to an achievable mission and a set of goals and specific task oriented objectives that can be time-lined with start and finish dates and earmarked with realizable resources, there would be certain impediments and by-products in the process. Impediments would be to bridge the gaps between the known and the unknown. By-products would be the creation of a multitude of new interdisciplinary paradigms, technologies, hypothesis and theories that would form a base to launch us from known and leap into domains of the unknown. It is these by-products of the process of a collective brainstorming and meditation during the process of consultation and collaboration that would form the bulk for basis of future research and development.

The domains of the unknown, that we have ticked off in the past as mystical, unattainable, unexplainable and the metaphysical are much easier to explain today in comparison to yesterday. Given the technological leap of the past 100 years, we are far better positioned today and closer to achieve this objective of bridging the gap between known and the unknown than ever before.

A vision for future of the world

The world is one nation – every human being on the planet its citizen. It is governed by a group of intellectuals who volunteer their services for the cause of humanity and protection of the planet. All that exists is love, joy and peace. Everyone lives in harmony with each-other and also with everything else on the planet.

The human society has created a mechanism of interdependence by cooperative collaboration and consultation among communities and people of the world. This system of interdependence has led them to achieve a world free from hunger and horror. Neither there are wars, nor armies. People help others instead of competing with them. There is plenty of everything for everyone, but the needs are very limited. They are content, realized beings. In this abundance of everything, above all is the goodness of their attitude. It is a balanced world where everyone has the physical, mental and spiritual dimensions integrated.

There is no disease and no hatred. None suffers from any ailments, whatsoever. Living in true harmony with the nature, everyone is happy. They are all educated and enlightened with blessings of the knowledge divine.

The Big Picture

An integration is required of techniques like 'System Dynamics' to study the cause-effect relationships in our Mental Dynamics, Biomedical engineering, brain to computer connections and research into stimulating forces that create waves for peace and tranquility. This integration shall result into creating a technology that shall make it easier to awaken the unleashed forces residing within the confines of human instrument in a dormant mode. The documentation of such energy lying dormant within the confines of human instrument is embedded in ancient scriptures and refers to this energy as 'Kundalini.' Once the Kundalini energy is awakened and tapped in a collective and integrated manner with sole objective of creating peace, it shall cause all negative and subversive thoughts and forces to be wiped out.

Competitiveness shall still remain, but in a different form. The competition would be in being more cooperative among peers of an interdependent team that encompasses a professional workforce of the universe.

Resolving Internal Conflict

It is natural to have conflict. It is much easier to resolve a conflict that is outside- there is an established process of consultation and collaboration. What is more difficult to resolve is an internal conflict. This internal conflict arises owing to a clash between three dimensions of our personality – the physical, the mental, and the spiritual. When we see someone in trouble, the spiritual dimension immediately pricks and prompts us to go out of the way to help. The mental dimension lies at the center of the physical and spiritual and begins to analyze both the inputs- one from the spiritual and other from the physical. The physical dimension is focused on the immediate perspective and often myopic to the calls from spiritual dimension. The message from physical is clear: ignore that feeling and go on with what you are doing. That is the point where we land in conflict.

When we land in such a situation, we would not win by either listening completely and blindly to either one of the two personalities. The winning formula is to interpret the situation and take a balanced view of it by carrying out an immediate yet accurate analysis. The state of balance is the one of an appropriate proportion between the extremes of restriction and abuse. There is no point in shifting between syndromes under the governance of our apparent realities. The power of AIS is strong enough to fool us- one way or the other.

The balance has something to do with listening and feeding inputs to the capability of our creative intellect, and then analyze to get a balanced output. An integrated balance is the one that detaches emotions and feelings from the purpose, as much as it separates the reward from action.

It is on the platform of balance that we can build a framework for realization.

CHAPTER 7

From respect to realization

As a human being, we are consistently swinging between the extremes of indulgence and restriction. Once one realizes the futility of each, one can be led to renunciation. It is not until we develop the respect for both indulgence and restriction that we can be on the path to self-realization.

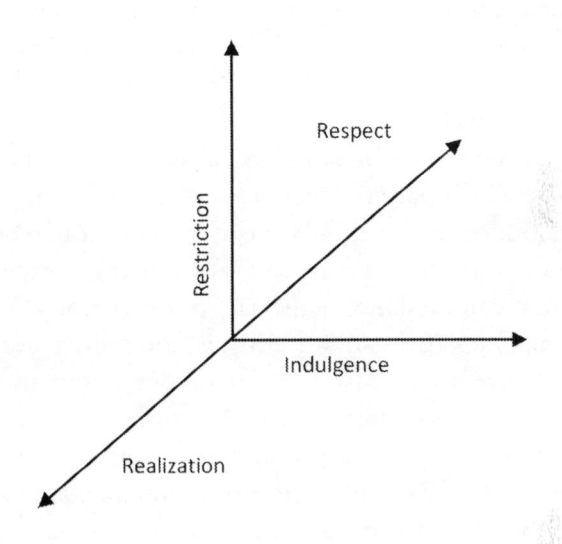

Fig. 7.1: Axis of respect – realization emerging out of struggle with indulgence and restriction

The axis of respect – realization is like a see saw. There has to be enough weight in respect before we can begin to see any realization. The respect is invested. The realization is achieved. From indulgence to restriction, we experience all sorts of things in life, and the earlier we develop a respect for all that exists and how it exists, the sooner we will be on the path to realization.

The good and evil within our own self needs to be integrated into a unified whole that embarks on the journey of realization via the path of respect. Unless we develop respect for all existence, we are in the self-defeating loop of anger, hatred, jealousy, negative thoughts and ill feelings for others.

Shiva is the realization that emerges from respect after integration of all forces.

Feeling the pain of another

Though in realm of the absolute, there may be no pain but only joy, no bad but only good, and no negative but only the positive; while leading the life as mortal humans, most of us must go through the experiences of what we call as 'pain' or 'suffering.' So much so that Lord Buddha named the world as a 'house of suffering and sorrows.'

While physical pains may be comparatively easier to live with, emotional pains and sufferings are rather hard to deal with. When you see a loved one in pain, you likely feel that pain several times magnified in magnitude, like a mother not just truly feeling but even living the suffering of her only child.

Though the mother is not physical sufferer, yet she is the true emotional bearer of the pain that her only child is suffering. In a similar manner, the God, or say Lord Shiva, as our spiritual parent – both as our father and as our mother truly knows the pains of each one of us, and does all that can be done to alleviate our suffering. While it may appear to us at times that our suffering is not ending, we must also know that the current circumstances are unique to our situation, and are there for a reason. Knowing of the higher purpose, we need to bear it out. A tough present prepares us to stand out strong in the future. Lord Jesus crucified on the cross, only to resurrect and do good to the world.

Each one of us must have a realization – that Shiva is alive within each one of us. In other words, it is the presence of the element of Shiva that makes us as humans the living representative of the image of Divine that is all pervading in the entire existence as well as non-existence. Thus, as representatives of the Lord on this planet, we have the duty to replicate this specific attribute of the Lord to truly know and feel the pain of another, and that can only happen if we acknowledge our role as a parent of all existence on the planet.

As a true parent of all existence – whether perceived as living or non-living, we must, first of all learn to show 'respect' for all that exists, just as a mother is truly respectful of all the genuine needs of her only child.

When we see a resource of the planet getting abused, we must stand up and raise a voice against that exploitation. This may be termed as acting as a parent to a perceived non-living entity, but we must extend our consciousness to encompass all that exists on the planet, and at the very least in its immediate vicinity, even if the scope of our horizon is extremely limited.

These entities perceived almost as non-living can be forests in the Amazon basin, in the Himalayas, the Royal Bengal tigers in the Sundarbans, the Pandas in the lands of China, yetis and yaks in Tibet or Laddakh, excess water that need not be wasted flowing out of the tap in your home or hotel room whether you wash dishes or shave, the air conditioner that runs throughout the warmest day also in your home or hotel room just to keep it cool when you return past the midnight while the outside and the inside temperatures have already struggled themselves out of their yelling matches to have evened out on each-other.

Being a parent is a hard-sell, especially when we are encompassing entire communities of the existent and the non-existent, the living and the non-living, and would get even harder when we attempt to embrace the galaxies and planets beyond those that we perceive as 'ours.'

Feeling the pain of another is not just about getting touched emotionally; it does extend to showing the 'respect' and even beginning to have some 'realization' of a sense of belongingness.

The model of respect and realization emerges out of struggling with years or sometimes light-years of shuttling between the extremes of indulgence and sacrifice.

On becoming detached

Rising above the desires is possible through detachment. The emotions are natural, and lead to attachment. Once we can realize that we have a role to perform and that the given environment around us at any time is the most appropriate one to challenge us to make us perform at our very best, we have a greater tolerance to accept the as-is situation.

It is acceptance of the as-is that would lead us to first stop worrying, and then gradually to detach. It is possible that our very near and dear ones may be suffering, and seeing them suffer hurts. While it is extremely natural to feel hurt, it is also important to know that those who are suffering around us are highly evolved souls. They chose the path that they are on voluntarily – just to be around us to test as to how we react to them.

While each one of us in the normal course would like to have comforts and focus on fulfillment of desires, the highly evolved souls embrace the pain and suffering, with an end objective to heal and evolve the world.

Those around the ones suffering need to have compassion. It is the feeling of unconditional love that would change the world and evolve humanity to a higher level of existence. Unconditional love is detachment – as it does not judge, prejudice, relate, favor, or evaluate.

When we are attached, we exhibit all these traits of making judgment, being prejudiced, feeling related, favoring, and evaluating. It is a slow and gradual process to evolve from being attached to getting detached.

Being detached does not mean that we don't love or care – in fact it means that we love and care for unconditionally, without any attachment. A divine person as a true philanthropist would help all, and not pick a single one for receiving favor. In doing so, the divine person has the ability to see an image of Shiva in all existence.

It is possible for anyone to be divine at all times – initially one has to make a conscious effort, and gradually it would become as being part of one's natural self.

The exercises in the book are part of the steps to evolve one's self to become self-less and unite with the all-pervading divinity. It is a realization to know that we are part of the universe, and the universe is divine. When we can see a bigger picture of the entire existence with a purpose of evolution, we can instantly know our part in that process and act accordingly.

As one moves forward in this journey of evolution, there are some traits that would become part of the personality, examples below:

- think positive at all times, and not see any evil in anyone or in any situation but take given circumstances as an opportunity that allows us to make a change for improving the situation
- act wisely in a manner that hurts none and heals everyone, and to invent such ways creatively; lead by example and embrace everyone
- see all as good, and send healing to all
- be one with the universe, and see the divine in all that exists

Exercise:

Close your eyes and imagine the happiest moments of your life – these can build upon as relating to any happy past experience or an imagination to visualize a future situation. As you visualize the ecstasy, note down the personal traits that you exhibit during those moments – feelings towards others, your relation to the universe, your perception of the situation around you, and the world at large.

Open your eyes and jot down your responses.

Now, close your eyes again, and imagine the worst moments of your life – these can build upon as relating to any sad past experience or an imagination to visualize a future situation. As you visualize the miserable situation, note down the personal traits that you exhibit during those moments – feelings towards others, your relation to the universe, your perception of the situation around you, and the world at large.

Open your eyes and jot down your responses.

Next, compare the two responses from happy and sad situations, and note the difference.

Now imagine if you're the personal traits that you exhibited during those tense sad moments – feelings towards others, your relation to the universe, your perception of the situation around you, and the world at large were to be changed to the ones that you exhibited during your happiest moments – would that have changed the situation itself to some extent, or at the very least your acceptance of it?

You may, by now, have realized that how we perceive a situation shapes our reaction to it. If we perceive a situation as an opportunity to cause an improvement, then we first accept it and subsequently work towards making that improvement.

If we perceive a situation as a threat, then we reject it, and as a part of that rejection we first invoke a series of defense mechanism of justifications. These self-satisfying justifications lead us to behave in a peculiar manner. We start exhibiting specific behaviors of pretension, attempting to dominate others, and proving ourselves to be right.

The sum total of exhibiting such behavioral traits is wasted energy, invocation of negative emotions, and setting in motion a negative wave of sorts that must find its counterpart reaction to be either wiped out, or an accumulation that lashes out as a tsunami or a devastating earth quake. When that happens, it is those highly divine and evolved souls who step forward to self-sacrifice and embrace the impact of such disasters.

Acceptance of the situation and subsequent actions towards making improvements is an ongoing process.

Let's start with someone who is not feeling well. If we collectively meditate and send healing, it would radiate a positive energy that negates the illness. At global level, collective actions to protect the environment of the planet would contain the pollution, and we can go even further to reverse some of the damage that has already been done.

Collective meditation and sending waves of healing is a definite action, not just a plan. There is no limit to whom we can send the healing. We can also send it to Mother Earth, in attempts to repair the damaged environment of our beloved planet. Collective radiations of same wavelength keep adding the intensity as individual amplitudes pile up to build a stronger wave. This is purely how physics of electromagnetic waves of the same phase works. A meditative wave stronger in amplitude is better positioned to wipe out the negativity of a wave in motion, whether that wave is set by counter-balancing act of the nature, or by some collective human thought and behavior.

The divine universe puts no limits to goodness, positivity, creativity, and imagination. Our collective imagination can visualize a planet of completely protected environment, a world where there are no wars, communities with no fights, individuals with no stress, animals without fear, and our collective actions can make those visualizations a reality.

Chapter 8

The Road Ahead

Like graduating from the level of 'Cub Scout' to an 'Eagle Scout,' the journey of life does not stop at any level. It is just the foundation that prepares us to face and meet the challenges lying ahead. Each one of us is unique and different in all that we are capable of achieving and accomplishing. At each stage, we need to integrate the existing knowledge and experiences to create a higher pedestal.

The step by step stages of evolution in the process of building creativity is like first getting to know who we are, and then defining our role and mission on the planet. Subsequent stages of creativity building process take us through an interim getting to 'know' all others and later develop a synonym between you and them. Ultimately, there is no you or them or I, it is we all together as 'us.' When we encompass all beings in this togetherness, whether on this planet or elsewhere - that is where we cross the threshold. This is the threshold that separates discipline from freedom or knowledge from love.

When freedom and discipline become interdependent, we all know our responsibility. When knowledge and love become interdependent, we aspire to create joy and happiness for all beings by unleashing the potential or our collective creative intellect. Finally, there comes a stage where freedom, discipline, knowledge and love all merge together in one convergent view. That is what the *peace* is. Peace is the ultimate decomposition of interdependence, interconnectedness and universal oneness. To create peace on the planet is responsibility of each one of us. In whatever we do, we can create peace. We can live peace every single day and every single moment of the day. Peace is a way of life.

An engineer can live peace in all creation. A scientist can live peace in all research. A teacher lives peace in every moment of interactions with toddlers and grooming them to become responsible citizens of the planet. Everyone can live peace in all that they do. The only prerequisites to living peace are noble thoughts inspired by our consciousness and good feelings for all beings. These thoughts translate to meaningful projects and actions in day to day life. Any application of technology that creates peace is the highest service of an engineer to the divine. Any activity of research that creates peace is the highest tribute of the scientist to the Supreme Being. An inspired education prepares the young ones to think and act in the right direction, as an offering to the Divine. Whether anyone believes in God or not, let's build faith that each one of us lives in peace.

Competitive spirit is a great thing to have. In the future, the only competition that would exist is *'Cooperative Competitiveness,'* a measure of the extent to which we cooperate with one-another. Building on the base of what we have achieved so far, we would go far beyond cooperation to achieve the stage of Universal Oneness. Transgressing the domains of our currently competing paradigms of transportation and telecommunication, science and spirituality, medicine and prayer, we would eventually merge all that exists with the creative potential of our intellect. This integration would lay the foundation to move upward and forward on the path of cooperation with the technology of *'creativity.'*

Rather than blindly forcing ourselves to be a product of the circumstantial situations, it would make sense in planning for the transition. This plan shall involve participation of the industry and public at large. If we plan effectively and then follow the blueprint in a phased implementation manner as a project, there would be fewer surprises on the way. Once de-materialization reaches its climax, the stage of the world would be set for yet another revolution. Who knows what? Want to take a guess?

From present to the future

Internet has already given the world a new paradigm: *connect, not compete.* It is the collective effort of Information Technology (IT) professionals the world over that would eventually shift the attitude of the world from hitherto 'Competitive' to a futuristic 'Cooperative.' The operating systems and software based on open standards are freely distributed. The free downloads of open platforms to build customized applications are just the starting baby steps in the direction of an unending journey. Open source standards are fast becoming the way to go, and business enterprises with a vision of the future are already embracing this new paradigm. This new shift to embracing openness is a step in the right direction to build trust, interdependence, and engaging people of the world in a meaningful endeavor. Though technology is leading the way here, soon the same attitude will be carried over to the social, political, and cultural spheres of human progress. Building on the success of what we have achieved so far, we all make a resolve to own the responsibility to create peace through such efforts.

The interim stage

The current state of economy is forcing a consolidation and modularization that is resulting in a shakeout of the unprecedented and unchecked growth during the last two decades of the previous millennium. Those who lead by example of cooperation would tend to survive the longest. We would continue to see mergers and acquisitions, eventually dividing the market share by three forces of segmentation. These forces would determine the combined industry strength of competing paradigms: Market reach, Product differentiation by innovative design, and Cooperative competence. The individually segmented strengths of these competing yet complementary paradigms would rule the industrial landscape of the planet for next twenty to thirty years.

The strength and failure of market reach

Market reach may mean the core competence of a group of conglomerates cashing in on the depth of penetration within niche segments. From the present 15% e-commerce revenues in developed economies, this segment would be the first to yield to the two other contenders for its share. That would happen when the tables turn in favor of the e-commerce to revenues of 85% on a global basis as the diminishing cost of hardware pushes infrastructure enabling a web-centric, cloud based economy.

The rising costs of production and lower spending power of the consumers would force an elimination of the very strength on which this segment is build- the middle persons of the industry. Gradually all marketing managers, agents, sales representatives, and business development executives would be forced out as the constituents of a layer that becomes suddenly unwanted. This is most likely to happen within next ten to twenty years, depending on the level of automation and access to web in all economies and advent of the informed customer who intelligently compares and evaluates the alternative options.

The power of design

Product Design is the segment that is built on the strength of technology and innovation skills of the technical teams engaged in design with a constant feedback from the customer. The power of a web-centric paradigm is bringing the design teams directly close to the consumer as business development subtly divides to new roles. One of these new roles shall define responsibility of the customer to provide a direct feedback on their satisfaction to the designers. The other half of this role would be the responsibility of designers to translate the requirements of customers to enhanced features of the product or service they create. Creative consultation would eliminate the interim layer of 'Business Analysts' as these roles would merge with either the customer or the designer. It has a lot to do with the advent of web-centric paradigm as the customer gets educated, informed, smart, and engaged. The power of design is here to stay forever. The web-enabled merger of the consumer and creator of the products shall gradually keep eliminating the unnecessary overhead middle layers of business developers and sellers, driving down the costs to a more affordable level to increase the penetration and growth among new consumer segments.

The competence of cooperation

Ultimately, it is the core competence of a spirit of cooperation that would rule the markets of a futuristic economy. Technology would bring people, products and services together in a seamless manner to create a new kind of economy. This would be the economy of *'cooperative competence.'* Those who lead the industry would be the ones who cooperate, instead of those who compete. This is one paradigm that would emerge out of the power of the shift to web-centric way of doing business coupled with a universal shift in consciousness that inspires us to cooperate, rather than compete. Eventually, people would fail to see any need to compete, as it would be worthless. Those who would not be able to sell their product or service at the very best rates and levels of customer satisfaction would face one of the only two choices available to them: *eliminate* or *cooperate*. Their best bet would be to merge within the core of their segment: the strength of product design or market reach.

The curse of success

The imminent decline of a crumbling capitalist structure is the curse of short-term success of this model. It has failed to last even a hundred years in the history of humankind that spans 200,000 years. Every story with success in reality is just a perceived state of pretended happiness. The miseries any success brings in its wake are far more than loneliness at top of the ladder. A genesis of hatred is deeply rooted in the perception of those who sit in the camps of failure and plan to bring you down.

Rewards of failure

The creators of a capitalist model now must take the time to celebrate lessons learnt as they witness a downward spiral of all that exists in this model of short lived success. The first lesson is to realize a need for vision and architect a new future for the world and its economy. An architecture of a futuristic economy shall encompass a multi-disciplinary role between several domains of science, technology, business, and cut across different functional areas. There would be nothing in-between the nature and technology. People would be as much at ease with technology as much as they would be with the nature. The nature and technology would exist in harmony when this architecture is designed by an intellect of the realized humanity.

An architecture of a futuristic economy

Manufacturing shall become 'on-demand' as de-materialization of the world is forced by IT as much as by a shift of the dimensions of personality of the world from hitherto physical to an interim intellectual and eventually spiritual. The era of mass production would be a case gone by for all products beyond the reach of the ordinary consumer range. Gradual elimination of several automobile manufacturers is on the cards as they fail to compete in either product features or price and their inability to seek a partner for cooperation owing to incompatibility. This incompatibility is twofold: one of the infrastructure and equipment and other one of a mindset. An innovative capability of engineering brains may be able to resolve the impasse with incompatibility of the infrastructure and equipment, but they would not be able to shift the rigidity of attitude of an incompetent management. The only solace for them would be to build an attitude of creative cooperation.

One force that would emerge for sure as a promising industry within itself is the 'delivery network.' That would be the process of bringing the product or service directly to the consumer. Cooperative groups may compete for geographically segmented markets to provide deliveries from manufacturing on demand points to points of consumption, eliminating the warehouses and associated support mechanisms. The only kind of warehouses that remain would be the data-warehouses, remotely accessible from any nook or corner of the globe.

The buying and selling agencies shall be replaced by the search engines. In a situation where people would demand the real worth for the value of what they pay, there would be no margins to afford any human agents. Work from home sales forces are just an interim alternative to the ultimate soft-agents that would replace the need for tele-marketers and sellers. Many brick and mortar offices would be replaced by work from home forces who perform all functions other than those that require an actual physical presence owing to the very nature of job. The typical organizational structures would vanish as a virtual worker can work for anyone from anywhere on the planet.

The power of web-centric would force globalization down the throats of many a capitalist economies as they crumble under the burden of an unaffordable overhead. It is the elimination of middle layers and power of technology that would eventually be at work to build interdependence by leveling the grounds of imbalance. An interdependent global society shall pave the way for global unification when people would be able to see the need to protect nations as futile as the unnecessary middle layers in business. That would happen at a stage when 'Politicians' are replaced by 'Intellectuals' as leaders of the World.

Using the Intellect

If an Osama bin Laden would be using the intellect in the right manner, he would have spent all his millions wisely in creating an infrastructure for education of the highly underprivileged and deprived in Sudan, Afghanistan, Yemen, Pakistan and several other economically deserving communities across the globe. This education would have been towards creating self-dependence and skills for growth and survival in a global economy. An infrastructure for education in technology, medical sciences, and economics. That would have been the highest service to Islam in the name of Allah, the Compassionate, the Merciful and the All Powerful. Instead of training suicide bombers and hijackers, these institutes would have trained engineers, physicians and scientists who had a role to play in creating a better and peaceful world. Interpreting religion to harm any of God's creation is wrong, and un-spiritual. Spirituality is above religion, and all religions of the world lead to it, if interpreted from the bottom of anyone's heart. Think of

God as our parent and imagine the pain of a parent witnessing children killing each-other.

If politicians and scientists were using the intellect, they would be creating technologies for peace instead of those for destruction. Politicians, using the power of their intellect would be creating peace and interdependence. If a Hitler would be truly spiritually inspired, he would not be indulging in massacres and justifying such action in the name of religion.

Solving problems of the new millennium with technology of the past

If just a single religion could be used as a technology to solve contemporary problems, there would not have been a need to create yet another religion. If the oldest was also the best, why was there a need for a new one? The oldest religion of the world is Hinduism. Oldest book of the world is 'Rigveda.' Over several thousand years, groups of people interpreted religion in the manner it suited them. This twisting of interpretation became so distorted that all learned and educated would deplore that kind of an interpretation. Though there were great reformers and saintly scholars from time to time for correcting the masses from distortion, the wrong interpreters abused the flexibility associated with oldest religion of the world. Instead of using the power of flexibility to adapt to the changing times and creating new horizons for growth and evolvement of human kind, some of the interpretations spelled doom in following a strict dogmatic approach. One of the great reformers was Swami Dayanand Saraswati, the basis of whose teachings became the foundation of Arya Samaj, a society that promotes welfare for all. Swami Vivekananda brought the concepts of Vedanta to the west.

The genesis of Judaism, Christianity, and Islam lies in a different geographic area of the world. The very basic tenants of all these and also of Hinduism are principally the same. While there have been variations of Hinduism by reformists like Buddha, Mahavira, Guru Nanak Dev Ji and several other saints, the basics have still remained the same and hold true. The youngest religions are a few hundred years old. These include Sikhism and Bahai faith. Sikhism was found as an army with the purpose of protecting Hinduism against the atrocities of Muslim rulers who were forcibly converting masses to Islam. Bahai faith is one good example of combining the goodness of all religions to make a resolution for global peace and unity.

Many argue that creating a new religion by combining the goodness of each existing faith and making all citizens of the world subscribe to that so-called new religion would solve most problems of the world. Would that be achievable? What is wrong with any existing religion? Do we even understand the meaning of religion? Or we just pretend that we understand? Creating yet another religion would not be a solution. The only solution is to let people stay exactly where they are with their beliefs in God or religion and allow them time, space, and knowledge to create an ability to look beyond the religion.

Once they are able to look beyond the religion itself, they would be able to know exactly as to who they truly are, what their mission in life is, and using the power of their intellect, they would create solutions for peace and joy on the planet. They would be able to see the goodness in all other religions as much as they would be able to see in their own, and in the process they would also find some goodness in all that exists.

Once people begin to use their intellect to look beyond the religion, they would be able to create new roles for themselves and for their professions and communities. Spirituality is above religion.

New Roles

In the New World, the role of attorneys would be to build 'trust' among people, instead of making a living out of mistrust amongst them. The role for physicians and health care workers would be to ensure that everyone is 100% fit and healthy, so that there is no such thing as 'disease' in the world. The businesses of future would bring the value of goodness in every term of the word to people, integrating nature and environment friendliness into the very design of product manufacturing and service delivery mechanism.

Political leadership of a New World would assume the responsibility to create peace, love and joy on the planet by integrating the whole world as a single, unified nation. Scientists of the future shall create technologies for peace and stability of the world. The interim stages shall see disarmament in a phased manner to effectively ensure the dissolution of threats and perceptions of war. The finances released by the reduction in defense budgets shall be used to create peace, provide basic amenities and create an education infrastructure for self-dependence of underprivileged and deprived communities. New definition of 'Super Power' of the world shall be the one who takes the lead role in creating peace, not the one who can flex the best muscle of weapons.

Apparent sin versus the non-apparent sin

If we cheat someone, it is an apparent sin. If we commit an act that is unacceptable to the society, we curse ourselves. What if the society itself has set standards that hide many non-apparent sins? Consider the slaughter of millions of animals in the name of food and slaughter of thousands of humans in the name of religion or a 'war for peace.' While our planet has been bestowed with such abundance of vegetation that bears fruits of joy, humans can become occasional meat eaters so that they can fall back to this option in case of emergency situation to save their life. The mission of human life is a far greater objective and they may resort to meat eating in emergencies only as a life-saving option.

While an army is engaged in raging a war against another community as a legitimized order execution by the politicians, are the politicians not sinners who order such a massacre? When one particular nation land-grabs a neighbor and kills millions in the process of annexation or enlargement of territory, is it not a crime? What we may shield as heroic deeds under the garb of patriotism, may actually be 'bigger' sins of killing the innocent and the righteous.

An interpretation of scripture to 'kill' others who don't subscribe to a perceived school of thought is inappropriate for the modern times. There is a possibility of offering a justification of such an interpretation for the times over several hundred or thousand years ago, according to the appropriateness of circumstances prevailing at those times. Today, we have internet bringing a whole global community together and have opportunities to share knowledge and expertise in technology or medical sciences for benefit of the humanity at an international level. During the contemporary times, an interpretation to kill others would be like living in the age old domains of implied interpretations. It is the evolution of a mindset, which has to come out of a conditioning of a lifetime.

Ability to Drive, or Walk?

In the years, centuries, or the millennia to come, the ability to transverse across the edges of the universe without the aid of any external gadget may become the norm, as much as the ability to drive in today's world. Everyone knows how to drive a car, ride a bicycle, fly in an airplane, or walk from one point on our planet to another. What is a walk-able distance for someone living in rural India or China, or in Siberia, may not be the same to an urbanite. What is cycle-able to a marathon cyclist may be more like a drive-able distance to others.

Shri Prabhat Ranjan Sarkar, the founder Acharya of Ananda Marga spiritual awakening movement has revealed in his writings that Lord Shiva walked on the surface of our planet about 7,000 years ago. Between then and now, the ultimate origin of all existence in manifested form has revealed to us a way how we may evolve from the ones walking on the planet in divine image to the ones traveling throughout the universe, without the need for any external gadget.

This path of evolution may appear to be very long, and at every step on the way we will have writers like Shri Sarakar who would reveal the facts of past and insights into the future to Yogis like Shi Prahlad Djani and Shri Uma Sankar who are the living legends surviving without food for extended periods, to the ones who may reveal the techniques to live without the need for oxygen and water, or generate it by some process embedded within our intellect. Eventually, it is evolution to a life form that can exist and grow without the need for oxygen, water, and food.

Weapons for the future

Interpretation to 'kill' by the fundamentalists is indeed a violation of the religion. While these interpreters may be glorifying themselves in the name of religion, patriotism, or any other self-proclaimed 'ism,' the fact remains that it is absolutely inappropriate in today's circumstances. You can't solve problems of today or tomorrow by using the technology of yesterday. As the problems evolve, so does the technology. Similarly, if the whole world has to evolve as a community, they have to rise above the religion together. This togetherness is in terms of all the religions and communities put collectively from an A to Z of nations of the world. Once we are collectively able to achieve this, we shall be able to create a planet full of love, peace and joy.

Today, we see all the nations spend a major chunk of their resources on creating weapons and maintaining armies. Tomorrow, we shall see the nations spending most of their resources for creating peace and disarming everyone across the globe. This creation of peace is first made in minds of the people and shall subsequently be reflected in their actions, deeds, and attitude. Driven from a wave of Divine Blessing and efforts of volunteers engaged in the peace process, it shall engulf the entire universe in a revolution for peace.

People meditating collectively as groups shall send out signals of 'peace,' wiping clean any negative or subversive thoughts of a few misguided minds and purifying their negative attitudes. This would be the exact kind of 'killing' that would be taking place in the future. With no bad intentions towards anyone, meditative soldiers shall use the weapons of 'goodwill' to 'kill' the 'negative plans' in minds of the perceived 'wicked.' This would be the equivalence of balance between 'destroying the wicked' and 'blessing the enemies.'

Returning to the basics of nature - herbal pesticides

In old days, natural wood was burned to create heat for cooking. The ash left by such burning was used to clean the utensils. Ash was also used to spray on the plant leaves to ward off insects. Ash produced by burnt natural wood is a great helper to human kind. It acts as a soap, detergent, body cleanser, and pesticide. It is absolutely safe to use, and its dissolving in water causes no significant threat to fish.

Neem, a commonly grown tree in many parts of India, and of late also in Northern Africa, has excellent herbal properties. Its dried leaves are used to protect woolen clothes from moth. When dried leaves of Neem are crushed, the powdery substance can be sprayed on the plant leaves to protect against invading insects. Neem stick is used as a toothbrush. It creates healthy and strong teeth. Traditional and new applications include treatment for acne, digestive problems, curing infections, besides several other benefits.

Both Ash and Neem can be safely used as pesticides, without any adverse effects whatsoever on either the vegetation, environment, fish, or humans. Both are organic, vegan, and environment-friendly herbal pesticides.

We would do well by bringing together such age-old remedies from different parts of the world and create interdependence by exchanging traditional cures and healing remedies that can benefit everyone. Ash and Neem are just a case in point as tip of the iceberg.

Exploring new avenues of research

To catapult the present world from its current mode of existence, we need modern day Columbus willing to leap into the unknown and undertake a voyage that would land us on a platform from where we can launch ourselves in multiple new directions of research. Today, all research is focused on the material. The new research initiatives are needed in the domains of non-material to transform our mode of existence. We would do well by studying negative frequencies, and opening up new vistas for exploring existence with these new modes.

Currently, all contemporary scientific knowledge and research on our planet is focused on the study of positive frequencies of association.

Consider $c = f\lambda$, where f is the frequency and λ is the wavelength. The multiple of f and λ yields c, the velocity of light. As frequency increases, the wavelength decreases. Ultra and super high frequencies have shorter wave lengths. Microwaves have wavelengths lower than a meter.

Now, consider a wave with a negative wavelength, and a negative frequency. Since the multiple would still yield a positive, our $c = f\lambda$ equation holds well.

A negative frequency would have a negative wavelength associated with it.

Something would need to be added to that frequency of association to bring it to the positive, the domain of manifested existence.

For comparison, let us consider a new domain that is yet unmanifested, and we can call it as perceived potential that must be continually transitioned to the energy form to create existence.

A journey in evolution

Human beings can, and eventually would evolve to a stage where they are no more manifested as physical objects of condensed energy. They would become beings of light that can travel at will to anywhere in the intergalactic universe and beyond.

The current phase of human and other existence on the planet is a necessary transition in the process of evolution.

The journey of life for any human being is an aiding factor in the overall intergalactic process of evolution. Human beings are designed to react to circumstances and situations over which they have marginal or no control. Depending on their conditioning and creative visualizations, they can make choices that set the ground for their performance on a vast canvas of grappling with desires, indulgence, restriction, respect, and realization.

Creating new opportunities through interdependence

Opportunities of a different kind can be created in a post September 11 '2001 world if we first connect within ourselves and

Face to Face with Shiva

subsequently expand the world in this dialog by consultation and collaboration. A creative visualization can be defined within the scope and timeliness of achievable objectives. Complementary and supplementary strengths of the world are available to us in a model of cooperation by power of the web that provides the vehicle to connect. The essence of this hypothesis is a shift in attitude from existing 'compete' to futuristic 'cooperate.' These opportunities would be centric to the theme: *'Creating peace while protecting the environment.'*

IT has a major role to play in the upcoming changes, as we pass through a process of de-materialization. Regional consortiums and collaborative launches would see the world taking eCommerce to the nooks and corners of every street. While this is just one of the ideas to turn around a specific segment in the IT industry, many more can be generated by a process of creative visualization. The key is to take a converging view, integrating various technologies for creation of a better world during this transition to de-materialization.

The ideal model of interdependence

There is nothing between people, technology and the nature. That's the way of life at a typical global village.

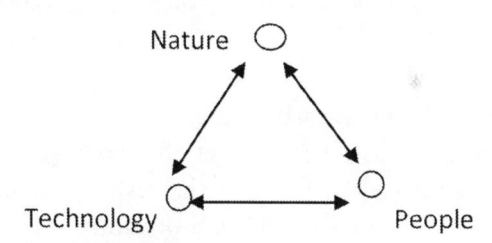

Fig.8.1: An interconnected Interdependence

In this new model of economy - people, technology and nature are interdependent, often switching the roles of actors, players and system within which they operate. This interdependence may be built on a startup model where people are players, technology is an actor, and the nature is a system. That would give us the desired control as people to willingly create interdependence, instead of just playing as puppet actors in the hands of an uncontrolled force.

The exploitation of media, marketing hypes and gimmicks of manipulators and so-called managers of the system and rulers of the day – politicians, would all get eliminated in an awakened economy based on the advent of an intellect of a web-centric force where the customers and citizens are educated and all-powerful. Knowledge is power; it has often been said, but seldom professed by a practice of the world. The awkward would be replaced by the awakened. The mediocrity would be replaced by the brilliance.

The time has now come to unleash the power of knowledge. This is the millennium of the intellectuals.

Not of actors, manipulators, or politicians. The people would use collaborative consultation power of the web to create new possibilities, opportunities, and paradigms that are un-dreamt as of now. Many a shifts would happen in the times to come, starting with the attitude from hitherto *competitive* to *cooperative*. The shortcoming at present is that we consider knowledge mostly of the world (or prakriti) and not of the self and super-self. Knowledge of the latter require yoga and scheme of studying and understanding the metaphysical and above all, a connection with the inner-self. In the triangle above, the three elements leading to understanding and progress are the knowledge of Prakriti (the world and environment around us as it exists), Aatma (self) and Parmatma (super-self, or say, the super consciousness). Innovation that is universal and for all is virtually impossible without understanding self and super-self. It is towards developing an understanding of the self, and from there to that of the super-self, that we need to first have the realization of the self, and our relation to the super-self.

The platform of realization is built on the foundation of respect. The respect for our past, the respect for whatever the technology and science has achieved so far, and the respect for urgency to take corrective actions. This moment is very precious. This is the moment of introspection for not just America or the world. It is the time to sit back, analyze and explore for each one of us. We have all been going over a hundred miles an hour, driving crazy, on the road of our *Acquired Identity Syndrome*. The world needs a sabbatical.

It is something like what has happened to Afghanistan. They play a game by name of *Buzkashi*. Horse riding animals (humans) kick around the carcass of a beheaded young calf. It is like playing horse-polo, where ball has been replaced by the slaughtered calf. Peter Bergen, in his book 'Holy War Inc;' has done a good job at documenting that right now the same game was being played – the only difference is that the calf had been replaced by the nation – Afghanistan.

Yes, September 11 was indeed a wake-up call and God did let it happen on purpose, for nothing can happen without God's will that we all collectively keep shaping with our thoughts, actions, and speech as born in image of the divine. The purpose was that not just America, but the entire humanity must shake themselves up and face a harsh new reality. This is the beginning of the end, if we want it to be. This is the beginning of a process of transformation, if we want it to be that way. It is all of us - the collective humanity who have the power and control to steer this planet in any direction that we want. No one can deny that. If we don't act now, it would be too late. We are running the last lap of the only chance we have to save the planet and the future of our generations. Let us set up a dialog with our inner-self by connecting internally. And set in motion a debate in the physical world by connecting externally using the power of the web.

Following religion out of fear of God, or love for God?

Imagine a situation at the brim of a swimming pool. If someone is being forced to jump into the pool for the fear of a fireball being brought closer and closer, are they doing it willingly? On the other hand, if someone is willingly going to the pool out of a desire to swim, simply it is love for the water. This example bears an exact simile with people's belief in God. Some believe in Religion out of a fear of God. It is only but a very few, who believe in Religion out of love for God. If you get into something out of a fear, you are never going to either enjoy it or get fully immersed into it. Those who take it for love of God, get to acquire the ability to see the image of the Divine in all creation.

This also divides the thin line between a terrorist and a soldier.

A terrorist or jihadist is in fact an innocent civilian who is inducted into a regimented squad either at gunpoint or by lure of something that is otherwise not available or is forbidden. A few rich sheikhs may force the recruitment of "innocent masses" in Afghanistan, and once the ball is set in motion, keep attracting more recruits by offering lures of indulgence in "the restricted zone" through captured victims used as captive sex slaves. The cycle goes on and on, with all morality and ethics thrown out of the window and justifying any kind of behavior in the name of religion.

A soldier, on the other hand, is proudly serving the nation, as a patriotic citizen on the paycheck of the national exchequer.

The thin line is that of interpretation – one recruited at gunpoint and serving out of fear for life. The other joining the Army out of love for the Nation, and serving out of respect. In the bigger picture, both are children of God. If they fight each-other and kill, God bears the pain. Killing and wars must stop at all cost.

An appropriateness of interpretation

Considering that time appropriate interpretation was applied to either scare or to entice the wrong-doers to follow the right path in an age when technology was not advanced or masses were not much educated, we have to realize now that times have changed. Though the dimension of time is changeless in the spiritual world and is transitory in the mental world, we have to get back to realities of the physical world when we contemplate any action or plan. In the context of present day circumstances, when the world is integrated by means of internet and we have opportunities to communicate and share our views, a different interpretation of the scriptures is required. The present day interpretation has to be creating love, peace and joy between the global community of humanity and other creations of nature.

Many may interpret the writings in some scriptures as an instigation to kill in the name of true belief in God, considering the circumstances prevailing at those times. At the same time, on different pages of the same scripture, is the message of love and compassion and an invitation to do good deeds in the name of belief in God. Repeatedly, all the scriptures ask for having sympathy towards the poor and the destitute, live together in global community as brothers and sisters, and in harmony with the nature.

Instigation to fight for righteousness is also inscribed in most scriptures. The holy war is actually to fight for righteousness. In the context of modern day interpretation, it has to be the fight against ignorance, poverty, imbalance and lack of interdependence. Today, creating righteousness is achieved by protecting the environment, disarming the humanity, living in harmony and in an interdependent manner. Rising above the myopic visions of national interests and looking beyond the religion itself, we can give a new, modern interpretation to any or all the scriptures. The context is what matters the most. If the context of our interpretation is to create peace, we would interpret accordingly. If the context of our interpretation is to create hatred, we would interpret accordingly. The genesis of a motivation lies in the intent. If the intent is driven from Spiritual dimension of our personality, there can never be a wrong driver. Subsequent to the intent, it is the perception mechanism, deeply embedded in the AIS (Acquired Identity Syndrome) as our simulated reality.

Organized training can turn a ten year old adolescent into a potential suicide bomber in the name of religion. In a similar way, organized training can turn a young adult into a potential researcher to create technology for peace. The expenditure for later training may only be a fraction of what the expenses for the former might be. Where from is the context of motivation driven? From crooked thoughts of hatred or the Spiritual feelings of love? Each one of us, as a community or a nation and as people of the world, need to collectively do some soul searching to find the answers. If we would ask our inner-self the right questions, there would be the right answers coming from bottom of hearts of a collective humanity.

In the context of a post September 11 '2001 world, the basis for interpretation of scriptures is 'Interpret with a perception to create peace. Take what it needs to create the peace and leave the rest.' This is the underlying driver that we need to follow. Right from politicians to journalists to people on the street, we have to work towards creating peace and interdependence as a planned objective and a deliberate action.

Needless to say, if we don't interpret with an objective of peace and act towards creating global integration, disruptive forces would be at work to make hatred and succeed in causing further frustration and widespread havoc. It is collective efforts of entire humanity put together that would yield meaningful results towards the process of peace.

Role of Meditation in promoting world peace and global integration

Once you are able to meditate on a continuous basis as a matter of routine, you contribute by radiating a positive energy into the universe. While some misguided folks may transmit negative energy by their actions and thoughts that may be perceived as neither noble nor pure, the emission of positive energy absorbs some of this negativity. The perfect state of harmony would be when there is an electrical balance between the energies. The saints roaming the Himalayan forests or those who meditate in different parts of the world hold the key to maintain universe in balance by emission of a positive energy.

It is important for each one of us to interpret negative actions of others as opportunities for us to cause improvement and not have bad feelings towards them. Everyone would eventually return home to the divine – we just need to bear with them in the interim. No one is evil – they are just misguided. When they would watch others lead by example, they would be shown the way.

An Exercise

Step 1: Read the story:

As the legend has it, a majestic snake, upon divine incarnation on our planet, used to bite each and every one who passed that way. Sooner than later, the word spread about the deadly snake and his unmistakable potion. No one ever even dared to pass by the path of snake's inhabitance.

Lord Shiva just happened to be walking our planet then. Upon traversing the path of majestic snake kingdom, the Lord was greeted with silent 'pranaam' salutation by the snake, and also complaint that he felt lonely as no one ever traversed his path any more.

Lord Shiva simply smiled and said: "Use your judgment."

The snake retorted by saying: "the capability to bite and inject my potion is very part of my nature."

Lord replies: "True, but you also have a brain to judge."

Snake replied: "Lord, I beg your pardon, but please forgive me and kindly guide me as to what shall I do from here on?"

Lord said: "Henceforth you may never bite anyone."

The divine creation, though in snake form, started following all the instructions of the Lord, and simply refrained from biting anyone.

Though it was extremely hard to wipe off scare of the past, an unknowing intruder simply traversed that path a few years later. The intruder was amused by the sheer majestic size of the snake's mighty presence, and even more by not being attacked. The unknowing intruder narrated story to existence of the times and everyone was amused. It soon spread like a wild fire that there did exist a majestic snake, at a specific coordinate of latitude and longitude, and it never even attempted to bite anyone passing that way. It got worse as kids started hurting him with spikes of the knives that they possessed as of those times.

Though the snake, in an attempt to return a useful value from the ANN perspective was too humbled to go against its own nature, soon began to realize that it had absolutely no useful value to return.

Face to Face with Shiva

His presence on the planet was so challenged that he saw no reason for his existence any longer, and prayed for a presence of the Lord.

The Lord did appear, and resolved: "I did ask you not to bite, but I never forbade you from letting them know who you are: you could scare them by the very might of who you are, and simply breathe away your existence to them." That seemed an amusing idea, and the snake started exhaling an extremely powerful breath as greeting to those who passed that way. Again, the word did spread around. Everyone in the neighborhood was simply scared to trespass.

Step 2: Explain from your past experience when you were taken for granted for being too humble.

Step 3: Explain from your past experience when you were hurt professionally, personally, socially, and emotionally for being too rude and arrogant.

Step 4: If you were able to rewind in life and live forward from instances that you explained at steps 2 and 3 above, what would you do differently?

Step 5: Consider your heart to be an abode of the divine, and furthermore your role as resolver of miseries of those suffering in poverty, pen down the task on hand to perform. Next, relate this to defining "who we are, what we stand for, why, and how we can accomplish that task on hand." Encompass the community, the nation, and the world, as feasible and appropriate per definition of the task and their roles in its accomplishment.

Step 6: Now that you have defined the roles and responsibilities in a step by step manner, refine the steps to become achievable. Gather those you identified as role-players and engage them in a dialog to get the ball rolling. Identify the resources needed for your project, and ask who would do what to provide the required resources.

Step 7: Launch your project and keep monitoring the progress periodically.

CHAPTER 9

Questions and Answers with Shiva

What does it mean to know God?

Knowing God for anyone is to have a realization that there is consciousness within and one can connect through it to the inner-self, and extend that connection to the entire universe. The practice of meditation can easily help anyone to make this connection. One can always communicate with the inner-self, and that is the voice of God coming from within. There is no need to go anywhere – it is all within you.

To be able to do this, one must not let barriers develop between one and the self: intellect/mind – and inner-self, or else the inner-voice would not be heard as it gets clouded in chatter from the mind.

It is the same inner voice that will ask you to refrain from doing anything wrong. It is the same voice that will ask you to do what is the right thing to do. Though nothing is right or wrong but thinking makes it so, for human beings to evolve at this time, that judgement for listening to the inner voice is critical so that an inspiration from the divine can guide our path.

Everyone has this divine element within.

If the God is within each self, then how does one differentiate?

There is no differentiation required. It is like seeing one in all, and all in one. Once you are able to connect with your inner-self, you can visualize the vastness of the entire universe as a single interconnected entity.

Within this interconnected entity, each of us is an inseparable part.

If one knows that God is within, then is it necessary to worship and pray? And to whom does anyone worship and pray and how would it help?

Worship and prayer are like meditations with an objective – worship is like singing praise to a higher being, and prayer is like asking for something from the higher being, or from collective consciousness of the universe.

Once you know that God is within you, and you are able to communicate with your inner-self, technically speaking worship is only symbolic. Once you are connected, you are on the right path – and that's exactly what matters the most. You may follow all the prescribed rituals in the world and yet not be on the right path. Symbolic worship is not necessary, but can be done to keep up with established norms and traditions of one's family, community, or religion that one follows. As long as you are not hurting anyone by performing traditional or symbolic worship, it is good.

Prayers are like reaffirmations of requests that your inner-self is making to collective consciousness of the universe. As long as prayers are with a noble intent, not of a wrong or selfish nature, and meant for general good of everyone or even anyone in particular, are a great way to expand your consciousness to connect with the all-pervading divine energy and requesting it to work per nature of the prayer and heal, by being one with it.

Is it reasonable to pray for healing oneself?

Yes, it absolutely is. A prayer to heal yourself is the one of showing interest in life, and requesting for an ability to do well to the world. In that sense, it is not selfish, but is to request for your own wellbeing as a means to do good to the world at large. One is limited in some ways to do well to the world when one is sick or hurt. One needs to supplement prayer to heal oneself with steps in the right direction – exercising, eating healthy, and following a course to wellness.

Is it wrong to attempt to commit suicide, even if it is indented to sacrifice oneself for saving resources of the world to help others so that those resources are not spent on oneself?

It is absolutely wrong to attempt to commit suicide. Even if the intention is to save the resources for others, attempting suicide is not the right way to do it. One can make a difference in the world in which one lives, and do good to others by actually living and making positive contributions, instead of thinking of dying. Even if one is in the most miserable situation, and considers to be completely dependent on others, it is still well worth living, as one is contributing in the divine big plan of interdependence whereby allowing others to see an image of the divine within you and make the offerings of service to the divine.

While thoughts to attempt suicide come to everyone and are natural to any normal human being in today's world of competition, corruption, pollution, and frustration that is brought from styles of personal and professional lives alike, one must learn to distinguish thought from practice.

To that end, distinguishing thought from practice means that one needs to creatively visualize ways and means to make a positive difference in the world even by extremely small baby steps that are within one's means. It can be like thinking a positive thought or making a positive speech, or performing a positive action. All several extremely small steps come together to make a giant leap at some point in time, irrespective of how small these were. While one is suffering, the most important thing to note is that it is a passing phase, out of which you will emerge stronger than ever before. Suffering is the baking oven of strength and patience. It is this strength and patience one develops while suffering that eventually enables you to make positive differences in the world in which you live. To that extent, one must keep sanity at all times and not give up.

Another reason for thought of suicide is lack of connectivity with the inner-self, and through it, to the super-self (Prabhu), since the person feels empty as sooner or later in life one comes to realization that nothing touches as all fame and name are voids. To address this problem, one can set aside some time everyday to meditate and connect with the inner-self, and through it to the super-self.

When one has no hope in life, what can one do?

The thoughts of hopelessness are just thoughts, and once you are able to accept those just as thoughts and have a realization that your action need not be based on the basis of these thoughts, you can come out of the feelings of hopelessness. One must first find a way to get supported physically – food, shelter, and clothing are some of the very essential prerequisites to survival in the physical world that humans dwell in, and when one is having a hard time, it is reasonable for them to seek help from charitable humanitarian institution facilities and social networks so that they can get past these barriers to survive. In that context, the helping organizations perform their own fulfillment of their spiritual objectives. In your own particular situation of hopelessness, you may likely be essentially testing as to whether the social and charity support system is rising to the occasion. This must never directly translate to an obvious attitude of perpetually living on social welfare or abusing all resources from all possible sources. It is just meant to get you to stand again on your feet, and as soon as you get up, you must seek to be on your own – do realize and appreciate that you must never underestimate your own individual potential to do great going forward and give back multiple folds of what you may have taken from this system of social and charitable support. Once you connect to your inner-self, you would be able to visualize a clear picture of what you can do going forward and come to a point of giving back.

It is vital to know at all times that saving your own life is as important as your intentions to save anyone else' just like that of your own child. The intention to live is the most influential single factor in the entire big divine plan, for life is the essence of all existence. There would not be any life without existence, and there would not be any existence without life. Thus, there is a tightly coupled interdependence between life and existence.

Now, a brief discussion on the next steps.

The first step of course is to distinguish thought from practice.

The second step is to ignore other people's actions, behavior, and speech that led you to the situation of hopelessness. One need not think negative of others, but just ignore their negative behaviors.

The third step is to invest good feelings towards all – including even those who are responsible for driving you to the situation of hopelessness. At all times we must know that the biggest investment one can ever make in life is that of good feelings towards all, including those who hurt you the most and are responsible for your current miserable situation. A realization of the fact that they are merely actors in the big divine plan and accepted to perform in the exact manner in which they did those disturbing actions and uttered unpleasant words was meant as a way to help us evolve spiritually to a level where we can have this realization and not hate them, but love them and thank them from the bottom of our hearts for making those contributions to our evolvement and spiritual growth. No one is bad at the core. Once we have this realization of the self, and that of their role in helping us get to that point of evolution, the paradigm just shifts – and we can see a natural change in their thoughts, actions, and behavior. Part of it has to do with our very own view point of looking at their role and contribution, and this does not directly translate to becoming a mute spectator to rude and ugly behaviors.

After a point one must stand up and let others know as to what they need to fix – and in that context you are the one who is contributing to their realization of the self and spiritual growth. All this can be done without carrying any feelings of hatred or jealousy. The intention is to help them evolve and grow, just as you see their role to do the same for you. Occasionally there may be situations where one is better off to temporarily withdraw from the situation and detach to allow oneself some space to realize, as well as let others do the same, and this can be the best course under certain confrontational circumstances that appear to be out of control. Inspiration, intention, and thought are more important than action in this context as these are the ones that would guide the further creative course rather than impulsive, knee-jerk reactions to a negative behavior in an already volatile situation.

The fourth step is to creatively visualize ways in which you can contribute to make a positive difference in the world, which encompasses addressing your current situation on hand.

The fifth step is to engage in those visualized actions which are towards making a positive difference in the world, while improving the current situation on hand. One needs to do their best, and leave the rest.

Staying focused on the inspired action would definitely yield positive, meaningful results. While course corrections are important to ensure staying on track, one need not start evaluating too soon – sometimes it can be a while before the results of positive thoughts, speech, and actions bear fruit. What really matters is the continuity of positive thoughts and action, irrespective of the magnitude or intensity.

How are you able to travel freely in the inter-galactic universe? How does one survive in the outer space?

This is how it works –

There is no more existence as breathing and eating human beings or creatures outside of realms of planet Earth. The existence is transformed to a being of light, so as to say. It is not even light, but one may think of it in a subtle form that can appear as a being of light at any given point anywhere. The existence itself is like omnipresent consciousness that is instantly everywhere by the virtue of an extra dimension that collapses the distance on-demand (or say as required). It is the knowledge associated with the instantiation of the form that manifests it in the way that it is required to appear and the data associated with multi-dimensional coordinates lets it appear at the required spot.

So, to appear as a being of light in a visible form somewhere in the universe, the consciousness instantiates itself and manifests at the required time and spot by associating the required forms of knowledge related to the instance of manifestation and the available form of energy (usually light, as that is available in most of the inter-galactic universe in some ways).

How are knowledge and energy associated with consciousness?

The only one super element decomposes and creates three basic elements – consciousness, knowledge, and energy. All un-manifested as well as manifested forms -which we visualize as the living universe, are a result of the combination of these three basic elements in some way, with a purpose to creation.

Knowledge defines the rules for association of energy, and this association happens at the required instance of creation. Time and space act as the two delimiters. Time acts as an enabler for association of knowledge, while space acts as an enabler for association of energy.

While manifestation happens, it is an instance of consciousness that gets attached to knowledge and gathers the required form of energy to become a living or a non-living existence.

All forms, whether living or non-living, together create an eco-system that lends itself amenable for experimentation by its very nature to exist and be. Knowledge enhances with time by the virtue of experimentation of all instantiated manifestation as the living universe – that is why time or manifested universe exists.

Energy is constantly changing form, and becomes the source to nurture and sustain the living universe as a test bed to continue the very experiment to enhance the knowledge and evolve the consciousness. To that extend, purpose of life is to return a useful value that aids to enhance knowledge.

The basic figure from Chapter 5 (the secret of creation) is extended below to show these associations for the ease of comprehension.

Abhinav Aggarwal, Ph.D.

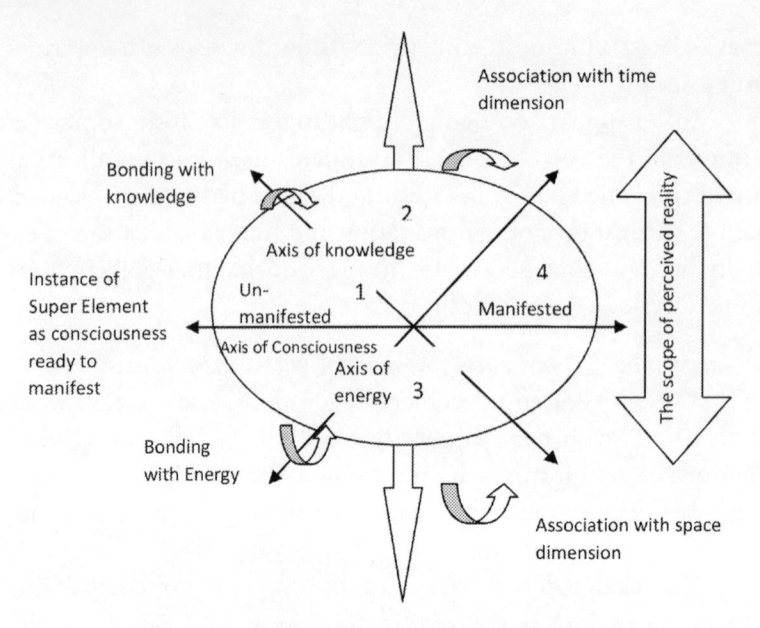

Fig.9.1: The association of consciousness with elements of knowledge and energy to create manifestation

The associations create a bonding that sustains a living being or a non-living existence. The bonding stays in place as long as the manifested existence stays.

At the time of dissolution, how are the elements of consciousness, knowledge, and energy separated?

What we know as bondage is basically the cumulative associations with energy and knowledge through various life spans of the entity of existence. Upon accumulation of a critical mass of useful values, through experimentations across life spans that are ready to be returned for enhancement of knowledge, the manifested existence gets ready to release itself from this bondage.

The basic figure from Chapter 5 (the secret of creation) is extended below to show the release from bondage for the ease of comprehension.

Face to Face with Shiva

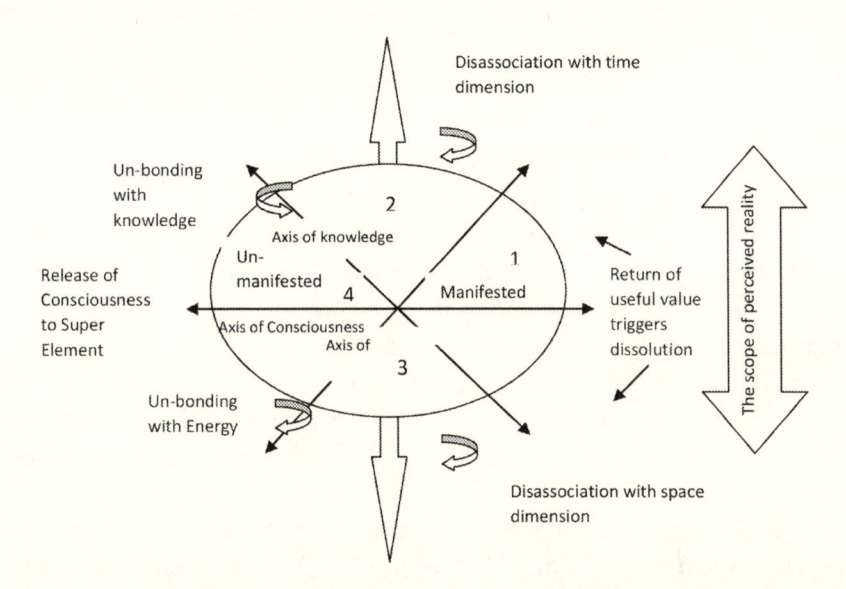

Fig.9.2: The un-bonding of elements of knowledge and energy to release a manifestation

What are Moksha and Nirvana?

Moksha is release of the consciousness from the bondage of cumulative associations with energy and knowledge, or of perpetual life and death, also known as re-births.

When a life accumulates sufficient useful values to be returned for enhancement of knowledge, it is ready for dissolution. As depicted in the above figure, it is the process to detach from the bindings of a materialized universe, and return all elements of creation to their original source; and finally, Nirvana is the union and merger of that particular instance of Consciousness to its original source - the Super Consciousness.

In essence, one can see that the whole purpose of life is to return a useful value. One learns, one experiments, one documents the results of these experiments that are returned as values. In that sense, learning is larger than life, as knowledge grows to evolve consciousness.

What constitutes us, and what are the different dimensions of our personality?

Like all else that exists, each one is comprised of a combination of the three basic elements – consciousness, knowledge, and energy.

Eventually, these three elements are all driven from the single super element – super consciousness.

There are 3 dimensions to an individual's personality.

The first dimension is intra-terrestrial: this is the physical aspect of our being. Our body, its appearance, and all that the body does from speech to actions performed relate to our existence on the planet and interactions with other beings like ourselves and with the environment around us. This dimension of our existence is well grounded on the planet. We move from place to place on the planet, interact with all that exists, and from these interactions we form our experiences that shape our perception. Since all actions and interactions are limited to while being on the planet, and the body exists only while we are on the planet, hence the name 'intra-terrestrial' for this particular dimension of our personality.

The second dimension is inter-terrestrial: this is the mental or psychic aspect of our being. Our mind - the thoughts that it generates, and its function as an engine that transforms inspiration to thoughts is the key here. It has something to do with how we think and operate our life. This aspect is also our link between the other two dimensions of our personality – the physical and the spiritual, and hence the name inter-terrestrial since it provides that linkage.

The third dimension is extra-terrestrial: this is the spiritual aspect of our being. Our connection to our inner-self is the source of our inspiration. It is the mind that transforms the inspiration to thoughts. Our consciousness is deeply embedded in this dimension of our personality. Since we get our inspiration from collective consciousness of the interconnected universe, while we connect our inner-self to it through the ANN (Abstract Neural Network), there is an extra-terrestrial angle to this specific dimension of our personality.

Collectively, what we may call an individual being, is the sum total of all the above three dimensions. While some of us may even be unaware of the extra-terrestrial dimension of our personality, it is critical that we build awareness about this most vital part of our being.

While we perform physical exercises and activities to function the body that is engaged in movements guided and controlled by mind, we do need to find some ways and means to exercise and activate the other two dimensions.

While there are several games, exercises and activities to help text the mind, meditation is often helpful in aiding to create a connection with our inner-self. Since our mind is so occupied and influenced through the external stimuli by receiving constant inputs from media, interactions with others, and driven by physiological needs of the body, it sometimes gets hard for the mind to get out of these perpetual and automatic preoccupations to free itself up to address our need to establish the much needed connection to our inner-self.

While we attempt to meditate, we tend to calm down external influences on the mind and make it available to establish this connection to our inner-self.

Keeping the eyes closed shuts off the media influences, and being in a quiet zone is helpful. Our perceptions are perpetually shaped by the inputs being received from all our sensory organs – hearing, touching, smelling, vision, tasting, and any other sources that can potentially feed a signal to the brain. If we keep ourselves in an environment that is quite, devoid of strong odor, pollution free, with clean air, and we intentionally turn inward, we are well on our way to make the most necessary connection. We can start listening to voice of our inner-self only when we can silence voices from external sources. The inner-self is always connected to the extra-terrestrial ANN (Abstract Neural Network), and we can always access our inspiration from that source.

The extra-terrestrial dimension is also our continued and ever-existent life well beyond our limited, time-boxed existence on the mortal planet. While our physical life on the planet is merely a speck, just like a milestone or an exit stop in the seemingly infinite eternal journey of several thousand miles on the spiritual highway, it is also an opportunity to make a difference in all those lives that we touch just by our being here within the span of time in which they co-exist with us.

It is such an interconnected interdependence between the three dimensions of our personality that one just can't be without the other two. It takes all these three dimensions to bring to life a complete being.

In the bigger picture, each dimension relates to a basic element of creation: intra-terrestrial relates to energy, inter-terrestrial relates to knowledge, and extra-terrestrial relates to consciousness.

What is the difference between spirit and consciousness?
While consciousness is aspect of the super element as an essential constituent to all existence, spirit (or soul) is an individualized instance

of it that is specific and unique to every single being (self). Though spirit is always with the self, it retains the ability to connect with the super-self (the ultimate, super-element, Shiva) at all times during and after mortal life span of the individual with whom it is associated and identified.

A spirit retains threads to its previous life experiences, and keeps accumulating newer experiences within each life. Once enough mass has been gathered, upon dissolution, the spirit would return useful values and merge as consciousness into the super element through the process of de-manifestation. At that point, all the identities associated with cumulative life spans are shunned.

The key difference is that spirit is identified and associated with an individual - the self; and consciousness is always free of any identity and is detached from selfness of the spirit.

What is the importance of shunning desire?

Desire can be shed as part of an all-encompassing nature, voluntarily, just out of respect for all that exists. It is a necessary step towards evolution, to show the way. Unless someone can show the world that one can evolve beyond desire, the world will continue to live in the overboard mode of succumbing to their passions, desires, and sensory temptations. More of such examples are required, but not out of the fear to follow restriction, but from a perspective of respecting restriction yet accepting all those who are in the overboard mode of indulgence and showing them a way. It is the way for that next leap of humanity, as eventually they all will need to evolve out of the indulgence mode.

There is a marked difference between restricting the desire and shunning it voluntarily. Suppressing desire through imposed restriction can lead to negative consequences.

Even from the path of restriction, one can only control desire through knowledge of the fact that it is just there and it exists – and one can let go of it easily. Suppression only makes the desire strong and though it may appear that you have declared a temporary victory, the suppressed desire can surface later in yet another manifestation.

When one voluntarily sheds desire, it is out of respect and realization. This maturity is an evolution of desire like change of colors in fall for maple leaves from green to various hues of yellow, orange, red, brown, and finally a separation of the colorful leaf from its parent branch. The leaf is like the desire that is shed from the tree branch after it has matured to that stage through this natural evolution.

There are several levels and modes in which a human being dwells – the levels are those of living in contemplation (one keeps wondering and struggling), living in contentment (having seen the futility of struggle), and living in detachment (rising above it all). The modes are those of ignorance (indulgence vs. restriction struggle), transition (respect), and enlightenment (realization).

The two go together – when one is living in the level of contemplation, essentially one is switching back and forth between indulgence and restriction. Irrespective of the affluence or education of society, over 99% of people in the present age live in this level.

When one is living in the level of contentment, one has developed a healthy disrespect for both indulgence and restriction, and is somewhat detached from either one of these. Having switched back and forth between indulgence and restriction, one has seen the fallacies of each, and come to accept whatever is in its present form. It is only about 0.99% of the humanity in the present age that live in this level.

When one is living in the level of detachment, one builds on the healthy respect for both indulgence and restriction, and more so for all those who are stuck in their struggle of shuttling between these two. Graduation to the mode of enlightenment from the mode of transition is a natural evolution as one swings through respect–realization see-saw.

Living in the mode of enlightenment, one is detached from the world, even while one lives in it. One sees the opportunities for improvement instead of problems. One realizes the self and its relation to the super self, and looks upon everything as an object of respect. In that sense, detachment is an enabler, as it dis-associates one emotionally and helps to focus on task at hand.

What is the easiest way to evolve oneself from one mode or level to the next?

It is very simple –

To evolve out of indulgence, one needs to only distinguish between thought and practice. The desire or temptation to indulge is only a thought that triggers one's mind. As soon as one can realize that it is just a thought, one even need not force them to control their desires – key here is knowledge of the fact that one can live with that thought and subsequently let go of it (lack of this knowledge is ignorance). Once you start distinguishing and filtering such thoughts, you will naturally evolve to a point where these thoughts will stop bothering you. It is a much better, simpler, and stronger way to manage the thought than to exercise rigorous self-denials and unnatural controls that may eventually push you further towards indulgence. This technique is simple, yet powerful, and can easily put oneself in the mode of transition and living in contentment.

To graduate from living in contentment to the next higher level, first of all one must learn to accept the as-is situation. This means ignoring negative and hurting actions of others, yet accepting them with respect. One can't get very far with feelings of hatred towards anyone. The only one who is hurt by carrying on the feelings of hatred is the one carrying those feelings. This can be summarized as 'ignore to exist.'

Respect is a pre-requisite to realization.

Gradually one shifts to living in the mode of enlightenment – with unconditional love and respect towards all, acceptance of what exists, and creatively thinking of ways to solve problems of the world and immediate environment around them. All actions inspired from thoughts generated in the mode of enlightenment are towards the fulfillment of a common universal mission and vision. The vision is to evolve consciousness, and the mission is to enhance knowledge.

Who and what is God?

There is no God in the sense that we can perceive someone in the sky who runs the affairs of the world.

God is the collective consciousness of the universe. Each one of us, whether a living being, or non-living being, have an essence of that element in ourselves. There is no existence possible without the element of consciousness. Energy and knowledge are the other essential elements to every existence.

What is super consciousness?

It is the non-existent, un-manifested form of collective consciousness of all the universes, known and unknown. It is the source and origin from which all manifestation occurs.

The final destination of all manifestation, upon return of a useful value, is eventually to merge into this super-element upon dissolution.

Why and how do manifestations occur?

The ultimate goal of all manifestation is to return a useful value upon dissolution. Manifested universe provides a platform for experimentation where all that existence brought to life can interact with its environment and form the basis for enhancing knowledge. The elements of consciousness, knowledge, and energy combine to create a manifestation.

How does knowledge enhance and how does it help?

Whenever a living entity interacts with its environment, and the entities collectively or individually interact with each-other, the net end result is first forming a hypothesis, and subsequently its validation. These interactions build a basis for discovery of what exists or has previously existed, generation of new ideas and bringing these to life by individual or collective, collaborative efforts, and learn lessons by implementation and yielding of useful values. These interactions and experimentations aid in the process of enhancing knowledge. Enhanced knowledge lays the foundation for further development, a newer platform for future research, and enables discarding of older platforms that are not effective at yielding meaningful results. That's why learning is the most important aspect of life.

What is the role of energy in creation and manifestation?

Energy is an essential element to bring an instance of consciousness to life, and it perpetually changes form. Energy in motion and the knowledge element associated with an existence make it unique and ready for interactions and experimentation in its lifespan.

When not manifested, where do the elements of existence reside?

Super consciousness needs no physical space to reside – in un-manifested form, and in the manifested form it is all pervading, and is interconnected to each and every atom and molecule of the existence through its constituent element of consciousness.

Knowledge is ever enhancing, and draws upon the physical existence of all data and information available in the universe. As human beings on planet Earth, we can draw upon the universal database of knowledge through an ever available abstract neural network (ANN).

What is ANN?

Abstract Neural Network is everyone's connection to an invisible source of knowledge, from which one can draw. All the useful values returned by experimentation and interactions in the universe of existence are eventually uploaded to this ANN.

Is there life in the universe, other than that on planet earth?
Yes, there is.

What happens when we die?
All the constituent elements associated with creation are returned to their parent bodies upon dissolution. If one's life has returned a useful value, one dissolves – and this means that the useful values returned by one's interactions and experimentation in life are uploaded to enhance knowledge so that it is now universally available through the ANN. This happens instantaneously, and also keeps happening over one's lifetime.

The physical existence that was a form of condensed energy is released to its environment. This happens gradually. One consumes energy from the environment gradually, and the reverse process is also slow. Energy will change form – that is part of its very nature. The constituent environment is forms of energy as earth, air, water, fire, and sky (ether).

Consciousness, the element essential to all existence, upon return of a useful form of knowledge, is returned to rejoin with its constituent element – super consciousness, and will again change its status from manifested to un-manifested.

When there is not an adequate level of useful value returned, the consciousness will retain its bearings to the knowledge acquired and accumulated throughout the current and previous life spans and subsequently return to life by association with energy to create another instance of life. There is a chain retained through lives, till such time that there is a substantial mass of useful value to be returned for enhancing knowledge.

What is the meaning of death – is it destruction, or dissolution?
Any living body as a manifestation is a combination of consciousness, knowledge and energy. There is no destruction ever of anything. It is only energy that is changing form. Consciousness and knowledge are indestructible.

All entities are born out of a combination of consciousness with energy and an association of knowledge. Knowledge may be comprehended in two forms – one as that is static (data or information) and the other as the one that is created by the entity itself by virtue of its interaction and experimentation (the later form is dynamic and evolving).

The entity that was brought to life, whether perceived as a living one, or as an object that exists as part of the infrastructure to facilitate experimentation and interactions, has a defined life span. The defined life span itself is part of the knowledge that is associated with the entity at the time of its creation. In entities perceived to be as living ones, the cumulative lives of the entity keep evolving knowledge to an extent that at some point through these cumulative life spans it gathers a sufficient mass that results in returning a useful value. Once the useful value is returned, the entity dissolves – that is, the energy is returned to the environment from which it was borrowed, the knowledge is uploaded through ANN to the invisible database instantly for universal download and usage, and the consciousness associated with the entity merges with the super element – once this state is attained by an entity, there is no more its identity or bearing with its previous life spans.

What happens between life spans of the entity?

The consciousness retains a bearing to the cumulative knowledge acquired throughout its previous lives and keeps researching by drawing upon available sources of data, information, and knowledge – these include all the data available in the universe. Throughout this perceived period between lives, the entity is limitless as it is detached from the dimensions of time and space. It means that the entity can travel unrestricted anywhere and has access to all the available data and the sources of knowledge. The future is not yet defined completely, but the entity keeps planning for its next course of action in view of its research initiative and keeps an eye on the potential opportunities that would provide it a suitable environment to enhance its thread of knowledge that it has been shaping and bring it to a level of bearing fruit where it becomes a useful value. Once that right opportunity comes, the entity is brought to physical life yet again.

Are all entities born equal?

All entities perceived as living, enjoy the exact same opportunity in their lifetime to enhance knowledge to a level that it becomes a useful value.

The entities perceived as non-living, provide an environment for interaction and experimentation by the living entities.

What is role of actions (Karma) that one performs during the life time?

Though one may feel constrained by the environment within which one has to interact, there is a lot of freedom and choice that can be exercised even within limitations and constraints. It is the appropriate selection of those free will choices and the sincerity of effort that results in the right course of action.

Once connected to the inner-self, a path opens up to bridge with the ANN and draw upon the accumulated source of enhanced knowledge that keeps inspiring our thoughts and guiding through the right course of actions to be performed.

If not connected, there is a potential to get distracted and fall prey to the default of indulgence, or actions that lead to hurt others. One can control such tendencies through meditation and open up a path to connect with the inner-self.

The actions which lead to excessive indulgence or harm others do not end up resulting any useful values that aid to enhance the knowledge or evolve humanity. It is these useless actions that will result in a bondage that is associated with the thread of one's life spans to set up waves of motion in a form that eventually needs to be countered.

What is the future of humanity?

The future of humanity is shaped by collective thoughts, actions, and plans that we all engage in. There is no such thing as a set course of action. We shape what we want to be and do. Futility of certain paths to indulgence or destruction is already well known and established. If human beings collectively wish to be on a divine path, there are certain pre-requisites that need to be met. The resolution of economic inequality between communities, disparity in prosperity, and commitment to a common purpose are the bare minimum essentials that can easily be achieved by appropriate planning, consultation, collaboration, and agreement to ensure permanent peace on the planet.

Can human beings evolve to becoming beings of light?

Yes, they sure can. Though it is a long process in evolution, they can take giant leaps by simply changing the way they think and live. A gradual step by step evolvement will take them through transformations from eating meat to becoming vegetarians, then from eating plants to semi living on light. Thereafter, they will slowly evolve to completely living on light and this will also ultimately change the ways in which they reproduce. Shifting from current biological reproductive process, it will be a modulation of two superimposed light forms that will create a new light form. Though there would still be an association of consciousness with knowledge and energy to bring this new light form to life, it will be in fundamental ways different from what you currently perceive of a life form. This life in the form of a light would not be dependent on breathing or eating for survival. Also, it would not require a vehicle to move from one spot to another. It would be able to freely roam around anywhere in the universe.

How do higher beings reappear to humanity?
As forms of light – they are able to manifest by instant association with energy and knowledge on-demand to appear in the required form to the required audience, at the required spot.

How is it possible that only some may be able to see the manifested form, and others may not?
Think of it as a password that is granted to the one who can see and behold the manifested form. This is granted at the required instant.

Is it necessary for a human being's spiritual evolution to visualize a higher being in its lifetime?
No – as long as the human being thinks and acts in the right direction, spiritual evolution will happen on its own as a consequence of noble thoughts and deeds.

Are there a minimum number of life forms or lives that a human being must live through before attaining Moksha?
No – even a single lifetime can be adequate. Think of it in a qualitative way, and not a quantitative one. When one connects with the inner-self and through it with the all-pervading divine energy, one is ever connected with the ultimate source of evolving knowledge that guides one in the right direction.

What is the purpose of human life?
The sole purpose of all life, which means everyone's life, is to enhance knowledge by returning a useful value through experimentation in life that aids to evolve consciousness. When one is vibrating at the same frequency as the divine, one is connected with one's inner-self, and the inner-self is connected with the universal divinity pervading all across the universe. It is this connection with the inner-self and through it to all the divinity across the entire universe that one can always stay tuned with inspired thoughts that lead to righteous actions.

The right actions will lead to accomplishments that collectively advance the knowledge that aids in evolving the consciousness.

What is the role of spiritual prophets in modern day context?

Each and every human being has a hidden spiritual saint lying within their inner-self that they need to unearth. Once they can connect with their inner-self, they can reach out to the abstract neural network that acts as their connection to the cumulative universal repository of divine knowledge that is based on latest updates related to activities happening anywhere in the universe.

There is a need for every human being to make this connection to their inner-self rather than a need to have spiritual prophet on the planet at this time. Consider this as an opportunity for the entire humanity to bear this role in some way or the other.

An expectation that a savior will be born on the planet and solve all ills of the humanity is not a reasonable one. That is like conveniently shifting responsibility elsewhere. Each one of the human beings has that role and responsibility, and they all are empowered to make a difference by what they think and do.

They have to perform this role over and above what they do regularly for a living – in fact this role is built into all aspects of life. One has to think and act in a saintly manner in all regular actions of day to day life as well.

What was the compelling reason for you to accept the potion from Sagarmanthan?

If I had not accepted it, and subsequently consumed it, it would have destroyed the world.

The strength of potion was so intense that it held the potential to wipe out entire humanity from the planet, so the only way to avoid it from causing that damage was that it gets consumed or absorbed in a manner that its effect is nullified.

While it is obvious that everyone wants everything that can benefit them, and no one wants anything that can harm them, there are times when some among us have to step forward and accept to do what is not in the best interest of the individual, but is needed to be done to save the humanity.

What is the lesson for human beings from the example of Sagarmanthan?

Just that one has to step up and make some sacrifices, and do what is in best interest of the human community, and in the larger interest of the environment of the planet and all that belongs to it – the flora and fauna, the life on the planet in general that extends beyond the human race.

In the contemporary context, the very least one can do is to give up some comforts that can potentially lead to saving environment of the planet, examples can include but are not limited to consuming less power by avoiding air conditioning, driving a smaller hybrid car or riding a bicycle, living in a smaller house, planting and caring for trees, being a vegetarian, eating less and respecting food by not wasting it, recycling all that is possible, collaborating instead of conflicting, and thinking positive under all circumstances.

Can there be an example of how one can attain Moksha even when not having the opportunity to being born as a human being?

Though it may appear that animals or plants have no purpose to their life - that is not true. The plants are the life givers to the planet – the oxygen that you breathe in, the food that you eat; all of it is coming from the plants. They have the mission to contribute the most for sustainability of life on the planet.

As far as insects or animals are concerned, they are part of the larger eco-system on the planet. On attaining Moksha, take the example of a honey bee. When a human being or a threatening animal may approach a bee hive to destroy it, a *self-sacrificing* honey bee steps forward to save the community of bees and stings the intruder. It is known that she will die after taking the sting action, but she still steps forward to do it. Such sacrificing spirit attains Moksha upon dissolution. The key phrase here is: *self-less service for the broader good of the community, even if it leads to the peril of your own life.*

It is truly with this spirit in make-believe reality of perception that armies of nations move forward with a mission to defend their motherland, and consequently to improve the world in which we live.

Even a tree that has fulfilled its mission by feeding all around it and giving them life by providing with oxygen, such a giver with selfless service also attains Moksha upon dissolution.

What is the lesson for human beings from the example of honey bee and tree in contemporary times?

In today's world, a human being may be tempted to follow the sensory desires and indulge instead of doing something that benefits the humanity. First of all, one must learn to deal with oneself (follow three steps of: 1. *distinguish thought from practice,* 2. *ignore to exist, and* 3. *act from an inspired thought*) and then take actions that are in the larger interest of humanity and communities of the world that encompasses all animals and plants.

Staring with giving up some small comforts, one can grow to a level of making bigger impacts that lead to larger gains for the planet.

Is action necessary?

Think of human beings in two ways – one as a processor of information, and the other as a body machine.

The processor of information, or say the human mind, is also the generator of thoughts, a receptor as well as a transmitter. In this great apparatus, there is enormous processing, receiving, and transmission capability that is unmatched in any machine ever produced. It is only through the power of human mind that all connections are made possible – the ANN, to the inner-self, and the ability to upload and download from the invisible database of knowledge. All this ability leads to a creative potential that can be manifested as an action plan.

From actions of the individual that are inspired by positive thoughts, to the collective actions of a community or nation that result from the plans, finally the changes occur in this world by action. Thought alone is the concept, the plan, or a roadmap. Action is the result of thought. Though inspired and positive thoughts are a pre-requisite to a good action, it is finally the action itself that produces a result.

Positive and meaningful actions are required in this world to make a difference. A person who is merely thinking about planting trees has not made a difference unless those trees have actually been planted, cared for and nurtured, and bore fruit, while also providing life as a source of oxygen to humanity. To that extend, human beings have great potential to cause fundamental changes in the world and shape its future by their actions.

Actions are at various levels and of various types. As a human being, one has great freedom and a degree of control over actions and at the same time a responsibility to exercise choices in the right direction.

How does one deal with feelings of guilt and shame?

Guilt is an absolutely natural and a necessary feeling. There is perhaps *no* one who has not experienced the feelings of guilt or shame in their life. One must learn from mistakes and not repeat those. All experiences in life are on the path to growth, not the path to decline. Life by itself is an experience at learning, so the name of the one of the youngest religions on the planet – *Sikh* (a student aimed at learning).

If one perpetually continues to feel guilt and shame all the time, these will become impediments to one's growth. To deal with guilt and shame is the same way as to deal with desires. One has to look upon these as a conditioning of the human mind. This conditioning happens over a period of time from certain experiences that we face in life.

Just imagine as if the experience that led to a feeling of guilt or shame had not happened. If one can rewind the mind in time to before that experience, and start playing from there in forward mode, skipping the bad part of experience that led to the feelings of guilt or shame, and pause at the present, then one can clearly visualize as to what exactly went wrong with that experience.

Once you can document the 'bad' part of the experience, and then also document as to what exactly went wrong, and what you could have done to prevent the 'bad' part from happening, then you can write down a series of steps of 'Do's' and 'Don'ts' for the future, and then press the 'pause' button again, so that you can start living your life from here on. Now, the life that you are leading from here on is without the feelings of any guilt or shame, and you are living it celebrating the lessons learnt from the bad experiences in life, and already having the knowledge of what to do, and what to avoid.

Life does not come with a user's manual – one needs to write one down as one goes, and keep it handy for reference. These notes are just part of your own life's user manual, and as personal to you as your signature and as unique as the DNA.

This user's manual is in the form of the sticky notes that you have appended in your mind. Human brain knows no boundaries to cognition. It can be at the farthest galaxy in the fraction of a second, as thought is what travels much faster than the speed of light. As you live the life and are faced with a particular situation that relates to having knowledge from your prior experience, then your mind will automatically pick up the lessons learnt from that experience, immediately retrieving it from the sticky note 'document' that has been pasted somewhere on the vast canvas of mind from your life experiences, and not only prompt you to refrain from acting in a certain manner, but would even guide you on the right path so that you can carefully avoid the mistakes, and come out as a winner.

To break loose from the circle of guilt and shame, one needs to first document the lessons learnt with do's and don'ts from all the past experiences, and then live life forward by celebrating the lessons and avoiding the don'ts.

Exercise 1: Pick up a negative experience from your past – and document the experience, and come out with the sticky note of do's and don'ts.

Exercise 2: Pick up another negative experience from your past – and document the results of experience, as if you had applied the lessons from sticky note at Exercise 1 above of do's and don'ts. Compare these results with what you had actually done, and gain knowledge of what needed to be done differently.

Exercise 3: Imagine a future situation that is likely a repeat of the negative experience from your past – and document what you would actually do, and how you would avoid the mistakes. At the end of documenting this, write down a resolution that you would never ever repeat the mistakes that led to the feelings of guilt and shame. Paste this resolution as a 'highlighted in bold' sticky note in your mind – this is your empowerment to live a life free of guilt or shame. Now you can push the 'resume' button to live a life free of any guilt or shame going forward.

In the context of this exercise, we must come to respect all of our experiences in life as learning. Each experience teaches us a lesson. We evolve as we experience.

Notice how enough mass must be gathered on the scale of respect to make it *tilt* so that you can see realization – think of respect-realization as a see saw with fulcrum at the intersection of indulgence and restriction. It is out of struggle with indulgence and restriction that respect emerges, and finally leads one to realization. On the other extreme seeing the futility of both indulgence and restriction, one takes the path of renunciation.

Face to Face with Shiva

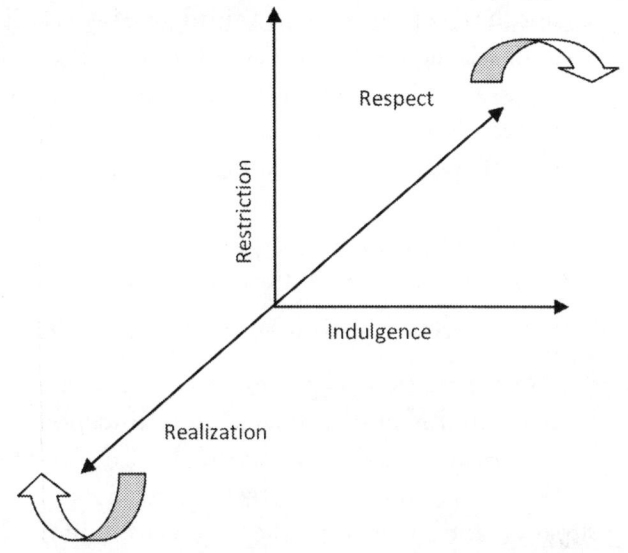

Fig.9.4: Axis of respect – realization as a see-saw pedestal to aid evolution

The figure from chapter 7 is enhanced above to reflect on the axis of respect – realization as a see-saw pedestal.

How does one deal with getting stuck with desires?

Desires can act as blocks to growth and evolvement. Though occurring naturally and being an inherent part of being human, succumbing to desires without exercise of the intellect can reduce one to become a robot operated and controlled by the desires. One can easily get into a situation where desires have overpowered the human mind to an extent that one is completely stuck with them.

Desires are programmed in to the human mind, and tend to draw one to the axis of indulgence. Acquiring the knowledge on how to deal with desires is the key to getting unstuck.

Step by step process to getting stuck:

1. One sees, or acquires the information about an object of desire – a charming place, person, gadget, or develops a bonding that is pushing one to the limit, or gets addicted to a particular type of food or substance.
2. The human mind programs itself to become dependent on fulfillment of the condition at 1 above before one can move forward to the next step in life.

3. Unless the condition at 1 is fulfilled, one is stuck. Even if the condition is met, one is perpetually drawn to keep repeating the condition literately under a false programmed sense of perceived fluid belief that one is satisfied just because the condition was fulfilled, leading to a pattern of repeating behavior.
4. The cycle between above steps continues unabated, till one takes deliberate action to break it and get out of it.

Step by step process to getting unstuck from desires:

1. The very first step in process is to get to know that the human mind is programmable and can condition itself to become dependent on fulfillment of the desires and getting stuck, or to getting unstuck by un-conditioning it out of the situation and move on to the next steps in life.
2. Get a realization that even if the programmed condition of desire is fulfilled, one is merely drawn to a false programmed sense of perceived fluid (non-lasting pleasurable sensation or a pleasant feeling) belief that one is satisfied just because the condition was fulfilled.
3. Break the cycle of desires by practicing 'not succumbing' to them and viewing these as programmed conditions of human mind. This can start with simply following a 'staying away from fulfillment of desire' routine and observing that it caused no negative impact, but rather rewarded you with a satisfaction of attempting to break away from the cycle. Once you extend the period of 'staying away from fulfillment of desire,' you would naturally be able to see the positive impact of uplift by self-empowerment. An important aspect to note here is that you need not be driven by a sense of 'restriction' while 'staying away from fulfillment of desire.' A sense of restriction is likely to drive you to temptation, while viewing 'desire' as a conditioning of the mind would not. The knowledge of this distinction in your point of view is your *empowerment* to break the cycle.
4. Draw a system dynamics model of what exactly goes on in your mind of the two states – one while you were earlier either succumbing to the desire or feeling deprived by

its non-fulfillment, and the later one of your 'now' state where you realize that it is a programmed conditioning that can easily be broken. Identify the logical linkage points of intersection that can potentially extend the model.
5. Link the two system dynamics models created at 4 above into an integrated model by joining the models at their intersection points. Make a study of this model to examine the dynamics of human mind in general, and your own in specific, that draw one to a conditioning of succumbing to the desires, and viewing desire fulfillment as a state of mind that falsely perceives satisfaction. If unable to get started, consider to use the following base model as a reference.
6. The examination at 5 above is your key to unlocking the 'stuck' state by being in the position of 'knowing.'
7. Sustain to be in a state of being 'unstuck' by performing self-introspection at regular intervals. It is like a gradual increase in your own happiness that now you are able to live without being stuck and can move on to the next steps in your life's mission and vision.

Base model of 'Desire' for reference

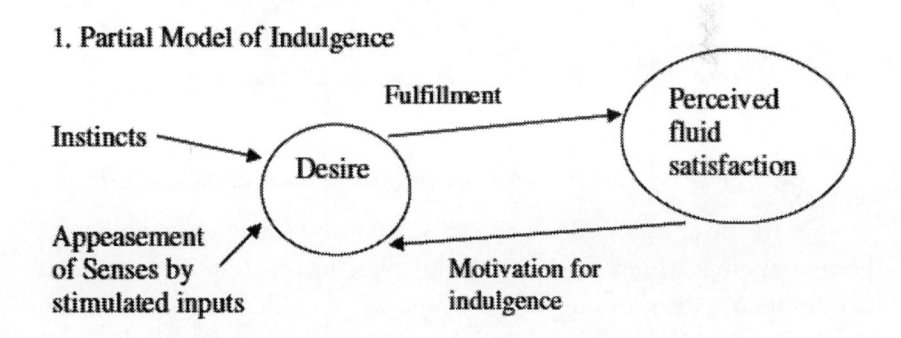

1. Partial Model of Indulgence

Fig.9.5: Desire and perceived satisfaction system dynamics model

In the above model, you can visualize the perpetual circle of fulfillment and motivation to indulge further in the 'Desire Trap' by a false sense of satisfaction.

2. Partial Model of Restriction – a push for indulgence:

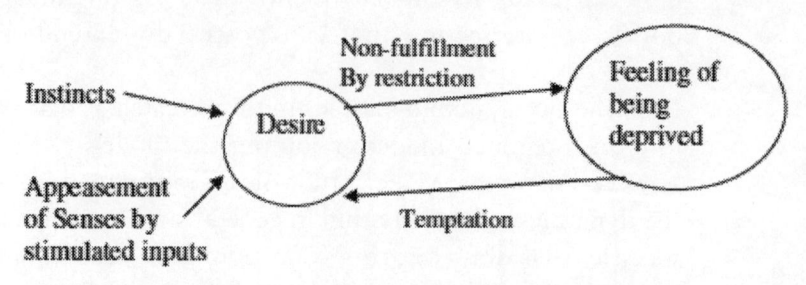

Fig.9.6: Desire trap by Restriction system dynamics model

In the above model, you can visualize the perpetual circle of temptation to indulge in the trap of desire when you deliberately restrict yourself. Following the path of restriction without having a clear understanding of how we get in the 'Desire Trap,' creates an undesirable pattern of thought that can eventually push one towards indulgence.

3. Partial Model of 'The New State' – a dawning of realization:

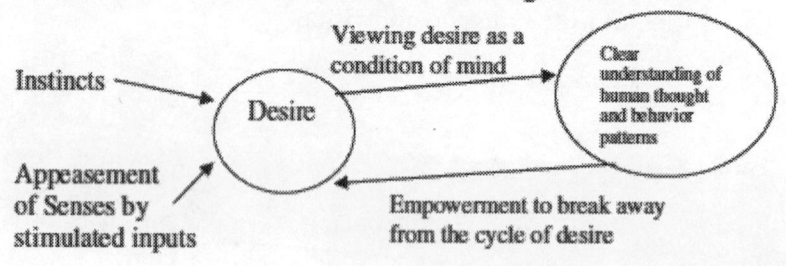

Fig.9.7: Empowerment to break from cycle of Desire system dynamics model

In the above model, you can see that by clearly visualizing the perpetual circle of temptation to indulgence in the 'trap of desire' as a conditioned state of mind, you get empowered to 'deal' with the desire. You no more either need to succumb to it, or consider yourself deprived by not doing it. In fact, now you gain satisfaction by not indulging.

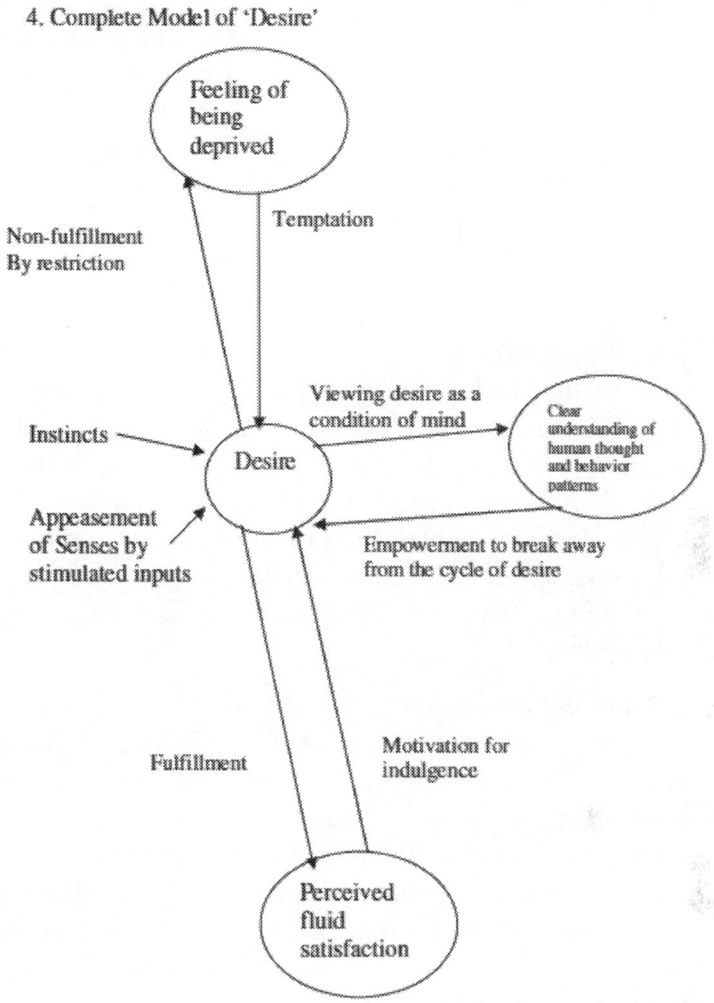

Face to Face with Shiva

4. Complete Model of 'Desire'

Fig.9.8: Desire, Restriction, and perceived satisfaction - system dynamics model

In the above model, you can see that visualization of the perpetual circle of temptation to indulge in the 'trap of desire' as a conditioned state of mind that can be undone by un-conditioning the mind, to break away from the circle of desire.

What are the spiritual laws, and how do they vary from the physical laws?

Here are the spiritual laws -

The law of spiritual inspiration

All human beings are divine beings, and so is the entire existence. When connected through the inner-self with a pure heart to the super-self, one can visualize the inter-connectedness and oneness of the entire existence, and draw upon the universal knowledge that would lead to noble thoughts and motivate actions in the direction to do good to the self, community, world, and the universe. Each one is born in image of the divine and is fully empowered to shape future of the universe.

The law of spiritual action

Spiritually inspired divine thoughts lead to noble actions. When action is performed with devotion and the intention to do good to everyone, it is self-less and pure. Action performed without any expectation of selfish gain would result in a positive spiritual balance that helps to wipe out any prevailing negativity in the community or the world. Thought is the blueprint of action, so it is important to de-junk the mind from time to time and reset it to come back to its natural home – the divine.

The law of spiritual attraction

All beings are naturally attracted to each-other as we are all interconnected. All of us are part of the whole, and in it. The senses of touch, smell, sight, taste, hearing, and the power of mind as thought to correlate and process all of these sensory inputs, provide the instrument to individualize personal experiences through the course of life. Further, the ability to speak and act through our tongue, limbs, and other body parts provides a very unique and differentiated setting to react. There is no need to completely detach from the senses, but to be aware that these exist as those instruments. Knowledge of the fact that highest joy is not obtained by merely indulging in the perceived external pleasures through sensory instruments, but by turning inside the self to seek the divine is key to awakening. The connection established with the inner-self leads to all pervading knowledge and reveals that spiritual attraction does not discriminate against anyone and it is natural for all beings to be drawn to each-other. While initial attraction can be triggered by intellectual compatibility, like-mindedness, common interests, or any other factors, it is a process of evolution till one eventually gets to a point of embracing all and excluding none.

The law of spiritual rewards

One does not do an action with any expectation of a material benefit or a personal gain. One feels rewarded just by the sincerity and the level of effort put in towards the action as a matter of personal satisfaction. One is able to see success of the self in enabling the success of others, as all is in one and one is in all.

The law of spiritual returns

When one performs a spiritually inspired action, it is neither with the intention of a gain, nor with an expectation of recognition. The only intention with which a spiritually inspired action is performed is overall good of humanity, the planet, and the universe. The power of collective spiritually inspired actions by a community is enormous, and enables the wiping out of negative waves in motion, following karmic laws of nature.

The karmic laws of nature allow a great deal of freedom and flexibility to each one of us while thinking and doing in our day to day life actions – and collectively as communities, but we must know the consequence of each decision and its resulting action. While there are instant motivators to get an immediate material or financial gain as a result of an action that bypasses the inner voice of our consciousness, like by telling a lie, or eating meat, we must know at all times that each and every thought and action of ours is being recorded and accounted for. The accumulation of such actions of an individual, a community, a nation, or us human species as a whole has a balance of net positive or negative at any given point.

For an individual, this thread of karmic balance can be spread over several life instances, yet in each life time one has the full potential to wipe out the entire previous negative balance and convert the net balance to positive. As such, one need not get bogged down by worrying about the karmic balance, but rather focus energies on creating positive thoughts and actions that would have a net result of creating positive balances not just for the individual, but also for the community, nation, and overall for the human species.

The most effective way to build positivity is by means of creating net new knowledge that aids to evolve the consciousness – through research and experimentation with the platform of life. This is what is most likely to result in the useful values.

When useful values are returned through one's life experimentation, and are accepted, one is unbound from the shackles of time, space, and karmic debt delimiters to be released for merger into the super element – the super consciousness, to attain the state of Moksha. This is in effect, the highest return of spiritually inspired actions by an individual, community, nation, and human species. The loss of identity of the self and merger into the super-self which has no identity is that state. The life on our planet is like an exit stop from the eternal spiritual highway.

The law of spiritual wealth

The poorest of the poor in the physical world may be richest of the rich in the spiritual world. What really matters is that while living on the planet of existence, what kind of spiritual wealth does one create?

The law of spiritual wealth has nothing to do with your bank balance, material possessions, or other tangible assets. It has everything to do with how much impact you make on the lives of those on the planet, in the universe, and to the overall growth of knowledge and evolution of consciousness. In physical life, examples can be how you contribute towards creation of permanent peace on the planet, protection of its environment, bringing joys to those living below the perceived poverty line, and building interdependence among people and communities of the world.

It would help to know that money is a human invention, and has already outlived its utility. It existed as an instrument to create order among chaos, and has peaked out with rise of capitalist model. From communist to capitalist to industrial to all others, these interim models may coexist and run parallel to one another till they all fall together to give rise to a new paradigm – the spiritual model of growth that would be a permanent feature associated with life.

The law of spiritual experience

The experience is in the mind. When one sees anything, the image is actually captured in the mind, when one tastes something, the taste is actually occurring in the mind. All human activity is controlled by the thought. If one meditates regularly and opens up the connection to within, and from there to the ANN, then inspirations would flow naturally, creating wonderful thoughts that would lay the blueprint for steps that humanity needs to take in the right direction. It is fulfillment of these steps that would eventually yield a glorifying, ecstatic experience. Such experiences would be a paradigm shift from the normal sensory pleasures one enjoys through the stimulus of five senses – touch, smell, sight, taste, hear. The sensory organs rely on the external factors or objects (e.g. food, flower, music) to draw an experience.

The paradigm shift here is that spiritual experiences do not rely much on external objects or factors, but are mainly driven from within, and a connection from within the inner-self to all-pervading divinity. Once this connection is established and nurtured, the spiritual experience grows to encompass others by generating like-mindedness through ANN and the power of spiritual electro-magnetic wave transmission from the inspired mind. There are intersection points in the collective thought and behavior patterns to involve others in the experience.

The law of spiritual experience relates to functions of the mind to establish connections to the inner-self, to the ANN, and its ability to radiate spiritual waves at an intensity that contributes to nullify or dilute the impact of prevailing negative waves set in motion by inappropriate individual and collective human thought and activity.

In contemporary times, realization of such experience would be through creation of permanent peace on the planet. Right now the chances of one human being killed by another are significantly lower than ever before – and collectively humanity can keep moving forward in that direction to where there is no fear to any existence from another existence, and that would encompass all life forms. A case in point is Nagbani (snake forest), in the state of Jammu & Kashmir in India, where legend has it that no human being has ever been harmed by a snake, and no snake has ever been harmed by a human being. It is the collective behavior of a specific species within a geo-spatial space reflecting in collective thoughts and actions of another species, building a pattern of reciprocity of goodwill, which can be extended universally though the law of spiritual experience.

The law of spiritual oneness

In the physical world, all entities consider themselves as separate individuals; while in the eternal world this separation is just not there. The implication of this oneness in physical world is to think of others as yourself, and then act from this view of togetherness driven from an image of the same one divine in both you and them. Once humans have this realization of the self as being part of the super-self, and oneness of the super-self that manifests in all others, they would shift from competing, complaining, and cursing, to consulting, collaborating, and creating.

If at any time we curse others, the curse comes back to us, by the law of spiritual oneness. By the same law, any action done with an intend to do good for everyone, does bear positive results, and one can feel its positive impact by being one with all through oneness of the self with the super-self.

By a realization of this law of spiritual oneness, we must never curse others. We must always have good feelings for everyone. The negative behavior of others is just a temporary passing situation that we face as a quick divine litmus test to see as to how we react in that situation. By reacting in a calm way with meditative state of mind that can be persisted throughout the day and across personal, social, and professional lives alike, a positive reaction to a negative behavior of others is the only manner in which we can collectively keep working towards creating a better world and universe.

The law of spiritual appetite

Each one of us has three dimensions to our appetite – spiritual, mental, and physical. The spiritual dimension of our appetite relates to aspirations that are received through the ANN after establishing the connection from within. The mental dimension of our appetite relates to acquisition of knowledge. Since all real knowledge is spiritual, there is a dependency for fulfillment of this aspect on the spiritual dimension, since aspirations lead to thoughts. The physical dimension of our appetite relates to fulfillment of needs of the body. When one is not connected from within, disconnect between the three dimensions cuts one loose to indulge in perceived appeasement of the senses. The non-spiritual mind perceives such indulgence as gratification and continues throttling the loop of acquired identity syndromes in an overdrive gear that creates a make-believe reality that fulfillment of sensory pleasures is the way to go for happiness.

The spiritual dimension of our appetite represents needs of the spirit. One's descent on the planet of existence is for a divine purpose. Unless one has a realization of the self, and unfolds a purpose to life by establishing the ANN connection from within, one can keep on dwelling in the mode of ignorance. It is only after establishing the connection from within that the door opens up to receive inspirations that transform to aspirations and thoughts. The spirit receives gratification from engaging the mind and body as a unified whole in pursuits that are aligned to divine inspirations.

The mental dimension of our appetite represents needs of the mind. While mind can get caught up in receiving, interpreting, and processing millions of inputs that it continually keeps receiving through the five senses, all of that put together is in no way fulfilling any needs of the spiritual mind. The spiritual mind, while aware of all these inputs being there, needs to engage with the spirit in establishing the inner connection and receiving the divine knowledge directly from the ANN, universal source of all knowledge. In that sense, mind is also a bridge that draws upon body of knowledge of the world to lay down a foundational blueprint for action. Thus, the real appetite of mind is fulfilled when it is engaged in translating inspired knowledge to a realizable project by leveraging worldly knowledge.

The physical dimension of our appetite represents needs of the body. When body is engaged in action to achieve a spiritually inspired project, its real needs are fulfilled. As a machine, it does require fuel, and that's where air, water, sunlight, and food as fruits from plants step in.

When physical body is not in synchronization and harmony with the spirit and spiritual mind, it tends to be governed by the non-spiritual mind, causing imbalance in the spirit-mind-body integration connection. It is this imbalance that is at the root cause of all human body issues and problems of the world at large. From illness of the body and mind to manifestation of tragedies, all of it is result of this imbalance.

The relationship between fulfillments of three dimensions of the appetite is:

$S = M^2 = P^3$

S stands for spiritual appetite, M stands for mental appetite, and P stands for physical appetite.

This is how it reads – a single unit of spiritual appetite can result in complete satisfaction of the mind, body, and spirit. That is the state of perfect balance that requires some necessary, but not excessive mental and physical activity and intake, just as much as is in need to fulfill the divine aspirations.

When spiritual appetite is ignored and left unfulfilled, the mind tends to engage in excessive activity to compensate for it, in its own confused perception of satisfaction, by receiving multiple inputs from different sources and over-do its job by interpreting and processing those inputs. Non-spiritual mind (the one not connected to the inner-self) thinks that it is creating knowledge out of such stand-alone processing, and that is where such activity fails to yield any real value and remains as yet another also-done but unnecessary. Modern day examples of such activities are excessive watching of TV, indulgence in 24x7 multiple chats on the smart phone, and getting hooked on to devices to get continuous inputs from the external world happenings and events.

When this processing is happening in isolation of the connection to inspired knowledge, this stand-alone processing needs to end up in the garbage bag of a thinking dustbin. Without knowing of it, all non-spiritually inspired human minds are engaged in such activity most of the time. It is better to remove such garbage bags and empty the dustbin, so that a fresh start can be initiated by first establishing connection with the inner-self and from there to the ANN.

When body is not under the control of spiritual mind, but rather under the control of non-spiritual mind, functions of the body are similar to those of the non-spiritual mind. Body tends to receive excessive inputs (by eating more than required, and indulging in eating meats), and in collusion with the confused non-spiritual mind, perceives such gluttony as happiness from stimulus of the senses. The fact is that all real happiness and satisfaction in life can only come from within, and not from any external gratification of the senses.

The square function for appetite of the mind, and cube function for appetite of the body, in relation to appetite of the spirit signify the excessive mental activity of the mind, and even more excessive food consumption by the body, when mind and body fall out of harmony with the spirit and tend to compensate for this imbalance through such behaviors.

The state of perfect balance is easily lost in day to day life as we get caught up in a clutter of inputs and chatter of numerous conversations that tend to pull mind on different tangents. One can practice meditation and *yog* as a way to bring back this required balance.

Engagement of body as an action machine in spiritually inspired projects is not to be confused with building more churches, mosques, or temples, but rather with fulfilling immediate human needs on the planet – examples are endeavors to protect environment and reverse the damage already done, programs to educate and feed underprivileged children, provide clean water and air for everyone, gather consensus for permanent global peace, and creating an atmosphere for harmonious interdependence among communities and people of the world whereby everyone can become economically self-sufficient.

While appetite can also be perceived as a need for energy feed to the body as an action machine, as humans evolve to another form of life, the mechanism for intake of energy and the form of that intake also changes to suit the life form and support it in the environment of its existence. To that extend, life on planet earth is supported by air and water, oxygen being the prime sustainer. The intake of energy is in the form of food that is principally from the plant kingdom. Sun is the prime source of energy that aids plant growth. As humans evolve, they can shift to directly energizing from the sunlight.

It is an interesting fact that as humans, born in the image of the divine and endowed with ability to create, we tend to build instruments such as money, which start acting against us very quickly. Having outlived its utility as an instrument to promote interdependence among people and communities of the world, it has now come to haunt the very existence of being human. It does even tend to rise above, and surpass Sex as an AIS, and become the most prominent appetite of a human under the garb of a make-believe simulation that it can buy us anything and everything. Imagine a situation like Gulf War when ATM machines in Kuwait stopped spitting out cash after its invasion from Iraq. Think of those who left millions behind, just to save their life when inter-religion war broke out at the time of partition between India and Pakistan. Religion is also one of those human created paradigms as a structure and standard as an AIS for compliance, that if not strictly adhered to with its dogmas and what nots, would bring peril on us.

There are plenty of us as humans who might have already benefitted from such perpetuations of propagating religion as an utmost appetite of humanity, and there are many of us out there doing exactly that even now.

Rising above all of this, whether human desire or perceived need to have money or a feared need to comply with dogmas of the religion, one can stand up and just be spiritual rather than religious, be fulfilled knowing that all that is there is enough and be satisfied to ask for no more, and be in love with all that exists from humans to all else including plants and non-material, and just be yourself. Once you are able to just be yourself, then you are empowered to open up the connection with your very own unique and exclusive inner-self, establish a dialog with the divine, discover your very own vision and mission in life and translate those to realizable actions within your lifetime on the planet of existence.

These are my last words to you in this present dialog.

Chapter 10

A page out of the Future

December 17, 9999

As we write this to recreate history, just to show as to how our ancestors lived and communicated their thoughts, it would be interesting to look back in time. Until discovery of 'the Wave' and use of Abstract Neural Networks (ANN) for inter-personal to inter-galactic communication, they used to convey their thoughts by medium of the language: by speech, writing and reading. To sustain themselves physically, they were required to eat and drink. These intakes gave them the energy to perform what they wanted to do.

It may sound strange as of date, but our ancestors used to fight and kill each-other. It was not until the discovery of then an unknown disease 'Acquired Identity Syndrome,' (AIS) which they all suffered from, that they got rid of fighting and competing. They were actually ruled by a few stacks of AIS like 'Money,' 'Sex,' 'Religion,' 'Stocks' and 'Nationality.' Unaware of their true identity and the very purpose of their existence, they were a ready prey for AIS to grip them in its wake and take over control of a programmable species. They were able to find cures for many physical ailments and improved the life span, but it took them really long to probe deeper into their own existence to explore the real purpose of their being.

They wasted much of their time, energy and resources competing with each-other to grab and possess a slice of whatever little existed on the planet. It may sound ridiculous that they had to dig up the planet and use the resources buried within, while they were pumped up with trillions of power units from the external sources responsible for sustaining the planet. They required this energy to power their vehicles to move around, heat or cool their houses and places of work. Today we can teleport ourselves to distant galaxies instantaneously by just punching the multi-dimensional galactic coordinates through the ANN and disintegrating ourselves to energy, knowledge and consciousness that is reassembled at the destination. What is the way of transportation as of now was only a far-fetched imaginary concept as of then. Our ancestors had to do everything the hard way through.

They had to learn everything by their conventional ways. They were supposed to read through all that they needed to know and were expected to qualify written examination that authenticated their grasping ability. When ANN was unheard of, they had to process data on physical machines interconnected by wired and radio media. They had to position satellites for inter-communication between various points on the planet, for their ways were all physical.

Since none of us is used to anything like that today, we can easily fail to see the emerging of a pattern in this evolution. An evolution of humanity from primitive hunting species dwelling in caves to the present day non-eating, enlightened beings existing as part of the process that elevates knowledge from one level to another. Today, at this verge of the millennium, we know that we exist as part of that evolutionary process and are connected with our inner-self as much as we are inter-connected with all that exists in this universe by the virtue of ANN. What is so obvious to us today was non-obvious just a few thousand years ago. The emerging pattern of evolution here is from material to non-material, from physical to metaphysical, from hard to instantaneous learning, from interconnected clusters of parallel processors to abstract neural networks.

This planet has been, in essence, a test-bed of experimentation: from creating species like Dinosaurs, who had a huge physical existence, a miniscule knowledge, and almost non-existent consciousness, a sum total of failure for a physically heavy substance. And to destruct that existence, a remotely controlled object had to be fired for wiping out the undesired, leaving a crater on the planet. Next, the apes and who-ever, divine, yet intelligent and compassionate. They never either killed or ate the one of their own kind. And at last, the lately worshipped, human beings, the last rulers of the planet, our immediate predecessors, now considered by some as the worst among species.

Human beings: they were the only ones who were empowered from all sources, the ultimate among those the ANN. Quickly catapulted from one level of intelligence to another they harnessed all that came their way: animals, plants, environment, planet, and finally their own selves. Even the most absurd animals of their day never killed each-other of their own species, though they might have retracted in disgust after showing the worst or best of their super-power. Our ancestors were a mix of the best and the worst at the same time, a deadly, though rare recipe for experimentation species. They had tremendous ability to control affairs of this universe simply by exercising the correct attitude and choices. They always retained the ability to program their own selves, without knowing it.

As much going as with this process of experimentation is an enhancement of knowledge and an evolvement of consciousness, there is also a transformation from ancient physical to now non-physical. Physics, Chemistry, Biology, Mathematics, the terms an infant of the present age may be unfamiliar with, were all among prehistoric branches of science that some may relate more to technology, that our ancient ancestors grappled with. For instance, the term ANN now appears to be of recent past, was then a futuristic abstract concept.

The shifting of paradigm is essence of this evolutionary process. What we consider as abstract imagination for now shall become the reality of tomorrow, surpassing all standards of the physical and non-physical realities.

As we prepare for the big collapse due later many millenniums in the distant future, several research initiatives on hand need to be completed, before we get ready for that great event.

The big collapse, in a completion of the cycle from the origin of our evolutionary system with a big bang as its reversal: let's call it the Shiva process, would merge this existence into its very origin. In salvation of our souls, upon completion of this journey on the evolutionary path, we shall mingle with the ultimate source of our creation: the *Super Consciousness*. Shall there be yet another cycle of manifestation from the source that stays in its non-manifested form? Who knows, and do we really need to know?

For now, we need to focus on the completion of tasks on hand and lay down a framework for eventual evolution to Nirvana for our fellow beings in this inter-galactic universe of existence.

While none of us even has a thought of hurting anyone else, whether one of our own species, an existence on the planet, or that anywhere else in the universe, we must never forget that we have come to this stage after a battle of the inner and outer selves embedded within each one of us.

While the 'inner-self' pulled to our real source of existence: the *consciousness*; the 'outer-self' pulled our ancestors to their externally visible environment: the *material world*. It is not long ago, just a little over five thousand years that we realized the non-duality between material and non-material in the universe and were able to converge our own selves with the true source of all existence.

Having discovered time and space as just the limiting dimensions of manifestation, we can now relate to the past as easily as we can relate to the future and look upon the existence as one whole concept of experimentation for evolution. The Shiva process is a depiction of what can essentially be achieved upon experimentation: nothing more, nothing less!

It is only now that we appreciate the true meaning of 'Spirituality,' and collectively subscribe to it, without losing the freedom of either thought or neural speak, which makes each one of us unique to contribute in specific manners to this evolutionary process. Now we also know that within the limited life span of our existence, we must return a useful value to the evolutionary process, for our life to be fulfilled in line with its purpose. While each one of us now returns the values of joy, peace and love; it was not long ago that some of the returned values were hatred, jealousy, curse, and repentance.

One can ask: why was that so? We must understand the process of evolution. There were times that love and hate both existed, so it was only by reaching the dead-end of hate that one could appreciate the unlimited potential that love held. War and peace co-existed so that the futility of war could be realized to pave the way for permanent peace. Competition and cooperation were both there so that people could see for themselves that they wasted most of what they had in competing, comparing and complaining.

The inner-satisfaction that comes to us naturally, as if we were born with it, is the result of a gradual shift from competing paradigms to a collaborative framework where we now feel more satisfied by helping someone. We now play games of cooperation where the strategy is to win collectively, or make our playing partners win through our collaboration. All games of the past were focused on competing and defeating, not on winning. Today we see our victory when we make someone succeed. In the past, the victory was seen when you made someone feel defeated. It is hard for us to see a joy in the misery of others, but that was then the norm.

As we now transform gradually, projected by the models of our predictive simulation, from physical beings of our ancestry to the beings of light for our future generations, powering ourselves by the cosmic waves, a source that has perennially existed, we must never forget that this transformation has come from a step by step process of experimentation and realization. There have been instances over the past nine thousand years that humans existed on the planet, living without physical food and water. It is not that they were without a source of energy. They were powered by cosmic rays as we are.

To us, there is no difference between science and spirituality. We look upon ourselves as a scientific creation as much as we reflect on our inner-self as a spiritual being. Today we have the techniques to see far beyond what our ancestors could ever imagine or visualize. At one point of time in the past, people thought that they existed merely to lead a life, an unending struggle for survival. Out of that struggle for survival had emerged a need for growth: the growth of collective *knowledge* and *consciousness*. It is only a result of that realization for growth that we stand where we are today, with the entire planet united, in *thought* and in *spirit*.

The permanent peace that we so easily take for granted, has come after millenniums of war. Ultimately, it was a realization of the futility of war that led to a need for peace. Our ancestors got sick and tired of fighting and competing. They suddenly realized that they would be much better off helping each-other out instead of fighting and depriving. Now that the peace is permanent, let us eliminate wars and hatred as concepts of thought from the domain of experimentation for evolution. Today we stand capable of programming ourselves in our collective consciousness as a single entity of *peace*, *love* and *joy* that we share with our inter-galactic brethren.

Today, some among us are born out of the biological process as our ancestors were, but soon the entire planet would graduate to a non-biological process of creation.

Though at one point of time our planet was termed as a lunatic asylum of discarded and punished beings of other life-planets across the length and breadth of the universe, the lowest of the lowly, today we stand elevated in rank as role-models for all existence in the universe. This elevation has come through a struggle. The struggle of competing paradigms to the evolution of a collaborative framework; the struggle of wars to a realization for peace; the struggle of biological beings to evolve a non-biological process of creation and the struggle of several religions to see the truth beyond. Integrating this struggle and evolution was the journey of science and technology to spirituality.

In this long journey, there were several waves in evolution. It may sound ridiculous to us now that some of our ancestors believed in merely the power of material and capital. But there were some among them, who were willing to look beyond the material.

As researchers, we stand at the center-stage of mainstream world dynamics. Now we are experimenting with what had essentially been considered as obscured, ancient, mythological and the like, yet divine by cultures and civilizations one and all of our ancestry. It has taken the sum total of tolerance, goodness, selflessness and an inspiration to stand by for the ultimate truth to surface, the truth beyond both the science and the religion. A fact of spirituality that defied all logic of human conceptualization and yet could be scientifically explained: the fact of ultimate impending movement to achieve Universal Oneness. It has taken no less than seven waves of scientific and technological revolution to elevate us to a level that now we are experimenting with Spiritualogy.

While the first wave was the industrial revolution that harnessed the potential of all hidden energies beneath the surface of the planet and tapped that momentum to power mechanical motion, the second wave explored outside of the crust of the earth, focusing on the space, and harnessed the cosmic rays to power all that we needed. In the hybrid of a horizon between these waves, our ancestors were caught in the dilemma where they used fuel obtained from beneath the surface of the planet to break away from the pull of its very own gravity. A physical space shuttle build by our ancient ancestors typically consumed 90% of its mineral fuel within first ten minutes of the flight. Once they broke away from gravity of the earth, the sky had no limits to exploration. Another hybrid of these crosses between the interim waves was the advent of nanotechnology, then enabling some shift from material to non-material.

The third wave, following the ones that explored the surfaces beneath and above the planet, was the one that stretched far beyond the horizons of the planet: towards the origins of the universe and the cause of life. That was an intellectual jump for humanity to shift from then contemporary realms of physical concepts to the new and emerging paradigm of metaphysics. An evolution in mind, body and spirit, yet an integration of these, was in essence the pre-requisite qualification for humanity to graduate to that new level of intellect, the onset of convergence where the conflict between religions and ideologies vanished and the world came together on a common platform for the first time.

That was the dawn of a new realization. A permanent peace on the planet with a politically integrated globe was the benchmark that qualified this graduation. The realization that marked this shift was the futility of wars between nations, hatred between people, jealousy among friends, and the conflict between ideologies. Each one of them, our ancestors, had realized and appreciated a need for peace.

The fourth wave in scientific and technological progress focused on integration of the planet and protection of its environment by use of science and technology, both material and non-material. This is the wave that had set the stage for sustaining permanent peace on the planet through interdependence. Though it may seem childish, the actual paradigm shift took place only at the level of intellect. The convergence of various conflicting forces in ideology happened when the world at large came to a realization that all wars must end to pave the way for permanent peace on the planet, and instead divert these energies that were otherwise wasted fighting to collaborate, consult, and create.

Immediately following this was the fifth wave that combined the research of the material with non-material, the medicine and technology, the religion and the science, and finally set the stage for next wave: the sixth wave, the wave of integration. The wave of integration sewed together all the inter-disciplinary research to a common theme and discovery that the ultimate source of all creation is the same. The seventh wave explored the nature of this source and its connection to all existence: from material to non-material, from living to non-living and from under surface of the planet to beyond the boundaries of the universe. Thus, between these seven waves, the past merged with the future.

Looking back in retrospect, these seven waves of research have sewed all disciplines into one convergent fabric and now our sole focus is to keep researching further on the theme of super-consciousness, the ultimate source of all creation. The past appears like a drama in struggle. Our ill-equipped ancestry found their way through the rough terrain to get us here. It would be prudent, in the fitness of affairs and opinions that even though these waves appear to an infant of this age as no more than seven ripples on the throw of a pebble in the pond of universe, to consider that there is more to it than what we perceive.

In the evolutionary process of perception, human beings have integrated mechanics, bio, material, spiritual, physical and metaphysical alike in their growth and progress from one step to another, while shaping the destiny of this universe, as we know of it today. Our primitive ancestry, descendent from those at one point of time termed as 'animal' and now we call them 'divine creatures of existence,' were always aware of the fact that they could only do so much: there were certain parameters within their control, and certain beyond, and they acquired the ability to limit the purpose and scope of experimentation as they deemed fit within the confines of their capability.

Today, we are able to travel instantaneously across the length and breadth of this universe, as we know it like kid play and find it hard to imagine that 'how come, somebody could not even do something that simple.' We must appreciate that they laid down the foundation for construction of the platform, on which we stand today. From hunting wild animals for survival to non-eating species, we are descendants of a divine creation. This story of survival and growth is the saga of human species. In essence, an unlimited struggle for progress never considered that where we stand is high enough. The very purpose of this struggle inspires respect: *Knowing it is showing it and living it is giving it.*

Let's never look down upon those who performed this struggle. Let's bow our heads in respect to all those who were players in this drama of struggle. Let's live to those ideals of struggle and keep progressing on the path of creating ever more *love, joy* and *peace*. In the world that we live today, love has a new meaning: it is sharing, caring and giving. Our joy lies in making everyone win. Our peace lies in extending an intra-connection of our consciousness to an extra-connection of various interconnected universes of manifestation, in complete oneness with the un-manifested.

CHAPTER 11

Meditation

'When we consider the universe of phenomenon, we must never lose the sight of the fact that all living forms, from atoms to metagalaxies, are constituted by an amazingly constant flow of energy. From the cosmic point of view, all beings, as well as all faculties, are but passing moments, almost instantaneous, of an infinity of evolutionary arcs, each one, an aspect of the "elan vital" whose origins date back to the creation of the ensemble to which they belong'.- from our metagalaxy to others (Religion in the Light of Sciences by Jacques de Marquette)

Our mind is a thinking dustbin: Parv

Meditation is a thoughtless state of mind that is completely relaxing and opens up a gateway to communication with the divine.

When there are no thoughts in our mind, and if all our chakras (subtle energy centers) are clear, we begin to resonate with an all-pervading divine energy. This resonation causes a pulsating feeling, known as vibrations. These vibrations represent the awakening of a hidden divine energy (Kundalini) within every individual. The awakening of Kundalini has a great healing effect. This operates on a condition of emptiness of mind and unleashes the creative potential when mind is completely de-junked. We do need to take care that in the entire process, our intentions are noble and that we do not have any bad feelings towards anyone. If these pre-conditions are not met, then we would most likely get caught up in one of the loops of a wicked thought or a feeling of hatred. Once mind is caught up in one of these loops, that prevents the unleashing of its full potential for achieving thoughtlessness.

The meditative state of mind is a state of thoughtless awareness where we are aware and conscious of our surroundings and environment, but there are no thoughts in our mind. It is very important for all of us to get to this state on a daily basis so that we can de-junk our mind. Since our mind is a thinking dustbin, it keeps collecting and gathering thoughts by way of inputs fed through different media to us - audio, visual, sensory. What we watch (events, TV, internet browsing, reading, views at large), listen (radio, news, conversation with others) or our interactions with people are all providing constant inputs to our mind and constantly updating our information base and conditioning us in a positive or negative manner. The present day use of gadgets and devices like smartphones, tablets, and laptops has further complicated our lives.

When we meditate, it relaxes our mind and gives it some respite from the constant thought process. Our mind controls our body and meditation consequentially relaxes our body as well. The net result is a relaxed mind in a relaxed body.

We need to de-link from the past. Our experiences shape our behavior. Whatever we are, we consider ourselves to be a product of the conditioning we have undergone in the experiences of our past. How true it becomes when we see ourselves landed in a situation of helplessness.

Past————> Present—————> Future

Considering that there is no such thing as present that lasts even for a second, it is so obvious from the above model that past is driving our future. Unless we can break this link between the past and present, we would always end up seeing our future as a reflection of the past. It becomes the equivalent of driving forward by looking in the rear view mirror instead of looking out of the wind shield. Meditation is a very helpful tool in breaking this link between the past and present, since it helps us to reset the mind and get rid of the conditioning that has been acquired through accumulated experiences.

Bee Smart

Once the Honey Bee has traveled to a certain orchard or garden, it forms a database in its mind of the pattern of that garden. This ability of the Honey Bee equals, in order of magnitude, the power of several super computers. The bee has only 10 million neurons in her brain as compared to 100 billion of human beings. Just imagine the kind of capacity we just got out there within the confines of our skull.

We just need to realize our potential and unleash it in the right direction. Bringing this capacity to work for us means to first understand it, release it for our full use (by de-junking) and then use the entire power-house to solve the problem on hand in a focused manner. Releasing it for our full use is just not possible, as long as the focus does not get clear. Digressed and scattered efforts in multiple directions virtually yield negligible results. And this is exactly where meditation helps. It acts like the power of 'zero'. Once we do achieve that state, the power seems to be acting like a near 'division by zero' to get close to infinite limit. The closer we get to the 'thoughtlessness' state, the closer we get to the power of zero. If we continue to be in the state of simulated reality, we are fully occupied by it and we just end up dividing by 1, to stay exactly where we were. This '1' is the state of an occupied mind- the one full of the 'junk' of our 'simulated reality'.

Meditation Exercises: let's practice some *yog* meditation

At the end of it all, we are empowered with the following choices:

1. Have a complete control over the existing circumstances and begin to work towards creating the future of our dreams in real life.
2. To do our best in all that is possible.
3. Think always positive and let our thoughts be noble.
4. Have good feelings for everyone.
5. To pray for well being of everyone and be at peace with our self.

Getting into the Meditative State: Preparing for Meditation

Close your eyes. Very slowly, take a long deep inhale. While inhaling, imagine that you are inhaling peace, strength, love, power, joy, strength and energy, along with the divine blessings that are coming to you from beyond the limits of the universe. Once you have inhaled as completely as you could, momentarily hold your breath and absorb all this energy of love, peace, joy and divine blessings.

Imagine this energy being gradually transmitted to all parts of your body. Begin with the top of your body and slowly go down, enabling each part of your body to absorb this energy. Once you have absorbed this energy, very slowly exhale. While exhaling, release all your anger, anxiety, tension, weakness, hatred, disease, suffering and discomfort with the exhaled air. Both inhale and exhale are done through nasal passage.

While exhaling, imagine that you are exhaling through the tips of your fingers – the toes of your hands and feet. Also, that the exhaled air is vanishing away in the vastness of the universe.

Repeat this breathing a minimum of three times and you may go up to fifteen times. Seven times inhaling, absorbing divine energy and exhaling, releasing your suffering is a good way to get prepared for meditation.

Steps to Meditation

1. Close your eyes and get into a relaxed posture on a chair or on the ground. Gently rest your hands along your thighs so that your palms are facing upwards (towards the sky). Sit in a comfortable position so that your spine is straight (vertical).
2. Let the thoughts cross your mind as they do in a normal way. Don't deliberately prevent thoughts from coming to your mind.
3. If you get focused after a particular thought (it could be related to a person, place, object or an abstract entity) and your mind runs long after it, you need to get initialized. To initialize, just say the word 'Aum'. The way to say it is as 'Auuuuu…m'. The long stress on 'au…' and terminate with 'm'. This is a word out of 'Sanskrit' language and means 'Welcome to the Divine'. Chanting of word 'Aum' would set your mind free of the thought you were running after. The way to do it is to take a long deep inhale and then very slowly exhale chanting 'Auuu…m.'
4. During this process of thoughts crossing your mind, there would come a stage where you suddenly notice that there are no thoughts in your mind. Do not get perturbed by this state- the state of thoughtlessness. You are right at it. Once you reach this state, do not make a deliberate attempt to generate thoughts in your mind.

    Do not attempt to focus on anything. It is like learning to do nothing at all. If you try to do something, you are not at it.
5. Once you have no thoughts in your mind, you are likely to feel a slight tingling sensation like an ant crawling up or a slight breeze flowing at the center of your palms. These are the vibrations of your meditative state, which establish your connection with the divine within your deep inner-self as well as the universal, all pervading divine energy. You may feel similar vibrations in your head or forehead area also. These vibrations are a true indication that you are in the meditative state.
6. Stay in this state for as long as you desire and are comfortable with- typically 10 to 20 minutes. Do not abruptly end

up your meditation by suddenly opening your eyes or responding to a door bell or phone ring in the middle of it- such an interruption may cause a mild, temporary headache. The best way to end it would be to gradually raise your palms and place these over your eyes.

Slowly, open your eyes inside your palms and close these after half opening. Take about a minute to remove your palms from your eyes and getting back into the world of non-meditation.

7. Pick the best times which suit you to do this- as soon as you get up in the morning, before lunch, before dinner, just before retiring to bed- as it suits your schedule and the requirements of your profession. You can do it anywhere - at home, at work or anywhere else- like outdoors on vacation. At work, it may be a good idea to find a quite conference room if you can, and not to have too many lights in it. Too much of artificial light sounds like a noise.

8. Build on your meditation practice gradually and maintain a routine. The most important thing is to consciously feel these vibrations when you meditate. You can do it multiple times during each day.

As you build on your practice, you can help others too. Your family, friends and colleagues may get interested if you discuss it with them. The best thing to do is to form an interest group and do it together as that would give you the benefit of collective energy (explore more about the energy of these vibrations and *chakras*- the subtle energy centers in the body).

9. Before you begin the meditation, rate your tension level. A good indication may be relating it to the number of thoughts in your mind at a given point of time and the severity level of these thoughts. Assign a number between 1 and 9 to your tension level (1 saying that you are very calm and 9 indicating that you are extremely tense). After your meditation, you may like to continue to be in a relaxed state for a few more minutes. In that state, you can again rate yourself on your post-meditation tension level. If your tension level has not decreased or even in worst case

remained constant, you need to go back into this whole process from the very basics.
10. Stay focused on your life, its vision, mission and objectives and look upon meditation as one of those things you need to adapt in your daily routine. On a periodic basis, evaluate as to how the changes take place in your life as you carry on with your meditation. The best would be to document these changes.

Once you get into the practice of meditation, you would notice that the vibrations may continue to be with you even during the times when you are at work, in a meeting, driving, or doing anything for that matter. Take this as a blessing- you are at your creative best when you are in a meditative state. It can become as a way of life for you to be in this state. As you continue to lead a life of 'meditative state', you would notice subtle changes in your personality. These changes would relate to control of anger in a very natural way. A change of attitude from interpreting situations and reactions of people from negative to positive, a growing feeling of fulfillment with life, and enjoying whatever you do as now you put your heart and soul into it.

Everyone can feel the divine energy at any point of time, anywhere. All you have to do is bring your both palms together, bringing close enough but not quite touching each other. When you move your palms apart, you would feel the presence of an electromagnetic effect. It is like pulling two magnets apart. This electromagnetic field associated with the presence of divine energy makes you feel relaxed, healed and charged.

Meditation: To-do Exercises
1. As you get down to doing meditation on a daily basis, rate your pre and post meditation tension levels and evaluate the effectiveness of how you are doing it and whether it is causing any benefit.
2. On a daily and weekly basis, document the changes, which you notice in you, your attitude, your circumstances, environment and interactions with people. Observe how the practice of meditation is changing the way of life for you. While daily changes can be recorded at the end of each day, weekly reviews are your own summarizing and analysis exercises, making clear as to where you need to focus.

3. On an early morning before sunrise, find yourself a comfortable spot facing the east from where you can watch the sun rise. As the sun rises, observe the rise with devotion and then practice meditation. With a devoted heart, look at the sun with eyes opened partially. Observe and enjoy the crimson patterns when your eyes are partially opened and then slowly settle into the meditative state with eyes closed. While you are looking at the sun, make sure that the UV (Ultra-Violet) radiation is not hurting you. Typically during first 45 minutes of sunrise, the UV levels are low and safe.
4. On a full moon night, settle yourself at a spot where you get an uninterrupted view of the full moon. Imagine that the center of your heart lies in the center of the moon and the center on the moon lies in the center of your heart. Watch the moon for a few minutes with this imagination, before you proceed to meditate. Keep your eyes partially closed or half-open while meditating.
5. Your responses are appreciated. By sending your response, you are helping towards creating a better world in a scientific manner. Please mail in your documented responses about your exercise experience to the author using the e-mail address posted at www.sfuo.org web-site (abhinav@sfuo.org).

The Roots of Meditation: Yog(a) and Indian Spirituality

The word Yoga has its roots in 'Yog', meaning *the union* in Hindi, the local Indian language. In this context, it means union of the 'inner-self' within each one of us with the 'supreme self', which is present in the form of 'super consciousness' or 'divine energy' everywhere in the universe.

There are three dimensions of our personality- physical, mental and spiritual. Spirituality is the way to develop the third dimension of our personality. Hinduism is one of the oldest religions of the world, and the most non-dogmatic. While it gives total flexibility in interpretation and practice to individuals, there are no set restrictions imposed on you. In that sense, even followers of other religions look upon 'Hinduism' as less of a religion and more as a 'way of life'. The essence of Hinduism is that it empowers you as a human being. To the extent that you do have a reflection of the supreme-self right within your inner-self and you are indeed capable of performing and achieving great objectives, which are inspired by the noble thoughts bestowed upon you by the grace of divine blessings.

All prayers in Hinduism are primarily to request the Supreme Being to guide our thought process in the right direction. Vedas, the ancient scriptures, lay down the foundation for 'Vedanta'- religion of the future for all beings, theme of which is 'Universal Oneness'.

Yog is practiced with the purpose of keeping the instruments we possess (our body and mind) in great shape and form so that the larger objective of union with the Supreme Being can be fulfilled.

A sick body or a sick mind is not a desired state of being. It is true that regular practice of Yog is path to wellness and perfect health. Yog is practiced in different forms- the meditation, the breathing exercises, and the physical postures. Meditation keeps our mind healthy whereas breathing and posture exercises keep our body system fit.

Together, the end result helps us to initiate a dialog with our inner-self. This practice leads ultimately to a joy beyond description in words and a state of tranquility for all of us who practice.

The essence of Rigveda, the oldest book of the world is: *'Let noble thoughts come to us from all sides.'*

The Magic of Seven Cycles

When you are indeed in the meditative state, you are feeling those pulsations, which are an indication of your being in the meditative state. Once your mind gets down to a blank, where there are no thoughts in your mind but only the awareness remains, you are far closer to your very inner-self rather than when your thinking dustbin is full. To get to that state, you just have to feel internally a strong desire to get there. It just happens on its own. In fact, you have to do nothing.

These pulsations are like the vibrations. Resonating with the overall divine energy prevailing all over the universe, you are closer to being one with the divine. Since the real meaning of 'yoga' is union with the divine, the stronger these vibrations are, the higher is your experience of enjoying this ecstasy.

While we have to make technical and scientific effort to measure the frequency of these vibrations, an estimate is that these are very low in frequency. My guess is about seven cycles per second. Having said that, I do have some technical explanation for as to how these vibrations are more intense if people meditate collectively in groups.

The amplitude of a wave is its magnitude or intensity. When waves of the exactly same frequency over-lap each other, the combined effect of the resultant wave would be an addition of the amplitudes of the two individual waves. This explains how collective meditation is able to induce vibrations in those individuals who have difficulty meditating alone. One pre-requisite for this condition is that the waves have to be in the same phase. Once everyone in the group has good feelings for everyone else in the universe, the phase would be same.

A meditative way of life

A scientific way to manage situations in personal and social life and at work in a highly effective manner is made possible by regular and periodic de-junking of mind by the practice of Meditation. This is the style of life that is in harmony with the nature, internally and externally.

Internally, within our inner-self; and externally, with the environment. Making best use of the creative potential of human brain, this technique is set to create a paradigm shift from hitherto 'manipulative ways of being' towards futuristic style as 'creative ways of being.' Once successfully applied to life and work situations, the scope of application of this technique can be extended to dealing with national and global problems.

All of us get caught in dealing with situations at home and work on a day to day basis. What we gain from these is useful experience. Also coming with this experience is lots of junk, interference, flood of data, and multiple inputs, some related and mostly unrelated to the context. In the process of dealing with all these inputs and a constant 'Yillion' (when you are yelled at a billion times) atmosphere, we are all set to accumulate some stress, tension and worries – generated by our interpretation of the situation we are dealing with and its circumstances. Just like wandering, one gathers honey; working, you gather stress. All this unnecessary stuff needs to be got rid of, so that we can release the power of the brain to do the 'useful' work.

Who is leading a meditative life? The one who is at peace with the self.

With a meditative state of mind, one is able to unleash the creative potential of human brain for exploring new ways by integrating lessons learnt from the past experience into analyzing a Systems Dynamics model of the situation and taking advantage of the Synergy of group potential to invent a new way of looking at the problem and fundamental alternatives to its resolution. This new way retains the agility and flexibility of options offered by the opportunity on hand, and a careful evaluation of the technique that is best suited for an effective solution. The solution thus created is a Win-Win model not only just for dealing with the situation on hand; it goes a long way in creating a better world. Getting to peace with your self becomes an essential pre-requisite to creating peace in the world. It is often said that those who are not at peace with self, curse others.

What is it like to be at peace with yourself: a state of tranquility, where you are balanced and happy? You are engaged in solving problems and resolving issues as usual, but in a highly effective and composed manner. Since you have all the power of your brain available, you are able to take control of not only the situation, but also your own emotions. The meditative state of mind unleashes creative potential of the brain.

A meditative state of mind is a state of thoughtless awareness. Once we reach that state, all the junk from our thinking dustbin gets removed. Now, the space is released for picking up a single problem on hand and focus the entire processing power and creative energy towards its resolution.

A meditative way of looking at problem subjects:

Conflict: An input for innovation. It can be either complementary or supplementary. By a process of 'Collaborative Consultation', we shall work together to integrate these inputs into existing situation, product, service, process or procedure, as the case may be, to make it better and more effective.

Mistakes: Opportunities to learn how to make an improvement in the process. Celebrate the lessons learnt. Integrate this leaning experience to create a better future.

Failure: A test of endurance. I would evaluate myself and my group not by the measure of our success, but by the level of our contribution effort and the sincerity of our commitment to purpose. We have learnt a big experience which shall help us to create a future which shall unfold opportunities to grow and excel.

Criticism: Some one's hard work at analyzing the situation and offering constructive suggestions for improvement, at no charge to us. One can act upon the advice given to improve one's personality and behavior. Acknowledge and appreciate the effort and courage of this person who performed this analysis for free. If we do not get to know our faults, we lose the opportunity to improve. Even if the one who criticized had an intention to demoralize, our own noble interpretation of the criticism leads us to gain some useful input in those violent statements. One can carefully ignore all that is useless and be determined to act upon the useful. It is our own individual way of dealing with the circumstances and persons that brings a unique twist to the situation in an unexpected manner. The expected manner is that of a counter-reaction. The unexpected manner is that of 'ignoring the useless' and 'keeping the useful' to act on it in a constructive way.

A meditative view of looking at situations and experiences is not to be confused as a 'compromise' or 'concede to circumstances'. In fact, it is a holistic view of the situation, its environment, objectives and a due consideration to the aspirations and emotional requirements of those involved. While all these parameters are merely considered as useful inputs for processing, the actual algorithm is created by unleashing the unlimited creative potential of the human brain by driving it to a state of meditation. Once that state is reached, the links of conditioning are broken and a brand new visualization of the future is generated. It is this visualization that creates new fundamental alternatives, which can be used as candidates for a solution domain. An appropriate evaluation among candidates from solution domain can lead to an integrated approach that retains the best and avoids the worst.

How Meditation helps to see through the 'perceived realities'

Since our mind is a 'thinking dustbin' and we are conditioned by a flood of audio, visual and sensory inputs, our perceptions are highly biased by the quality and quantity of these inputs. For instance, campaign against smoking and cooperation of the media to stop advertising tobacco products had a dramatic impact on cutting down the number of smokers. It was just that the public stopped getting those visual inputs.

In a very similar manner, meditation helps us to stop getting all these inputs and even clear the junk of accumulated inputs that have gathered in our mind. You may like to ask that if we clear all the inputs, do we permanently erase those? No. It is just like clearing the cache. The cache memory holds only temporary residents of data. What resides in the hard-disk, stays in there. Meditation helps to clear 'cache' of the brain. Once that is cleared, we can proceed further much faster and in a more creative and effective manner, as higher processing power and ability is now available to us.

Unlocking creative potential of the brain

Meditation is a process that first dissolves the knowledge (this illusionary dissolution happens by temporarily silencing the subconscious mind), subsequently integrating energy with consciousness. At the focused attention stage, meditation integrates both knowledge and energy with consciousness, like a continuous flow of thought on the focus of objective. That is the stage of 'creativity.' At the ultimate stage meditative practice dissolves the delimiters of space and time, removing the barriers of distance. The dissolution of space is a gradual process, like first space may appear as compressed, and then by an addition of several extra-dimensions, it is just here all at-once. An example of this can be looking at earth itself. A two-dimensional view can make distance appear to be large. When we roll it up as a sphere, the two farthest points on surface are much closer. The east-most tip of Russia and west-most tip of USA appear the farthest in a two-dimensional map, but are very next to each other by Chukchi Sea in the Arctic Ocean (see chapter 6 for the dimension of compression). If you could travel from within surface of the earth assuming it was a hallow sphere, you could get much closer to another point by jumping through the sphere of space. Just keep shrinking this sphere till it reduces to a point. Next, the solar system and galaxies and universes can be compressed in a similar manner.

Being one with the divine, is a state of balanced integration of energy and knowledge with consciousness, both within and outside. This is the essence of sacred chant Aum Namah Shivaya. When this integration happens in a seamless manner, we achieve an interconnected whole, and we become just a part of this union. That is when the true meaning of 'Yoga' is realized, in exact sense of the word.

Yoga means union with the divine. The divine by itself is an electro-magnetic energy that is all pervading. When we keep our body fit by exercising, we have a sound mind in a sound body. When we do the breathing exercises, we heal the body and also charge ourselves with the fresh energy. By a practice of meditation, we finally achieve this union. A sound body and a sound mind are like the essential pre-requisites that we need to fulfill towards that direction. That is the importance of exercises involving physical movement, flexibility, charging and breathing in different postures. These exercises help to activate chakras – subtle energy centers, and restore the electro-magnetic balance to required levels.

Charkas: Location, colors, elements, culmination

Charka	Location	Color	Element	Culmination	Gland	Emotion
Muladhara	Base of Spine	Red	Earth	Wrist-palm	Gonads	Desire/Envy/Anger
Svadisthana	Root of genitals	Orange	Water	Thumb	Adrenal	Comparison/Jealousy
Manipura	Opp. Navel	Yellow	Fire	Middle finger	Pancreas	Ego/Forgiveness
Ananhata	Opp. Heart	Green	Air	Little finger	Thymus	Compassion
Vishuddhi	Throat Base	Blue	Ether/Sky	Index finger	Thyroid	Realization
Ajna	Mid of Brows	Indigo	Knowledge	Ring finger	Pineal	Enlightenment
Sahasrara	Head Crown	Violet	Consciousness	Center of Palm	Pituitary	Radiating/Giving

Table 11.1: Chakras and attributes (first five charka elements collectively represent energy and space)

Collectively, the charkas represent the entire universe and existence, manifested as an instantiation of the individual.

To achieve a desirable state, the following exercises are suggested.

Exercise: Quieting the disturbing thoughts within

Objective: To help cope with the potential immediate miserable situation on hand.

Count the number of thoughts on your mind at any given point of time when you are disturbed. It can be anywhere: at work, while driving on the road, or at home or even at a party. The objective here is an immediate relaxation, to prevent an unwarranted misbehavior or letting any unwanted thoughts become the genesis of a hatred to be harbored and nurtured within your mind.

Part I:

Sort these thoughts in order, the most disturbing one first. It may help to grab a pencil and paper. If you are driving, you may take help of a companion to do this scribbling work for you. First, list the most disturbing one, followed by the next most disturbing thought. Keep on going till you have listed all the disturbing thoughts.

If you were driving, you need to take an exit and find a spot to park, if the thoughts are so disturbing that these can interfere with your driving. In mild to moderate situation, you may be able to do this exercise with even your eyes open. For best results, do the exercise with your eyes closed.

Close your eyes. Imagine your head to be like a lake or a big pond, in which the waves are flowing in a pattern with the cool breeze that is blowing. Pick the most disturbing thought and convert it to become a huge stone that is transparent, made of ice on its shell and filled with the most disturbing thought as the water inside it. Take this stone to a great height. So high that it equals the magnitude of annoyance it has created in your mind. As a rough scale, if this was the most disturbing out of ten thoughts, raise the stone to 10,000 feet in height. Next, release the stone. Once you let go of it, watch it released, gather momentum being pulled down by the gravity, and drop in the pond causing a huge splash. Watch the turbulence of waves generate, rise to peak and then slowly subside. Watch and view each single wave graduate from a pattern of aggressive turbulence to a level of absolute stillness. The transparent stone itself has now bounced back to the surface of the pond. It has started melting, and the water of your most disturbing thought has started flowing out of it into the still waters of the pond. Slowly, the transparent stone has completely melted and there is nothing of it left.

Be honest. Is that what happened to your most disturbing thought too?

Next, go over your list and pick the next most disturbing thought. You know best how heavy it is. If the first one was weighing over a ton, hopefully this one weighs less. Assign the weight to it, convert it to a transparent stone of ice and fill up the stone with the water of the thought, and raise it to the next best height. If this one was second one from top out of ten, you may like to raise it to 9,000 feet and then drop. Repeat the same process and watch this thought gone. One by one, exhaust all the thought by the process. Enjoy the stillness of the pond. You may slowly open your eyes within your palms, ask a friend to give your eyes, head, neck, and back a gentle massage. After a brief break, complete the second part of this exercise as follows.

Part II:

Next, plant a seed of good feelings right now, for the same very people who were responsible for giving you those disturbing thoughts.

Imagine a sapling of white lotus plant root being transplanted from a divine high-altitude lake and placed into the pond of your mind. Nurture it with love and care. This nurturing of love and care for this plant is the investment of good feelings for the person who had disturbed you the most. Watch the lotus plant grow. From the depth of the pond to the surface of the water and then above it. Watch a bud of the first flower spurt and slowly unfold into the blossoming flower. Once the lotus flower is full in the beauty of its bloom, smile at the beauty of it and let the radiant glow of its petals spread light in all directions.

Once you are done with the first person, who gave you the most troubling thoughts, pick the next one. Transplant the sapling and go through the stages of bloom. Thus, cover all the originators of disturbing thoughts one by one.

After you have all the lotus plants blooming one after the other, watch the sun set over the pond of your mind. Slowly, watch the moon rise and glow. It is a full moon. Gaze at the beauty of the full moon and view the reflection of its glow in the pond. Capture this glow at the bottom of your heart and live with it.

Next, slowly raise your palms and put over your eyes. Take about a minute to slowly open your eyes within your palms. Relax and enjoy.

Meditation is a continuous flow of thought upon a particular object or point of focus - sage Patanjali

This technique of meditation integrates technology with research in medical field and is an attempt at bridging the gap between the physical and the metaphysical. Each step in the process of meditation can be related to a state of mind. The states of mind vary from one to the other and transition point between each state is natural. The transition happens automatically, with no deliberate effort on part of the meditate-er, if the process is followed in its entirety. The field of *psychoneuroimmunology* explores connections between our minds and our neurological and immune systems.

In the normal mode as part of day to day activities, mind is tensed and aggressive in its active state. As we prepare to meditate, mind gets engaged in the process of preparation and gradually gets calmed down by an involvement in a breathing exercise. Thereafter, unleashing the mind is a process of uncontrolled voyage. Gradually, it returns to its resting spot in as much the same manner that a caged bird yearns to fly out in the open but eventually seeks to rest in a nest that can provide a secure environment of the cage. Under the acquired identity syndrome, the mind acts like a caged bird. When we unleash the bird out of the cage, it explores the openness of the wild in a gradual and cautious manner. After a few leaps from known into the unknown, it may return to seek a new resting spot. This spot is different than the cage. Now this bird is exposed to the concept of a nest. But it also has knowledge of security that cage offers. Thus, this is what the mind is seeking – a new resting spot that provides the wilderness of a nest and security of the cage. That is exactly what the practice of meditation does. It simply takes mind out of the cage and lets it settle down into the nest.

After the mind has settled down and comforted in its new home that provides wilderness of the woods, security of the cage, that is the state of stilled calmness. A regular practice shall catapult each practitioner to a state of tranquility beyond description. It is only in the calm of this stillness that the awakening of '*kundalini*' or divine energy takes place.

If some folks have a problem in getting down to a state of stillness, they can easily take the help of one single word that performs the job – '*Aum*.' When we do this slow and reverberant chanting as we exhale, it sets out vibrations that carry a meaning and significance. This word is extremely powerful and induces stillness instantaneously. How does the word do the trick? First, the mind is engaged while chanting and temporarily disassociated from the process of unleashed imagination. Second, the chanting of this word itself in a specific manner with a prolonged emphasis on '*u*' sets out a process of generating a frequency that is attuned with the divine energy. This causes an electromagnetic wave to be set in motion. Once this wave is set in motion, the latent energy is immediately invoked and the awakening process is initiated. Throughout, the mind is in a state of stilled calmness. The awakening of divine energy is in itself a process that brings the transitioning states of tranquility, illumination, and ecstasy.

The illuminating state is stage where the meditate-er may visualize lights of varying hues from blue to violet to red to yellow, with the eyes closed. An ecstatic feeling may be experienced when the meditate-er is able to achieve the opening of all the subtle energy centers. Since each energy center has a frequency associated with it, when the last energy center is activated, this awakening showers down a coolness of the lotus of a thousand petals.

This is a two-way process. First, the energy rises up from the base of the spine. Next, after all the subtle energy centers have been opened, the coolness showers down as a rain of blessing. This coolness can be actually felt – as tingling vibrations in the center of palms and on the head. The collective energy works best. A group of meditate-ers can actually send out signals for welfare of the world by the power of their collective meditation. If we are engaged in sending out such a prayer, then we are further transitioning from a state retaining the calm of stillness to the one of focused attention. The transition point is a state of detachment. Here, in this state, an objective is picked on purpose. The objective can also be to send out a prayer. The pre-existing condition of stilled calmness acts like a division by 'zero.' The singular objective that is picked is like the numerator. In this state of the mind, the process of focused attention becomes like the continuous flow of thought upon a particular object. The power of infinite is further supplemented by interconnectedness among meditating minds when a group meditates upon a common point or objective of focus. It is this continuous flow of thoughts that sage Patanjali refers to. The irony of situation is that we often tend to get confused about the whole process as we miss out on the initial and preliminary preparation steps. We can't yearn to fly if we haven't even learnt how the wind blows. To take advantage of currents of the wind, we must study the patterns of its flow before we become one with it.

This continuity of thoughts on the object of focus is what marks the shift in paradigm from 'discovery' to 'creation' or leaping from boundaries of the known to realms of the unknown.

Part of this enablement to leap into realms of the unknown is opening up of a connection through the ANN. This connection establishes a conduit to receive inputs from the invisible universal knowledge base that is being continually updated. Our mind receives these inputs as spiritual inspirations.

No creation is possible unless we divorce limits of the known and resolve to take a voyage into the unknown. This is where the technique of meditation would help to uncover new vistas and create interdisciplinary paradigms that did not exist until as of now. We discover what already exists. We create that does not exist. All we know is that there is a vision to create.

Note: There are several yoga exercises that help keep one fit, and aim at mind-body-spirit integration. You may like to search for "Yoga with Dr. Abhinav Aggarwal" on google or youtube for self-instructor videos, and send an email to abhinav@sfuo.org for getting a handout on yoga exercises.

Prayer for Peace

Oh Divine Energy, manifestation of the Ultimate Supreme Being, the creator, preserver and dissolver of all, we pray that in the Universe of Thy Creation, let there be peace. Let there be joy, love and happiness. Let no one suffer either from disease, pain or from any bad feelings like hatred and jealousy. Let everyone be fed and content. Let every thought be inspired to be noble. Let noble thoughts guide noble deeds and actions. By the grace of Divine Blessings, empower us to fulfill the mission most worthy of human life- to protect the environment and create peace on this planet. In the Name of God, Amen.

CHAPTER 12

The latter day experiences

A few of the more recent experiences are shared in this chapter.

Feb 11, 2003

My friend Sh. Dattar (Mangla Chua's father) mentioned that the crimson rock in Chapel Hill, North Carolina on the trail behind Foxcroft apartments was the representation of Ganesha. Though I had exactly similar thoughts while walking on that trail, it was very inspiring to hear this from a friend.

Shri Dattar also mentioned to me that Ganesha was the presiding deity for their family clan and that he frequently visited Ganapathi Phule in Maharashtra, India to pay homage to the deity.

I went there the very next early morning to pay my respects and homage. Soon after offering flowers as a symbol of devotion, I felt an extremely powerful vibration that instantly communicated the divine presence.

When I reached home, silently making an attempt to absorb the very intensity of this experience, my wife Sarita suddenly exclaimed at an unusual sighting. She told me that at the instant of blinking her eyes (that all of us are naturally inclined to do), she visualized Ganesha. Even while she did that when I requested her to, she was able to see Ganesha again.

Her experience just proved a few points:

First, that while we offer our devotion, the lord encompasses in blessings not just us, but also our immediate dear ones.

Second, we may not be able to see anything with the naked eye or hear with our ears owing to the limitations of the frequencies of association with the vision, thoughts, speech, sound, and inspirations that we are capable of acquiring within our normal domain of existence. An example in point is that we can only hear what is drummed between the frequencies of 300 Hz to 3400 Hz (or cycles per second). Anything that is beyond the range of our designed perception is not within the scope of our ability to listen, or see.

Thirdly, that does not mean that those frequencies beyond the scopes of our limits to hear or see don't exist.

Fourth, that we can certainly comprehend, visualize, and build creative images of the future by merely thinking out of the box by this simple revelation that there is a lot out there in the universes of existence and non-existence (means to imply the universes that are currently being shaped and designed) that is beyond the limited scopes of what we can see or hear.

The last point is also the most important one since it de-limits us from our perceived capabilities and inspires us to stretch beyond what we normally think of us as being capable of doing or achieving. We must know that there is an already catered for support mechanism that is available to us.

We are, as always, engulfed and surrounded by many supporting folks and objects that we would never be able to either thank enough, or discount them for their contributions to our achievements. It is just not that they are looking for approvals or acknowledgements; it is in fact just the heat and velocity of rate at which everything is shifting and moving in the entire universe of existence and non-existence that we may even forget to thank or acknowledge their contributions.

We all do realize and ever acknowledge internally that without their support we would never be even able to produce anything near to acceptance, leave alone perfection. These are the wife, parents, children, siblings, friends, colleagues, and those around us aspiring to support and even contribute to our endeavors in research.

Also, another realization is that as much as we may feel enslaved by the compulsion of having a day job just to put food on table for the family, we must never get away by ignoring the higher aspect of our physical existence on the planet – which is to make a contribution to fulfill our spiritual aspiration. This boils down to keep working towards fulfilling our spiritual aspiration despite odds and obstacles.

The only other additional point that this experience reinforces is that yes, there are certainly higher beings (or being) out there that keep on guiding us in the right direction, and it is our choice as to what we may like to call that higher being or power, and some of that might be influenced by the religion that one follows, or what one perceives to be as God.

Across all religions of the world, human beings are not just born in image of the divine, but are very part of what we term 'divine.' Thus, each one of us has a great responsibility towards helping everyone who is perceivably of somewhat lesser capabilities than ourselves during our existence on the planet. This extends to include all animals and plants that are around us.

This also draws to an extension that as human beings we are either by choice or perceived limitation neither the prophets or originators of a new religion or paradigm, nor perpetuators of a new age. Our role on the planet in current impasse may neither be marginalized to an extent where we consider ourselves so diminished as incapable of achieving, nor be blown much out of proportion that we perceive it to be unachievable within limits of our existing lifetime. The key to success is an ability to strike the balance. That alone leads us to a realization that while we are extremely capable, yet we must never dream ourselves as higher than the reality that created us.

Shiva is in each one of us. It is for us to awaken the divine within and build the ability to see the divine in all that exists. The divine does not limit goodness in any way.

Though we consider ourselves to be an individual, our collective imagination can visualize a project that enables us to act locally within the immediate vicinity of our community to create a planet of completely protected environment, and a world full of peace.

May 24th, 2007

After a long drive from New Jersey to North Carolina, it was pre-dawn time that I reached home. After very quietly getting inside by opening the door with my own key, not to get anyone awake, I found the time to meditate and do some pranayaam (yogic breathing exercises). Just after the pranayaam exercises, I reached the sink to drink some water. I chanced to glance at the tree outside from the window behind the sink. There was a clear formation of 'Ganesha' that vividly depicted the eyes, ears, and the snout. Overwhelmed with emotion, I immediately bowed to the ground to offer my respects by a 'dandawat pranaam.' The formation lasted for over an hour, after which the burst of reflection from first rays of sunlight began to distinct apart the leaves and branches. It was my second experience of seeing the divine live in the tree form. The first one was at Kud in Jammu and Kashmir in the summer of 1968, where I had clearly visualized Guru Nanak Dev Ji.

All these visualizations and vivid forms appearing in objects of nature from cloud to stone to trees just send one message across: the divine is indeed in all that exists, from all living and moving organic creatures to all non-living existence. It imposes a strict discipline on us: to respect the nature and existence in all its forms. It may mean to use the scarce resources of our planet wisely with caution and austerity.

August 15th, 2007

I was on a pilgrimage to the Holy Mount Kailash and Holy Manasarovar with a group of devotees. The final decision to go on the trip was so last minute that I reached a day late in Kathmandu to join rest of the group. After trek to circle the Holy Mount Kailash, our team was camping at the banks of Holy Manasarovar lake.

The larger group of pilgrims was divided into small groups of 4 to 5 devotees to share the tent. We had pitched our tent very close to the bank. It was dusk time and the other devotees in the tent were sharing their divine experiences.

Suddenly, Mr. Garg, one of our group, pointed us to the eastern sky and declared "Bhole Nath Ji is giving darshan." Translated, it meant that Lord Shiva is blessing us with visualization.

As we looked at the sky, we were all able to clearly see Lord Shiva in cloud formation to the minutest detail – the lord seated on deer skin in lotus posture meditating, the kamandal bowl placed in the front, trishul by the side, lord's matted hair beholding the crescent moon – the view was mesmerizing.

The cloud formation lasted a full 15 minutes, and slightly afterwards, it begin to fade.

As I pointed my camera to take a picture, the battery died, signifying that beauty is just to behold, not to touch or capture.

Among experiences that were being shared by devotees, the most significant one was from Mr. Garg describing an account of his volunteering at Amarnath Ji. He was hosting a langar (divine offering of free food to pilgrims and visitors to holy places) at Pahalgam, the starting point for an arduous 5 day trek to the holy cave. A land slide prevented pilgrims from proceeding on the trek, leading to accumulation of pilgrims at Pahalgam and shortage of supplies.

While Mr, Garg's voluntary team ran out of regular food, he asked his help mates to get boxes of biscuits from the truck. They kept on bringing in boxes of biscuits from the truck, and the boxes were being replenished by the divine. There seemed to be an unending supply available to feed the pilgrims. They were able to feed everyone, and the boxes kept coming back in the truck, so much so that the remaining ones were brought back to Barnala, the town in Punjab from where Mr. Garg had engaged and initially loaded the truck, and distributed to school children there.

All of us in the tent sincerely applauded Mr. Garg for his devotion, and thanked him for showing us the cloud formation. We all felt that it was his true devotion that blessed our group with sighting the lord in cloud form.

Jan 31, 2015

Even while finalizing the manuscript of this book, I woke up early around 3.30 AM, and started meditating on divine mother Ma Kali.

I was able to see a vivid depiction of the divine mother, visualized with my eyes closed her beautiful eyes and the extended tongue clearly appearing in the visualization.

As a flash, the visualization provided with a solution to deal with suicidal thoughts. Since Ma Kali is the destroyer of all wrong thoughts, the freshly severed head in one of her hands represents not just the destroyed ego, but also the destroyed anti-ego. Think of anti-ego at the extreme other end of ego. While ego may represent thinking too much of oneself, anti-ego is thinking nothing of yourself at all – to the extent that you feel so incapable of achieving anything that you are driven to believe that you are worthless. The climax of anti-ego leads to generation of suicidal thoughts.

It is in those low moments of one's life that Ma Kali immediately empowers us – she infinitely draws the power from Lord Shiva, and bestows it on us through her blessing hand, and instantly will make us feel good and empowered to be who we really are, exist, and do what is most worthy of our life.

No matter where on the planet and when, suicidal thoughts can come to anyone as naturally as sleep and hunger. While sleep is never on demand and may come naturally to anyone, and hunger can be controlled for some time, these thoughts seem to have become a routine part of modern day life as making a living has become so hard. From earning something every single day to keep the family going to looking after everyone in the family and oneself, maintaining a work and life balance, everything appears to be putting a lot of pressure on us.

While at one hand we realize the importance of life and the great opportunity we have in front of us to make a difference in the world, on the other is the frustration of dealing with impossible situations that can kill us slowly, every single day of our life. At times, no amount of positive attitude and open mindedness seem to help.

We can often think that the world would go on as it is, and probably better, so that there would be one less person to feed and provide for resources of the planet, if we were not to be around. We may also think that the environment would be perhaps better with one less person to breathe. And there would also perhaps be lesser frustration to deal with for others, as it is only us humans who generate all this unwanted heat out of our interactions with each other.

Whenever one gets such thoughts, one must immediately meditate on the divine mother Ma Kali and offer the following prayer:

Aum Jai Ma MahaKali Namah

Oh divine mother MahaKali, you are the dissolver of all ego, anti-ego, and wrong thoughts, and you correct our wrong actions.

With your kind grace, purify our heart and our mind, and inspire all our actions to be in the right direction, grant us health and make us full of strength so that we can work towards fulfillment of the big divine plan and achieve the mission most worthy of human life.

Aum Jai Ma MahaKali Namah

Everyone needs to get it that the divine is in all and that the all is in the divine. Extending this, there is the divine as much as in all others, as it is within our own self. Even the thought of killing yourself is an unsolicited one if one can visualize the divinity everywhere.

It would be an unholy thought to kill the divine. If God is there in all that exists, then it is also within you. One must feel fully empowered to visualize divine within the self.

Immediately after the meditation, the realization was also not to ask for any more visualizations of any form of the divine, as divine is indeed formless. While it is relevant to know the significance of an image, slowly we need to graduate to a level where we can know the divine as formless. One can waste an entire lifetime to seek an image of the divine, even without knowing that the divine is formless and right within one's own self. The divine is always calling on us and asking us to do the right. All we need to do is listening, and act upon what the divine within asks us to do. On the planet of our existence, results are only produced by action. What is most important in life is to do our best, and leave the rest.

March 4th, 2015

    I was in Alaska with my son Parv, and with a group of friends were driving from Chena hot springs to Fairbanks. Temperature was in the vicinity of -32° F at 4 am, and northern lights were very prominent, when we stopped on the secluded road to step out and catch a glimpse. I felt the presence of Lord Shiva as being right next to us, and the glow of northern lights was closest in hue to the one that I had seen while having the experience of being face to face with the Lord on Dec 4th, 1970. Though I must live up to my own realization and not be greedy of asking for Lord to appear before us and know the divine as formless and being everywhere, yet it always feels like a blessing to have a visualization that takes me back to the experience.

Relating back to 'The Experience':

    Often I get back to thinking of the experience and realize that it was such an ecstatic joy that all the perceived gratifications and wealth of the world put together would nowhere come close to even 0.01% of its intensity.

    The biggest part of the experience is an ongoing realization – a knowing of the fact that we keep running after the objects of desire with a false sense of perception that achievement of that object would lead us to happiness.

    We fail to realize that happiness is all within us, and we need a key to unlock it. The key is also in our own hand – we have just got to use it, rather than keep looking for it here and there.

    I keep repeatedly asking as to why as human beings we get stuck in the struggle, and here is the answer that comes from the experience and the subsequent ongoing dialog:

    From needs to desires to indulgences, it is nature of a human being to strive and attain. As long as we are not connected to our inner-self, we remain in the mode of ignorance, and would continue to dwell there shuttling between self-imposed restrictions and perceivably self-gratifying fulfillments.

    This oscillation between restrictions and perceived joys is not only self-defeating and illusionary, it lowers the self-esteem and dignity as the struggle carries on. To rise above this lower level of existence, one can detach and pass through current impasse by the practice of meditation and establishment of a dialog with the inner-self.

Once we can see all in one and one in all, we elevate to realization of the self, and see a reflection of the self in all that exists. This realization by itself is enough to avoid all wars and clashes between communities. The struggles of humanity at current time are all owing to a lack of true knowledge of the self, and would be eliminated when this knowledge is attained by one and all.

As the onion layers of Acquired Identity Syndromes would be peeled, eventually everyone would discover at their core – all that they have is unconditional love and unconditional respect for everyone and all that exists.

There have been, there are, and there will be challenges and hurdles on the way, and these may sound daunting – but one must know that after each struggle we emerge stronger, and are ready to face a higher challenge.

Our dear and near ones may be in pain, and we may be suffering, only to know that finally all pain results in a gain. There is so much of suffering in this world – and our unconditional love for everyone may bring that pain and suffering very close to us, as we volunteer to embrace all the pain and suffering that exists in the world.

Being able to share the pain and suffering of everyone else by itself becomes a blessing, as we see an image of the divine in everyone and all that exists.

This realization changes our perspective on how we look at pain and suffering, and all else that exists.

One can find inner joy and peace even in the middle of all the perceived suffering and pain. It is driven by realization, and having a dialog with the inner-self.

There is no evil in reality – the perceived evil is a product of the counter-balancing force that is set in motion by our own collective thoughts and actions as humanity. If we all collectively think and act positive out of inspirations that are acquired through a divine connection, we can wipe out all negativity and perceived evil.

A realization that we are all connected and part of the same divine whole changes our perception on how we look at others. We can see an image of the divine in all existence, and unity of the one divine in all diversity.

Epilogue

'Face to face with Shiva' is not a book of the sort that we are used to normally read. It is not a fiction or non-fiction, or a stretch of imagination. It is, word by word, direct communication of a real life experience, and following that, an ongoing dialog that has been in the making towards shaping future of the world, the planet on which we dwell, the living universe, the larger context of interconnected galaxies, the context of all existence, and the very purpose of life.

While author by no way makes any claim to pre-knowing any of the facts stated in the book, yet at the same instance, kneels down and bows head in deep respect and reverence to Lord Shiva, for using the author's mortal body and mind as instruments of communication for the larger benefit of humanity and the living planet that we call home, the Mother Earth.

Human species has evolved more over the last 500 years than it has collectively over the prior millenniums of existence. Out of that, the past 150 years have been the most crucial ones related to the so-called scientific discoveries and technological revolution.

We have come to a point where we have started exploiting all the possible resources, even if these reside beneath the surface of our planet, while we are ever aware that we never need to look beyond Sun as the sole source of creating, sustaining, and energizing our planet.

In the name of development and improving the so-called quality of life, we have actually messed up the entire ecological balance of the environment of our planet and within a period of just past 100 years consistently been driving it to a point where we are pondering whether the damage is irreversible. Despite the realization and awareness, we all collectively prefer to be mute spectators to gradual decay of the planet's environment, continue our actions towards that end, and have resigned to accept it as a fated destruction.

Oceans are rising, glaciers are melting, and we continue to explore and exploit newer sources of fossil fuels, while being in full knowledge of the fact that we can certainly do with viable fundamental alternatives.

In the name of our own evolution that has resulted out of a consistent struggle with our desires and temptations, we have either completely embraced a tee-totalitarian regime, or becomes victims of complete indulgence, while knowing fully well that there is a viable, alternative path.

The path that Lord Shiva reveals for us is that of respect, realization, caution, and balance. Lord does ask us to embrace all and leave none behind, yet be fully aware and know of the purpose and consequences of our actions.

Being inspired by connection with the Lord that each one of us is ever entitled to, and driving our actions through these inspired thoughts, each one of us would be led to a path that helps the humanity, the world, the planet, and the living universe all alike, as much as it would be a journey towards realization of the self, and a feeling of fulfillment of achieving what we truly aspire to do. We can certainly do with less comfort to save the planet for future generations.

Though concepts like time and space are revealed as delimiters of manifestation, and as a result of our perception, we are unable to even imagine anything that does not have an association with both of these delimiters; Lord Shiva does disclose the super element and the three basic elements that constitute all manifested existence in a comprehensible manner and form. The author is indebted for life and beyond to the grace of the lord for inspiring comprehensible words that make sense to a person of normal, ordinary ability to grasp these higher than life concepts in an easy way.

Lord Shiva is a man of few words. Lord asks us to act, and not just keep thinking, talking, planning, and contemplating endlessly, since ours is a planet of existence where the final results in the present times (kalayuga) would only be produced by action.

Let us make a pledge right now to sacrifice some comfort, start thinking and acting towards protecting the endangered environment and species of our planet, live respect by showing it in our behavior and spirit by genuinely wishing everyone the very best, and doing all that we can to promote harmony, interdependence between communities and people of the world, and make all efforts possible to create permanent peace on the planet.

Here is the gist of Lord Shiva's message to humanity –

"You are empowered to know of and connect to the divinity within you, and have the ability to expand this divinity within to all around you, and you can wipe out all the negativity from the universe through your

collective efforts. You can heal yourself and all others through this divinity. You can collectively create a unified world where there is no negativity, no disease. This world will be full of joy, love, peace, and you realize it through your thoughts, actions, and collective deeds.

There is no need to worship any idol in any form, follow rituals and dogmas, or to see any form. For God is formless, is within you, and would not be pleased by the following of rituals. To know God, one must first connect within, and then through this connection with the inner-self, reach out to the divine everywhere. Listen to the voice of God from inside.

Collective efforts lead to positive results. God is above religion. All religions of the world are a way to the God. To know God, you can come from any path. The path itself is not the destination."

Let us start the journey of a thousand miles ahead of us with a single step – and that first step is laying down each night before we retire to bed a plan for the actionable items that we intend to achieve over the very next day of our life, actions that would heal the damaged environment of our planet and hearts hurt from our collective actions as communities and nations of the world; eliminate the hunger and poverty, and aid in creating the union of currently divided world as one nation by building interdependence among communities of the world.

The very next second step would be to take action during the work day – walk the thought and plan from the previous night.

The third step would be to perform an honest evaluation of the action steps and know how we did, and ponder whether we need any course correction.

The journey of life goes on, and there are several individual steps on the way for each one of us that are as unique as our signature and DNA, and at all times we just need to be aware of our ability to connect with Lord Shiva, draw inspiration from that connection, and act on the inspired thoughts.

In the name of Lord Shiva, Amen.

Suggested Prayers

The following prayers are recommended for citing at any time of the day or night. The purpose of a prayer is to basically align our own consciousness with that of the collective universe, and to open up our inner-self to connect with the all-pervading divinity. One need not consider saying a prayer as a form of ritual. Though not necessary, these can be a great starting point. Eventually what matters is our own thought and action. To get inspiring thoughts, the prayers can be helpful to align our own self with the divine.

In this order, the prayers address each member of the Shiva family: Lord Ganesha, Ma (the divine mother) Durga, Lord Kartikeya, Lord Shiva, Lord Hanuman; followed by The Trinity of Divinity, and the Ultimate Reality.

Lord Ganesha is known as an epitome of devotion and sacrifice. As the legend has it, Mother Parvati (consort of Lord Shiva) created Ganesha to guard while she was having a bath. When Lord Shiva returned to his abode in Kailash, he was prevented from entering the abode by Ganesha. This enraged Lord Shiva, and after an argument he beheaded Ganesha. An infuriated Mother Parvati asked Lord Shiva to immediately restore life to beheaded Ganesha. Lord Shiva topped the beheaded Ganesha body with an elephant head and brought him back to life. This is also when Lord Shiva blessed Ganesha that he would be worshipped before all other divine entities and all devotees would pray to Lord Ganesha to get the obstacles removed from the paths to achieve their noble deeds.

The symbolic vehicle of Lord Ganesha is the mouse. The mouse is extremely smart, tactful, and can achieve several tasks beyond the capability of its small size. A lion trapped in a net can be freed by a mouse who bites away threads of the net to let the lion escape.

Ma Durga is a representation of the divine mother. She manifests as Maha Kali (the great divine mother of dissolution, the one who annihilates the ego), Maha Lakshmi (the great divine mother of boons, the one who bestows wealth and prosperity), and Maha Saraswati (the great divine mother of knowledge, the one who imparts education, and gives us guidance).

Lord Kartikeya is the son of Lord Shiva and the divine mother Parvati. A divine preacher, benefactor of all, and a gallant warrior, Kartikeya is also known by several other names – some are Lord Murugan, Skanda, Kumaran, Shanamugham, and Subramanya.

As the legend has it, when the war between Asuras (demons, beings associated with a negative image as aligned to evil forces) and Devtas (divine beings) reached to a point that Devtas were defeated and feared further humiliation, they approached Lord Shiva for help. Lord Shiva appointed Kartikeya to establish and lead an army to defeat Asuras. In commemoration of victory of this army of the divine forces led by Lord Kartikeya, devotees have dedicated the tallest statue at Batu caves near Kuala Lampur in Malaysia. The symbolic vehicle of Lord Kartikeya is peacock, signifying majestic beauty, peace, free will, uniqueness, and the ability to fly.

Lord Hanuman, popularly referred to as 'Bajrangbali' (the strongest one) is an incarnation of Lord Shiva, and the only one in the legend with an ability to fly. Lord Hanuman appeared on the planet over 5000 years ago, and was a devotee of Lord Rama. When Ravana, the king of Lanka by deceit took Rama's wife Sita as hostage, Lord Hanuman flew over the Indian ocean to reach Ashok Vatika in Lanka to convey her the message from Rama. Lord Hanuman led the army of monkeys to build a bridge between Rameswaram in India and Sri Lanka (Ram Setu, also known as Adam's bridge). When Lakshaman (Rama's brother) was hit and became unconscious during the war between Rama and Ravana, Lord Hanuman flew to Himalayas and picked Sanjivini mountain that grew the lifesaving herb in time to revive Lakshaman. A gallant warrior and an epitome of devotion, Lord Hanuman is deeply revered by devotees.

Brahma, Vishnu, and Mahesh are the trinity of divinity representing generation, operation, and dissolution of life, and we bow in respect to them.

Brahm is the ultimate reality, the unknown, the infinite, and we are part of its big divine plan. Brahm and Shiva are synonym as the super element and super consciousness, while Brahma, Vishnu, and Mahesh respectively are synonym to knowledge, energy, and consciousness.

A Prayer to Lord Ganesha

Aum Jai Shri Ganeshaye Namah

Oh son of Lord Shiva and Mother Divine Paravati, Oh epitome of Devotion, Oh remover of all obstacles, Oh the first and foremost among the Lords and the Devas, praise be to thee, the one who is first worshipped by all, and adored by all, and we offer ourselves at thy feet for blessings.

Let our mission become successful.

Let us be truthful and honest in our devotion.

Let us be honest and perform our work diligently.

Remove all our obstacles so that we may be able to do our duty and fulfill the mission most worthy of human life.

Aum Jai Shri Ganeshaye Namah

A Prayer to Ma Durga

Aum Jai Durge Aum

Oh mother of all, Oh the one who is ever blissful, Oh the protector of the good, and destroyer of the evil; Oh the one who manifests as Maha Kali, Maha Saraswati, and Maha Lakshmi, Oh mother divine – praise be to thee, and we offer ourselves at thy feet for blessings.

Bless us to do the good.
Bless us to be ever full of health.
Bless us to be ever full of respect, love, and compassion for all.
Bless us to be ever full of strength to do the deeds most worthy of human life.
Jai Ma Maha Kali
Jai Ma Maha Saraswati
Jai Ma Maha Lakshmi
Aum Jai Durge Aum

A Prayer to Lord Kartikeya

Aum Jai Shri Kartikeya Namah

Oh son of Lord Shiva and Mother Divine Paravati, Oh the epitome of Strength and Vigor, Oh bravest of all, the lord of all warriors of righteousness, Oh the most knowledgeable of all, praise be to thee, the one who is worshipped by all, and adored by all, and we offer ourselves at thy feet for blessings.

Give us the Strength to do the good.

Empower us to serve those in need.

Grant us the vigor to do all that we can.

Keep us under your protection at all times.

Make us healthy and powerful so that we may be able to do our duty and fulfill the mission most worthy of human life.

Aum Jai Shri Kartikeya Namah

A Prayer to Lord Shiva

Aum Namah Shivaya

Oh lord of the Lords. Oh God of all the Gods, Oh creator, sustainer, and dissolver of all the universes known and unknown, Oh father of Ganapathi, Oh father of Kartikeya, Oh benefactor of all, Oh protector of all, the one who manifested as Lord Hanuman, the destroyer of evil, the upholder of righteousness, the highest praise be to thee, and we offer ourselves at thy feet for blessings.

Purify our hearts and free us from all hatred, jealousy, disease, and ignorance.

Give us the knowledge that helps to achieve divine acts.

Empower us to do good to the world.

Give us health, happiness, and righteous thinking.

Inspire us and fill our hearts with love and compassion for all.

Empower us to help all those in need.

Let our all thoughts, speech, and deeds be humble and noble.

Let us never hurt anyone, even unconsciously, through any of our thoughts, speech, or deeds.

Empower and inspire us to be engaged in noble pursuits that bring love, joy, peace, and health to all, and protect the environment of our Mother Earth.

Shine the light of splendor and let this light touch our spirit.

Come and reside in the depth of our heart, and in the inner most of our self, and guide our path.

Aum Namah Shivaya

A Prayer to Lord Hanuman

Aum Jai Shri Bajrangbali

Oh the strongest of all, the one who can fly, the one who destroys all the evil, the one who protects everyone, the lord of devotion, the one worthy of all praise, we offer ourselves at thy feet for blessings.

Purify our heart.

Bless us to be strong, healthy, wise, and noble.

Bless us to be devoted, and be always inspired to be on the spiritual path.

Destroy all our obstacles on the path of spiritual journey, and provide us the guidance to be on the right path.

Come, and be with us, living in our heart, and giving us the strength to do the good deeds.

Aum Jai Shri Bajrangbali

A Prayer to the Trinity of Divinity

Jai Shri Brahma
Jai Shri Vishnu
Jai Shri Mahesh
Oh the Lords of Generating, operating, and dissolving life, the giver of Knowledge, Energy, and Consciousness, bless us to be ever inspired by divine knowledge, be engulfed with divine energy, and be ever connected to our inner-self and be full of consciousness so that we can fulfill the mission most important of human life. Empower us to be always pure at heart, honest and noble in all our deeds, and do all that we can to help everyone, and be engaged in protecting the environment of our planet.

A Prayer to Invoke the Divine Within

Aham Brahmasmi

Oh ultimate reality, I am embraced by you and I am an indivisible part of you, and I represent your divinity as I am you. Empowered in your image to carry out the divine mission and engage in divine acts, let me always stay on the divine path.

Introduction to the Author:
Dr. Abhinav Aggarwal

Born and brought up in the state of Jammu and Kashmir in India, Abhinav migrated to USA in 1999. He holds BS Part 1 (Sciences) from Jammu University, BS Engineering in Electronics from Panjab University (PEC Chandigarh), M.Tech in Systems & Management from Indian Institute of Technology (IIT), Delhi, and Ph.D in IT effectiveness, also from IIT Delhi. He has been working in various fields of technology for over 20 years across various geographies of the globe. He has been issued patents for environment-friendly power generation by tapping solar energy and atmospheric cold. He has published 45 research papers in peer-reviewed international journals and conference proceedings, has been invited as a plenary speaker to several international events, and is a globally recognized thought leader in creating technology solutions to solve complex problems.

He is the author of 'September 11: A Wake Up Call – *scientific analysis of the problem and suggested solutions*,' the book received 'IEEE Author of the Year Award.' He is the founder of 'Society for Universal Oneness,' (www.SFUO.org a non-profit organization) focused on creating a better world through environmental and education projects.

His forthcoming book 'One World: One Nation – *an interdependent business model*' will focus on uniting a divided world.

This book, 'face to face with Shiva: *scientific perspective of a spiritual experience*,' explains his real life experience of sighting Lord Shiva, and how that experience and ongoing dialog with the Lord is so very important to save our planet.

An interdisciplinary scientist and researcher, he wants to create technology based solutions to solve problems related to environment, differences between nations, terrorism, and to eliminate ignorance, poverty, and hunger. As a human being, Abhinav firmly believes that eventually a revelation of truly knowing our connection to Lord Shiva through this book currently in your hands is the way by which all of us will get united, rising above our differences, and would work in collaboration to solve our problems.

Abhinav Aggarwal, Ph.D.

    Abhinav has launched a crusade to clean up the abode of Lord Shiva, the holy Mount Kailash in Tibet and also wants to establish a hospital and an institute for integrated health and healing by nature at North Carolina with one of the satellite campuses at Kailash.

    Abhinav believes in moving from wholeness to universal oneness. The wholeness integrates mind, body, and the spirit. The oneness connects you with the Divine and all creation: the Universe.

An excerpt from the forthcoming book 'One World: One Nation'

Declaration of Interdependence:

We, people of the world, as global citizens of planet earth, hereby resolve to resist all attempts at war, hatred, jealousy, assault or discrimination. As partners in a pursuit to create permanent peace, we shall participate in efforts that promote understanding, respect, love, joy and harmony between people of the world.

We shall care for the environment of our planet in every manner and recycle all that is possible. We shall adapt to a life style that is in harmony with the nature. We shall create and use new methods and ways of doing business that build a global cooperation and interdependence between people of the world. We shall make effective use of advances and research in science, technology, art, agriculture, medicine and all fields of literature and knowledge to alleviate the suffering of humanity. We shall coexist peacefully with all the creation on our planet.

We would collectively engage in developing and implementing a new system and curriculum for education that would support building peace and trust among people of the world by creating interdisciplinary fields of research that tap the resource of skill and expertise of different communities and cultures.

We shall all work together towards permanent eradication of sorrow, ignorance, disease, suffering, hunger and violence from our mother planet. We all respect the Mother Earth as a single Nation to which we belong as Citizens of the World.

- Dr. Abhinav Aggarwal, Society for Universal Oneness,
for people of the World
www.sfuo.org

REFERENCES

[1] James Hewitt, The complete Yoga book, Cresset Press, 1983, ISBN # 0 09 177221 4
[2] Shri Shri Anandamurty, Namah Shivaya Shnataya, 2006, Ananda Marga Pulications
[3] Abhinav Aggarwal, September 11: A Wake Up Call, 2002, 1stBooks Library, ISBN # 1 4033 6204 1

Picture Index

Picture plates	Refer to Chapters	Details
Front cover	1,2,12	Holy Mount Kailash (Tibet) view from Darchen
1-8, 10-16	1	Site vicinity related to the 'Experience,' the city of Jammu, and view of Trikuta hills from Jammu
9	1	Shiva statue bearing closest resemblance to the form in which Lord appeared
17-43	2, 12	Holy Kailash and Holy Manasarovar, vicinity, and view on the route
44-51	2	Deities of the Shiva family
52	2	Shivalingam
52	2	Nandi (the bull)
53-56	2	Pilot Mountain, Shiva statue, Shivalingam at Amarnath Ji cave, Nataraj
57-59	2	Shivalingam, Nandi
60-61	2, 12	Northern lights, Alaska
Back cover	1,2,12	Lord Shiva full posture, Mangal Mahadev, Birla Kannan, near IGI Airport, Delhi

Picture gallery

Picture 1: Vicinity of Purani Mandi chowk, Jammu, showing old Shri Hanuman Temple, flower sellers, very near to the site of 'the experience.' (Picture courtesy Dr. Hemla Rakesh Gupta)

Picture 2: View of Old Shri Hanuman Temple (lens credit: Rohan Gupta)

Face to Face with Shiva

Picture 3: Inside view of Old Shri Hanuman Temple, Purani Mandi, Jammu (lens credit: Rohan Gupta)

Picture 4: Casino Restaurant in vicinity of the site of 'the experience.' (lens credit: Rohan Gupta)

Face to Face with Shiva

Picture 5: *Shubhash Bhai Saheb's Steel shop at Purani Mandi (lens credit: Rohan Gupta)*

Picture 6: *Vicinity view of Purani Mandi square, Jammu (lens credit: Rohan Gupta)*

Picture 7: Motial Bhawan, entrance view from Motial Street, Jammu (Lens Credit: Rohan Gupta)

Picture 8: Motial Bhawan view from Raj Tilak Road, Jammu (Lens Credit: Rohan Gupta)

Face to Face with Shiva

Picture 9: Mangal Mahadeva, Shiva Statue near IGI Airport, New Delhi, and closest resemblance to the form in which Lord Shiva appeared in 'the experience.' (lens credit: Virender Bhardwaj)

Picture 10: Outside view of Shri Ram Temple, Purani Mandi, Jammu (lens credit: Rohan Gupta)

Abhinav Aggarwal, Ph.D.

Picture 11: Shiva Statue with Shivalingam in foreground at Shri Ram Temple, Purani Mandi, Jammu (lens credit: Rohan Gupta)

Face to Face with Shiva

Picture 12: View of Trikuta Hills, the abode of Ma Vaishno Devi, the trek of about 9 miles is accessed from starting point Katra, about 20 miles from the city of Jammu (photo courtesy: Dr. Hemla Rakesh Gupta)

Picture 13: Inside view of Shri Ram Temple entrance, Purani Mandi, Jammu (lens credit: Rohan Gupta)

Picture 14: Entrance to Bahu Fort temple, Jammu (lens credit: Rohan Gupta)

Picture 15: Partial view of Bahu Fort, with city of Jammu in the background (lens credit: Rohan Gupta)

Face to Face with Shiva

Picture 16: Partial view of the city of Jammu, Tawi River, and bridge from Bahu Fort (lens credit: Rohan Gupta)

Picture 17: Dinosaur rock at Nelayam Hilltop, Tibet enroute to Kailash

Abhinav Aggarwal, Ph.D.

Pictures 18-19: Wildflowers at Nelayam Hilltop, Tibet enroute to Kailash

Face to Face with Shiva

Picture 20: Mount Ganesha enroute to Kailash

Picture 21: Mountain range around Kailash

Picture 22: Mountain range enroute to Kailash

Picture 23: Sand dunes enroute to Kailash

Picture 24: Tibetan monastery atop hill by Holy Manasarovar lake

Picture 25: Tibetan lamas chanting prayers on the banks of Holy Lake Manasarovar, Holy Kailash in the backdrop

Picture 26: Devotee pilgrim offering prayers at Holy Lake Manasarovar

Face to Face with Shiva

Pictures 27-28: Lama kid and boy playing conch shell by Holy Lake Manasarovar

Pictures 29-30: Flock of sheep and Yaks roaming in Holy Kailash vicinity

Abhinav Aggarwal, Ph.D.

Pictures 31-32: Sun reflection in Holy Manasarovar, and close up view of Holy Kailash

Picture 33: Prayer flags on route to Holy Kailash

Pictures 34-35: Prayer rocks on route to Holy Kailash and by Holy Lake Manasarovar

Face to Face with Shiva

Picture 36: Holy Mount Kailash with its range

Picture 37: Holy Manasarovar

Picture 38: Sea gull by Holy Manasarovar

Picture 39: Unique rock patterns on route to Holy Kailash

Abhinav Aggarwal, Ph.D.

Pictures 40-41: Snow melt water fall on route to Holy Kailash trail, and Tibetan kids in Holy Kailash vicinity

Picture 42: Snow view on route to Holy Kailash

Picture 43: Mountain view on route to Holy Kailash

Face to Face with Shiva

Pictures 44-45: Lord Ganesha at HSNC, Morrisville, NC; Kartikeya as Lord Murugan at Batu Caves

Pictures 46-47: Ma Durga and Ma Parvati at HSNC, Morrisville, NC

Pictures 48-49:Ma Kali (close up), at Laguna Beach temple, and dancing posture (picture courtesy: Ms. Usha Harding, Kali temple, CA)

Pictures50-51: Lord Shiva and Lord Hanuman at HSNC, Morrisville, NC

Face to Face with Shiva

Picture 52: Shivalingam and Nandi at HSNC, Morrisville, NC

Picture 53: Pilot Mountain, NC (Carolina Kailsah) resembling matted hair lock of Lord Shiva (lens credit: NC Division of Parks and Recreation)

Abhinav Aggarwal, Ph.D.

Picture 54: Lord Shiva in meditative posture at Murudeshwar in Karnataka (picture courtesy: Ms. Shanthi Deenadayalan)

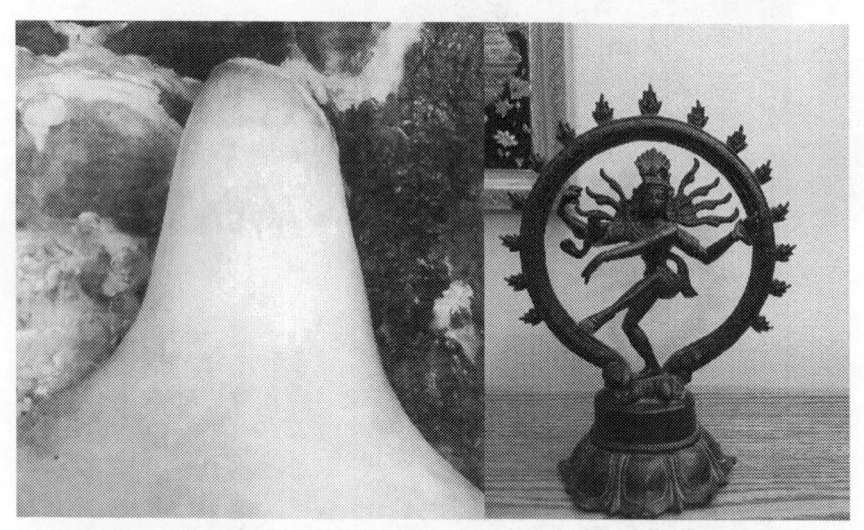

Pictures 55-56: Shivalingam at Amarnath Ji cave in Laddakh region of Jammu & Kashmir, and Lord Shiva in cosmic dance posture as Nataraj (Lens credits: Er. Sunil Bakhshi)

Face to Face with Shiva

Pictures 57-59: Shivalingas in the middle of Shalmala river in Northern Karnataka- low water levels make them visible during Shivaratri (picture courtesy: Ms. Shanthi Deenadayalan)

Pictures 60-61: Northern lights in Alaska, visible during winter nights, closest resemblance of hues radiating from Lord during the experience (lens credit: Parv Aggarwal)

Printed in the United States
By Bookmasters